Excel 2003 Programming

A Developer's Notebook™

Excel 2003 Programming

A Developer's Notebook™

Jeff Webb

O'REILLY®

Beijing · Cambridge · Farnham · Köln · Paris · Sebastopol · Taipei · Tokyo

Excel 2003 Programming: A Developer's Notebook™
by Jeff Webb

Copyright © 2004 O'Reilly Media, Inc. All rights reserved.
Printed in the United States of America.

Published by O'Reilly Media, Inc., 1005 Gravenstein Highway North, Sebastopol, CA 95472.

O'Reilly books may be purchased for educational, business, or sales promotional use. Online editions are also available for most titles (*safari.oreilly.com*). For more information, contact our corporate/institutional sales department: (800) 998-9938 or *corporate@oreilly.com*.

Editor:	Simon St.Laurent
Production Editor:	Reg Aubry
Cover Designer:	Edie Freedman
Interior Designer:	David Futato

Printing History:

August 2004:	First Edition.

 This book uses RepKover™, a durable and flexible lay-flat binding.

ISBN: 0-596-00767-1
[M]

Contents

The Developer's Notebook Series

So, you've managed to pick this book up. Cool. Really, I'm excited about that! Of course, you may be wondering why these books have the odd-looking, college notebook sort of cover. I mean, this is O'Reilly, right? Where are the animals? And, really, do you *need* another series? Couldn't this just be a cookbook? How about a nutshell, or one of those cool hacks books that seems to be everywhere? The short answer is that a developer's notebook is none of those things—in fact, it's such an important idea that we came up with an entirely new look and feel, complete with cover, fonts, and even some notes in the margin. This is all a result of trying to get something into your hands you can actually use.

It's my strong belief that while the nineties were characterized by everyone wanting to learn everything (Why not? We all had six-figure incomes from dot-com companies), the new millennium is about information pain. People don't have time (or the income) to read through 600 page books, often learning 200 things, of which only about 4 apply to their current job. It would be much nicer to just sit near one of the uber-coders and look over his shoulder, wouldn't it? To ask the guys that are neck-deep in this stuff why they chose a particular method, how they performed this one tricky task, or how they avoided that threading issue when working with piped streams. The thinking has always been that books can't serve that particular need—they can inform, and let you decide, but ultimately a coder's mind was something that couldn't really be captured on a piece of paper.

This series says that assumption is patently wrong—and we aim to prove it.

A Developer's Notebook is just what it claims to be: the often-frantic scribbling and notes that a true-blue alpha geek mentally makes when working with a new language, API, or project. It's the no-nonsense code that solves problems, stripped of page-filling commentary that often serves more as a paperweight than an epiphany. It's hackery, focused not on what is nifty or might be fun to do when you've got some free time (when's the last time that happened?), but on what you need to simply "make it work." This isn't a lecture, folks—it's a lab. If you want a lot of concept, architecture, and UML diagrams, I'll happily and proudly point you to our animal and nutshell books. If you want every answer to every problem under the sun, our omnibus cookbooks are killer. And if you are into arcane and often quirky uses of technology, hacks books simply rock. But if you're a coder, down to your core, and you just want to get on with it, then you want a Developer's Notebook. Coffee stains and all, this is from the mind of a developer to yours, barely even cleaned up enough for print. I hope you enjoy it... we sure had a good time writing them.

Notebooks Are...

Example-Driven Guides

As you'll see in the "Organization" section, developer's notebooks are built entirely around example code. You'll see code on nearly every page, and it's code that *does something*—not trivial "Hello World!" programs that aren't worth more than the paper they're printed on.

Aimed at Developers

Ever read a book that seems to be aimed at pointy-haired bosses, filled with buzzwords, and feels more like a marketing manifesto than a programming text? We have too—and these books are the antithesis of that. In fact, a good notebook is incomprehensible to someone who can't program (don't say we didn't warn you!), and that's just the way it's supposed to be. But for developers...it's as good as it gets.

Actually Enjoyable to Work Through

Do you really have time to sit around reading something that isn't any fun? If you do, then maybe you're into thousand-page language references—but if you're like the rest of us, notebooks are a much better fit. Practical code samples, terse dialogue centered around practical examples, and even some humor here and there—these are the ingredients of a good developer's notebook.

About Doing, Not Talking About Doing

If you want to read a book late at night without a computer nearby, these books might not be that useful. The intent is that you're coding as you go along, knee deep in bytecode. For that reason, notebooks talk code, code, code. Fire up your editor before digging in.

Notebooks Aren't...

Lectures

We don't let just anyone write a developer's notebook—you've got to be a bona fide programmer, and preferably one who stays up a little too late coding. While full-time writers, academics, and theorists are great in some areas, these books are about programming in the trenches, and are filled with instruction, not lecture.

Filled with Conceptual Drawings and Class Hierarchies

This isn't a nutshell (there, we said it). You won't find 100-page indices with every method listed, and you won't see full-page UML diagrams with methods, inheritance trees, and flow charts. What you will find is page after page of source code. Are you starting to sense a recurring theme?

Long on Explanation, Light on Application

It seems that many programming books these days have three, four, or more chapters before you even see any working code. I'm not sure who has authors convinced that it's good to keep a reader waiting this long, but it's not anybody working on *this* series. We believe that if you're not coding within ten pages, something's wrong. These books are also chock-full of practical application, taking you from an example in a book to putting things to work on your job, as quickly as possible.

Organization

Developer's Notebooks try to communicate different information than most books, and as a result, are organized differently. They do indeed have chapters, but that's about as far as the similarity between a notebook and a traditional programming book goes. First, you'll find that all the headings in each chapter are organized around a specific task. You'll note that we said *task*, not *concept*. That's one of the important things to get about these books—they are first and foremost about doing something. Each of these headings represents a single *lab*. A lab is just what it sounds like—steps to accomplish a specific goal. In fact, that's the first heading you'll see under each lab: "How do I do that?" This is the central question of each lab, and you'll find lots of down-and-dirty code and detail in these sections.

Some labs have some things not to do (ever played around with potassium in high school chemistry?), helping you avoid common pitfalls. Some labs give you a good reason for caring about the topic in the first place; we call this the "Why do I care?" section, for obvious reasons. For those times when code samples don't clearly communicate what's going on, you'll find a "What just happened" section. It's in these sections that you'll find concepts and theory—but even then, they are tightly focused on the task at hand, not explanation for the sake of page count. Finally, many labs offer alternatives, and address common questions about different approaches to similar problems. These are the "What about..." sections, which will help give each task some context within the programming big picture.

And one last thing—on many pages, you'll find notes scrawled in the margins of the page. These aren't for decoration; they contain tips, tricks, insights from the developers of a product, and sometimes even a little humor, just to keep you going. These notes represent part of the overall communication flow—getting you as close to reading the mind of the developer-author as we can. Hopefully they'll get you that much closer to feeling like you are indeed learning from a master.

And most of all, remember—these books are...

All Lab, No Lecture

—Brett McLaughlin, Series Creator

Preface

There are a number of books that include good introductions to programming Excel, but this is not one of them. I assume a couple of things about you: the first is that you're already somewhat familiar with Excel and Visual Basic; the second is that you've got a programming problem to solve.

Excel 2003's new features solve problems dealing with teamwork: collecting and sharing data, programming across applications, and maintaining security. In researching this book, I noticed that most of the newly published Excel books touch on these topics but don't explore them in depth or put them in context. So that's where I focus my efforts.

Each chapter is organized into a collection of labs, each of which addresses a specific programming problem. You can follow along in the text to complete the lab on your own, or you can jump ahead and use the samples I've built for you. Often one lab builds on another, so it's a good idea to skim earlier sections if you are jumping ahead in a chapter.

I don't expect this book will be your only resource, so I include a lot of references in each chapter. I've also included those references as hyperlinks in the sample workbooks (see the Resources sheet). Mostly those links deal with very specific issues related to the topic, but they also include links to toolkits and other software that may be required.

Don't Force It

If you get stuck, there are a number of ways to resume your progress:

- Try turning on macro recording (Tools → Macros → Record a New Macro), perform the task in Excel, then turn off recording and examine the code that Excel generates.

- Search MSDN (*http://www.microsoft.com/msdn*) to see if Microsoft has addressed your problem.
- Search newsgroups (*http://groups.google.com/groups*) to see if someone else has solved your problem.
- And, of course, you can always check *http://www.oreilly.com/catalog/exceladn* or *http://www.mstrainingkits.com* to see if I've solved the problem!

If something still seems too difficult, examine your approach. In that situation, I generally go fishing and come back to the problem later. If you don't live somewhere with good fishing, I guess you're just stuck.

Get the Samples

The samples for this book are at *http://www.oreilly.com/catalog/exceladn*. You'll need them, so go get them now. They are available as a Windows compressed folder (.zip), which you'll need to expand on your computer.

The samples are organized by chapter, and some chapters include subfolders for Visual Studio .NET projects. Each chapter uses one main workbook (ch01.xls, ch02.xls, etc.) as a starting point to provide instructions and navigation.

Font Conventions

This book follows certain conventions for font usage. Understanding these conventions up-front makes it easier to use this book.

Italic
Used for filenames, file extensions, URLs, application names, emphasis, and new terms when they are first introduced.

`Constant width`
Used for objects, methods, variables, properties, data types, database elements, and snippets of code that appear in text.

`Constant width bold`
Used for commands you enter at the command line and to highlight new code inserted in a running example.

`Constant width italic`
Used to annotate output.

How to Contact Us

Please address comments and questions concerning this book to the publisher:

O'Reilly Media, Inc.
1005 Gravenstein Highway North
Sebastopol, CA 95472
(800) 998-9938 (in the United States or Canada)
(707) 829-0515 (international or local)
(707) 829-0104 (fax)

We have a web page for this book, where we list errata, examples, or any additional information. You can access this page at:

http://www.oreilly.com/catalog/exceladn

To comment or ask technical questions about this book, send email to:

bookquestions@oreilly.com

For more information about our books, conferences, Resource Centers, and the O'Reilly Network, see our web site at:

http://www.oreilly.com/

Acknowledgments

Thanks to David Lazar and David Fries at Microsoft as well as Steve Orr, Matthew MacDonald, and Jeff Maggard for reviewing parts of this book. The folks in the developer's community and those who downloaded draft versions of these chapters from my site have also contributed by asking questions that I then had to answer.

I'd also like to single out Simon St.Laurent and John Osborn, my editors at O'Reilly. Simon is a writer in his own right and it was a pleasure working with him. John is a fellow Wombat from DEC and he got this title rolling.

My family helped, too: Trish through her patience, Dorian and Sophia by laughing at my jokes, and Joey by taking me on walkies.

Program the New Excel

You've probably seen Microsoft's TV spots where the office workers are cheering, sliding down the hall on their knees, and otherwise celebrating their fantastic achievements. The message I get from that is not what Microsoft Office can do; it's what the team can do together.

You may or may not like those ads, but their point is valid: Office 2003 isn't really about features, it's about cooperation. This book is an Excel programmer's guide to that way of thinking.

Dude, Where's My Data?

Not long ago we were hearing how software helped us work with data; now it's how software helps us work with others. But where did the data go? More and more it's hiding behind a web page.

Folks know how to use web pages: they click a link and go to a new page, they click a button to add something to their shopping cart, type in their payment info, check out, and then get confirmation in email. Those actions now seem so natural they need little explanation.

You can do the same thing with your office processes: click on a link, fill out an expense report, and click a button to submit it for approval. These web-based processes replace the document-based approach. Instead of .doc and .xls files flying around you've got a single data format shared between the browser, email, database, and Office applications: XML.

Think of all the information where you work as a giant stream of XML data. You navigate the stream using your browser and you use Office applications to reach in and get, add, or change things (Figure 1-1).

Figure 1-1. Rider on the stream

How the Pieces Fit

The preceding analogy isn't as silly as it looks. To break it down a bit, consider the pieces that make up the new Excel features:

- Workspaces and lists are documents and document fragments that you create in Excel and share through SharePoint services.
- Lists exist as XML data which is imported or exported through Excel.
- These pieces all interoperate by means of web services.
- Finally, InfoPath is the form engine that collects data and stores it as XML.

Figure 1-2 illustrates how these pieces fit together. The XML flowing between each piece is called a *data stream*. Figure 1-1 is not really off the mark.

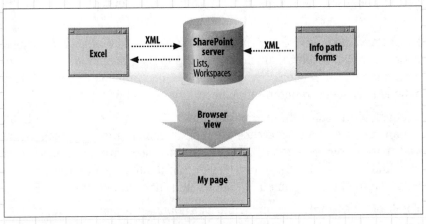

Figure 1-2. XML-based features cooperate behind the scenes

Underlying this interaction are two pieces that I don't know how to fit into Figure 1-2 legibly:

Things that make life easier for some often make things more complicated for someone else (in this case, us). Understanding XML and its related standards is a major undertaking. Fortunately, Office often lets you take a high-level view.

If you explore a SharePoint server, you won't find any list, workspace, or even XML "files" – it's all stored in SQL! In fact, that's the way the next generation of Windows works; Longhorn is backed by SQL.

- You can program Excel and these other components using Visual Basic .NET. You can still use VBA in Excel, but VB.NET provides a better programming platform for working with XML, web services, and InfoPath.
- Security controls access throughout the system. Office 2003 uses established techniques, such as digital signatures, and introduces permissions through Information Rights Management (IRM).

Try It

That's the grand vision, but even if you don't intend to install SharePoint or build a web-based interface to your business processes, you can still make use of the new Excel features. Table 1-1 is a guide to the new Excel features, where they are located in this book, and how to use them.

Table 1-1. Guide to Excel 2003 features

Feature	Look here	Use to
Workspaces and lists	Chapter 2	Share workbooks and ranges of cells. Sort and filter ranges of cells. Control user access to shared items.
XML	Chapter 3	Transform spreadsheets into HTML and other formats. Transform XML data files into workbooks. Map XML data to ranges of cells.
Web services	Chapter 4	Get dynamic results from the Web. Control remote components, such as SharePoint lists, through VBA code.
.NET programmability	Chapter 5	Build .NET components to use from Excel. Work with Excel from VB.NET. Create Excel .NET applications.
Security	Chapter 6	Password-protect workbooks and ranges. Control user access to ranges. Restrict permissions on workbooks. Digitally sign workbooks and macros. Distribute Excel security settings.
InfoPath	Chapter 7	Create XML data entry forms. Link a form to a database or web service. Validate data entries. Convert from data to HTML. Program InfoPath forms in VBScript or VB.NET.

Is Excel 2003 a big deal? On the surface, not much has changed — there are a handful of new objects and the user interface of Excel is largely the same. Underneath that are fundamental shifts implied by the new features: Lists, XML, web services, .NET, and InfoPath build a framework for entirely new ways to exchange data with Excel.

If you get stuck trying to follow along, open the sample ch01.xls to see how I did it.

The following sections provide quick tutorials on using the new Excel features together. There is more detail in the chapters, including how the new approaches compare to features from earlier versions of Excel, but let's not get bogged down in those details here. This is a great place to get up and running quickly, as well as get a top-level view of what's new.

Kick-Start Lists and XML

To see how Excel's list and XML features work, start Excel and follow these steps:

1. Choose File → Open, type *http://www.mstrainingkits.com/Excel/ExcelObjects.xml*, and click OK. Excel asks you how you want to open the file (Figure 1-3).

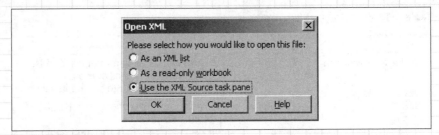

Figure 1-3. Opening an XML file in Excel

2. Choose Use the XML Source task pane and click OK. As shown in Figure 1-4, Excel asks if it's OK to create a schema.

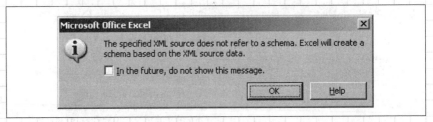

Figure 1-4. Excel offers to do some work for you

3. Click OK, and Excel reads the XML file and generates a view of the data it contains in the XML Source task pane, like that in Figure 1-5.

4. Drag these elements from the object folder to adjacent cells in a row: introduced, topic, name, and docString. Excel creates a list on the worksheet (Figure 1-6).

Chapter 1: Program the New Excel

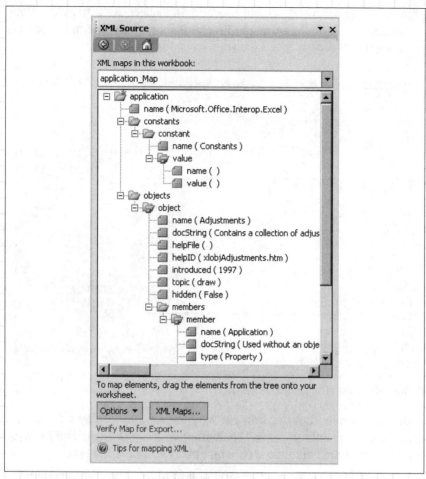

Figure 1-5. The XML Source task pane in Excel

	A	B	C	D	E	F
1						
2						
3						
4		introduce ▾	topic ▾	name ▾	docString ▾	
5		*				
6						
7						
8						

Figure 1-6. An XML-based worksheet list in Excel

5. Choose Data → XML → Refresh XML Data. Excel downloads the list of Excel VBA objects from the file.

6. Click the introduced column heading and select 2003 from the drop-down list. Excel filters the list to display only the new objects (Figure 1-7).

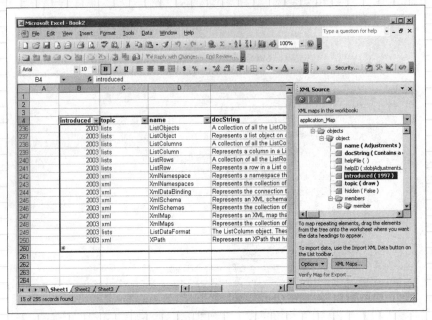

Figure 1-7. A list of the new Excel objects

That's pretty neat, but docString is way too long to display on screen. I like using Comments to display multiline text in worksheets and because we're all programmers here, you won't mind writing a little code:

1. Start the Visual Basic editor and open ThisWorkbook in a code window.

2. Select Workbook from code window's the object list and AfterXmlImport in the event list and add the following code:

```
Private Sub Workbook_AfterXmlImport(ByVal Map As XmlMap, _
    ByVal IsRefresh As Boolean, ByVal Result As XlXmlImportResult)
    Dim cel As Range, ws As Worksheet, rng As Range
    Set ws = ThisWorkbook.Worksheets("Sheet1")
    Set rng = ws.ListObjects("List1").ListColumns("name").Range
    For Each cel In rng
        If Not (cel.Comment Is Nothing) Then cel.Comment.Delete
        cel.AddComment cel.offset(0, 1).Text
    Next
End Sub
```

3. Return to the worksheet, select the docstring column, and then hide it (Format → Column → Hide Column).

4. Update the list from the source XML (Data → XML → Refresh XML Data). After Excel refreshes the list it runs the code you wrote to add comments cells in the name column (Figure 1-8).

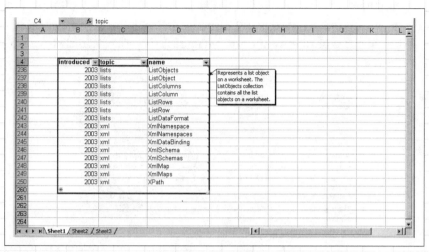

Figure 1-8. Descriptions display as comments after a little code

Kick-Start SharePoint

Wow, you're so proud of your work you want others to be able to use it. To share the list, publish it to a SharePoint site:

1. Click anywhere on the list and then choose Data → List → Publish List. Excel displays the first step of the Publishing Wizard (Figure 1-9).

If you don't have SharePoint, look ahead to Chapter 2 to find out how to set one for a free trial online (it only takes a few minutes).

Figure 1-9. Starting to publish a list to SharePoint

2. Specify the address of your SharePoint site and give the list a name and description. Click Next. If you aren't logged on to your site, Excel displays a sign-on dialog box for you to enter your user name and password.

3. Once you're signed on, Excel displays the columns that make up the list, along with their data types (Figure 1-10). Click Finish to create the list.

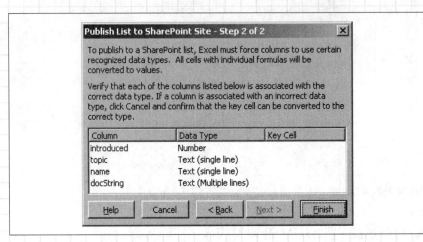

Figure 1-10. Choosing types for SharePoint

4. After SharePoint creates the list, it passes the address of the list back to Excel, which displays it in a success message (Figure 1-11).

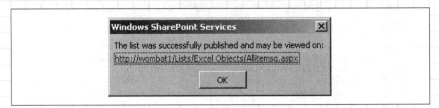

Figure 1-11. Success!

5. Just to make sure that it worked, click on the link in the previous success message. Excel displays the list on the SharePoint site in a browser window, as shown in Figure 1-12.

The published list looks different from the way it did in Excel. For one thing, the code you wrote is gone. Only the data remains, but authorized teammates can edit that data, sort and filter it, add attachments, create new views, and export the list to documents.

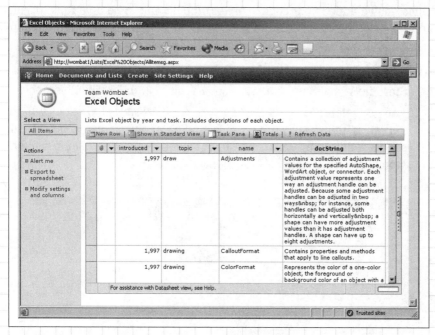

Figure 1-12. Publish the list to share it on the Web

Kick-Start Web Services

Perhaps you've looked at the object list in Figure 1-12 and thought what it really needs are code examples for each object, and hey, why not make them easy to cut and paste? You could add another column to the list, but since samples tend to be long it makes more sense to add them as attachments.

Adding attachments to a SharePoint list is straightforward: double-click the column with the paperclip icon on the row where you want to add an attachment. SharePoint displays a dialog box that lets you add file attachments, like the one in Figure 1-13.

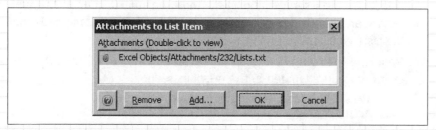

Figure 1-13. Attachments in SharePoint

If you don't have the Web Service References menu option, you need to install the Office Web Services Toolkit. See Chapter 4 for more information.

Once you've added your code samples, you'll want to be able to get them from your workbook, but there's no Excel object or method that lets you get list attachments. To do that, you'll need to use the Lists web service.

To see how this works, follow these steps:

1. Start the Visual Basic editor. Choose Tools → Web Service References.

2. Add a reference to *http://server/_vti_bin/lists.asmx?wsdl*, where *server* is the domain name of your SharePoint server. Figure 1-14 shows adding a web reference to my local SharePoint server, wombat1.

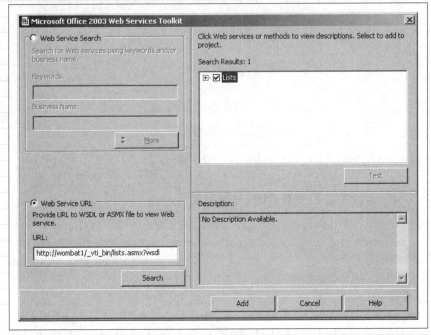

Figure 1-14. Adding a reference to a SharePoint server using the Office 2003 Web Services Toolkit

3. Select the Lists service and click Add. The toolkit queries the web service and builds a proxy class that you can use to call methods that the Lists web service provides.

4. Make the following changes (shown in **bold**) to the AfterXmlImport event procedure created in the previous section:

```
Private Sub Workbook_AfterXmlImport(ByVal Map As XmlMap, _
    ByVal IsRefresh As Boolean, ByVal Result As XlXmlImportResult)
    Dim cel As Range, ws As Worksheet, rng As Range
    ' Create Web service object.
    Dim lws As New clsws_Lists, xn As IXMLDOMNodeList, rowID As Integer
```

```
Set ws = ThisWorkbook.Worksheets("Sheet1")
Set rng = ws.ListObjects("List1").ListColumns("name").Range
For Each cel In rng
    If Not (cel.Comment Is Nothing) Then cel.Comment.Delete
    cel.AddComment cel.offset(0, 1).Text
    ' Get row ID
    rowID = cel.row - rng.row
    ' If row ID is between 1 and the # of items in list
    If rowID > 0 And rowID < rng.Rows.Count - 1 Then
        ' Get the list of attachments through SharePoint Web _
            service.
        Set xn = lws.wsm_GetAttachmentCollection("Excel Objects",_
            rowID)
        ' If there is an attachment
        If xn.Item(0).Text <> "" Then
            ' Add a hyperlink for the attachment
            ws.Hyperlinks.Add cel.offset(0, 2), _
                xn.Item(0).Text, , _
                "Click to view sample", _
                "Code sample"
        End If
    End If
Next
End Sub
```

5. In the workbook, refresh the XML data (Data → XML → Refresh XML Data). The code adds hyperlinks for each attachment in the SharePoint list (Figure 1-15).

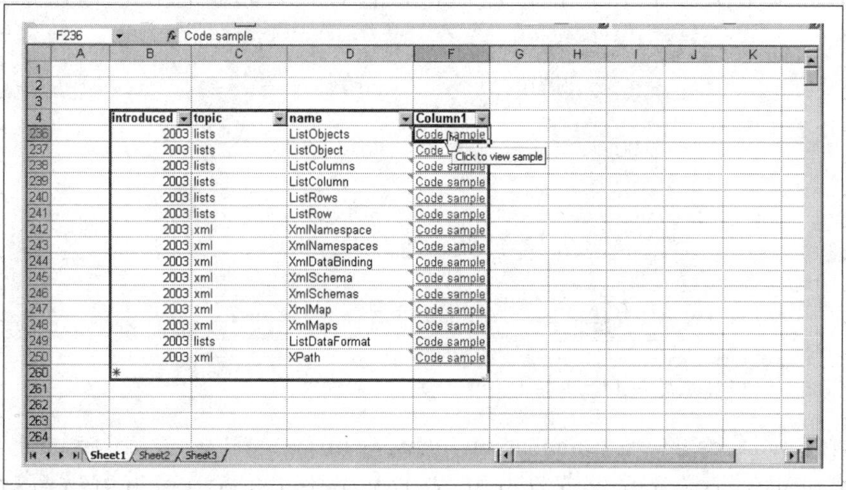

Figure 1-15. Using the Lists web service to add hyperlinks to attachments in a SharePoint list

Clicking on any of the links in Figure 1-15 displays the attachment from SharePoint in the browser, as shown in Figure 1-16.

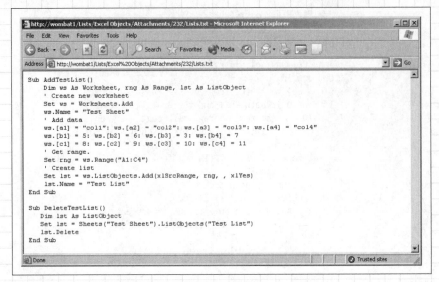

Figure 1-16. Click the link to view the code sample from SharePoint

Kick-Start Security and .NET

If you save and close the workbook you just created, you'll see the warning in Figure 1-17 the next time you open it:

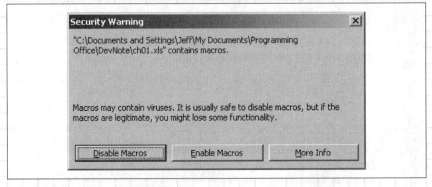

Figure 1-17. Macro security warning in Excel

You're probably very familiar with this warning, and you also probably know that if you digitally sign the code from within the Visual Basic editor, you can change the warning to look something like Figure 1-18.

That's a little less frightening, and if you (or your users) select Always trust macros from this publisher, Excel will automatically enable macros

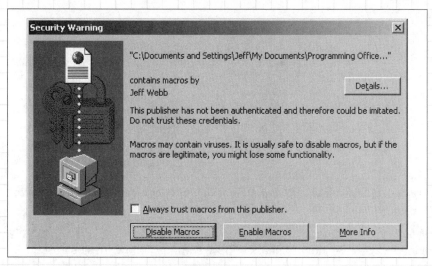

Figure 1-18. Signed macro security warning in Excel

that have your digital signature without warning—at least under the default security settings.

With Excel VBA, digital signatures are the only way to grant or deny the permission to run code on the user's machine. VBA code is distributed as workbooks, templates, or add-ins and the code in each of those files must be signed before it is trusted.

There are some problems with this approach: users may choose to trust a publisher who isn't trustworthy—trust is an all-or-nothing proposition—and updating macros means sending out new files to all users. Excel 2003 addresses these problems by allowing you to program workbooks using the .NET Framework and code-behind assemblies. The .NET Framework uses a different security model, based on levels of trust that can be assigned to locations, such as a folder on a public server where assemblies are stored.

When you program Excel 2003 in .NET, no code is stored with the workbook. Instead a special custom property tells Excel where to load the code from (Figure 1-19).

Since the workbook in Figure 1-19 contains no VBA code, the user never sees the macro security warning. And, if there are changes to the .NET code, the new assembly can simply be replaced on the server. Users get the new code the next time they open the workbook.

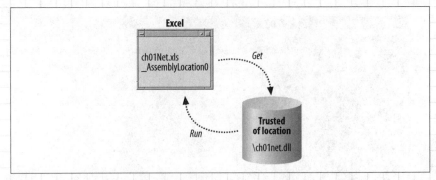

Figure 1-19. Excel loads .NET assemblies from trusted locations to perform automated tasks

Whether a location is trusted is determined by the user's .NET security configuration. To view or change these settings, follow these steps:

1. From the Windows Control Panel, choose Administrative Tools → Microsoft .NET Framework 1.1 Configuration, then click the Configure Code Access Security Policy link.

2. Expand the User, Code Groups, All_Code, Office_Projects treeview items, as shown in Figure 1-20.

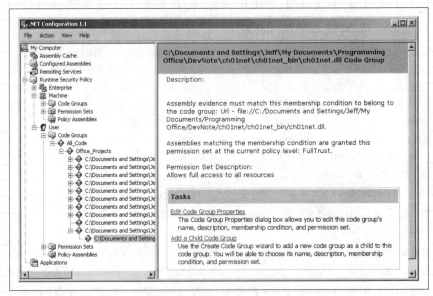

Figure 1-20. Configure .NET security settings to create a trusted location

3. Click the Edit Code Group Properties link to see the security settings for the group (Figure 1-21).

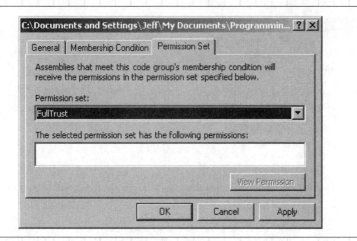

Figure 1-21. Grant FullTrust to allow all .NET code to run

To see how programming Excel from .NET works in practice, you'll need Visual Studio Tools for Office (VSTO). VSTO is purchased separately from Office. If you already have VSTO, you can follow these steps to implement our previous example in .NET:

1. Start Visual Studio .NET and choose File → New Project. If VSTO is installed, the New Project dialog box displays Excel Workbook as one of the project templates (Figure 1-22).

2. Create a new project using the Excel Workbook template and base the project on a new workbook. VSTO creates a new folder containing code files for the project.

3. Start Excel and open the workbook created by VSTO. Repeat the first procedure in "Kick-Start Lists and XML" to create a list from *http://www.mstrainingkits.com/Excel/ExcelObjects.xml*. (Don't write any VBA code, though.)

4. Save and close the workbook.

5. In VSTO, choose Project → Add a Web Reference to add a reference to the Lists web service at *http://server/_vti_bin/lists.asmx?wsdl* (Figure 1-23).

If you don't have VSTO, browse these steps to get an idea of whether VSTO is something you should buy.

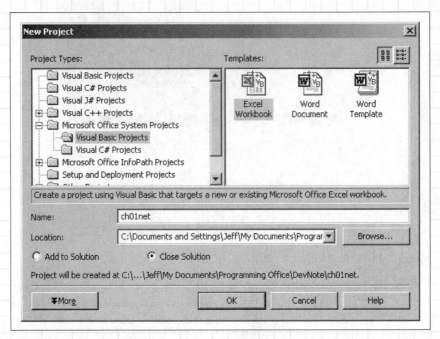

Figure 1-22. Project templates

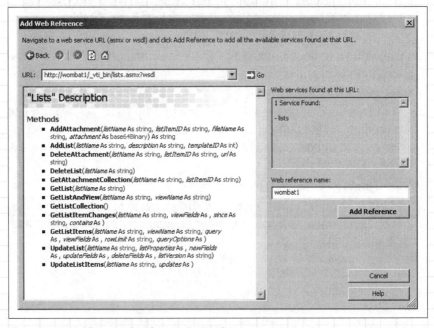

Figure 1-23. Adding a web reference in Excel

6. Open ThisWorkbook.vb in the VSTO code window and create the following event procedure.

```
Private Sub ThisWorkbook_AfterXmlImport( _
  ByVal Map As Microsoft.Office.Interop.Excel.XmlMap, _
  ByVal IsRefresh As Boolean, _
  ByVal Result As Microsoft.Office.Interop.Excel.XlXmlImportResult) _
  Handles ThisWorkbook.AfterXmlImport
    Dim cel As Excel.Range, ws As Excel.Worksheet, rng As Excel.Range
    ' Create Web service object.
    Dim lws As New wombat1.Lists, xn As System.XML.XmlNode, rowID As Integer
    ws = ThisWorkbook.Worksheets("Sheet1")
    rng = ws.ListObjects("List1").ListColumns("name").Range
    ' Pass Web service this application's credentials.
    lws.Credentials = System.Net.CredentialCache.DefaultCredentials
    ' Change from For Each because of problems with Excel's Range
      collection.
    For rowID = 1 To rng.Rows.Count - 1
        ' Get the single-cell range object for each row in the name column.
        cel = ws.Cells(rowID + rng.row, rng.Column)
        If Not (cel.Comment Is Nothing) Then cel.Comment.Delete()
        cel.AddComment (cel.offset(0, 1).Text)
        ' Get the list of attachments through SharePoint Web service.
        xn = lws.GetAttachmentCollection("Excel Objects", rowID)
        ' If there is an attachment
        If Not IsNothing(xn.Item("Attachment")) Then
            ' Add a hyperlink for the attachment
            ws.Hyperlinks.Add(cel.Offset(0, 2), _
              xn.Item("Attachment").InnerText, , _
              "Click to view sample", _
              "Code sample")
        End If
    Next
  End Sub
```

7. Run the project (F5). Visual Studio builds the assembly and then opens the associated workbook in Excel.

8. Refresh the list in Excel (Data → XML → Refresh XML Data). Excel runs the code in the .NET assembly to add comments and hyperlinks.

You'll notice that the .NET code is only somewhat similar to the VBA code you created earlier. Visual Basic .NET is really a different language, with significant improvements over earlier versions of Basic. If you perform the tutorial, you'll also notice a number of gotchas that I should warn you about:

- VSTO only works with Excel 2003 and Word 2003. Earlier versions are not supported.

- If a .NET procedure fails, Excel just ignores the problem. To break on errors in VSTO, choose Debug → Exceptions, select Common Language Runtime Exceptions, and then select When an exception is thrown: Break into the debugger.

- You can't make changes to .NET code while you are debugging. You must rebuild the assembly for changes to take effect. (This changes in the next version.)
- The Excel Range object isn't always recognized as a collection in .NET. To work around this, replace For Each loops with For...Next loops.
- Web service methods are called somewhat differently than in VBA. The .NET web service tools allow you to specify security credentials for the user and provide slightly different objects as return values.
- The .NET code runs more slowly than the VBA version. Each call between Excel and the .NET assembly crosses a process boundary, which imposes overhead.

These aren't trivial problems, but if you can deal with them .NET provides a more advanced security and deployment model than VBA. Also, .NET provides a single development platform for working with other applications, which I'll talk about next.

Kick-Start InfoPath

The list we just created on SharePoint isn't perfect. Some of the items in the topic column are inconsistent and the docstring text could use a bit of a rewrite. You can edit the list directly in SharePoint or Excel, but those tools aren't best suited to editing paragraphs of text or maintaining consistency among entries. A better solution is to use InfoPath to create a data-entry form for the list's XML.

To see how this works:

1. From Excel, export the list as XML data (choose Data → XML → Export). Name the exported file *ExcelObjectList.xml*.

2. Start InfoPath, choose Design a Form then choose New From XML Document or Schema in the task pane. InfoPath starts the Data Source Wizard.

3. Specify the file you just exported, click Next, then click Finish. InfoPath creates a new empty form template with the schema generated from *ExcelObjectList.xml* displayed in the task pane.

4. Drag the name, introduced, topic, and docstring elements onto the form as shown in Figure 1-24.

5. Right-click the docstring field on the form and select Text Box Properties. Set the display properties to allow paragraph breaks and wrap text (Figure 1-25).

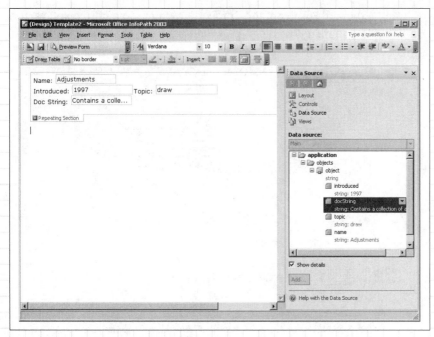

Figure 1-24. Creating a form in InfoPath

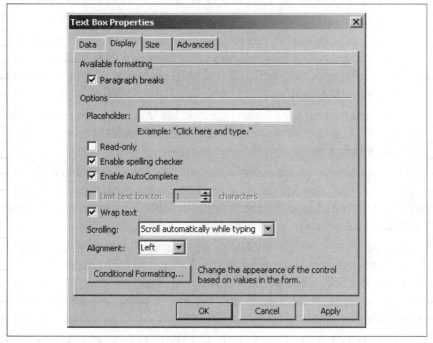

Figure 1-25. Setting text properties in InfoPath.

6. Click Preview Form on the InfoPath toolbar. InfoPath displays the XML file (Figure 1-26).

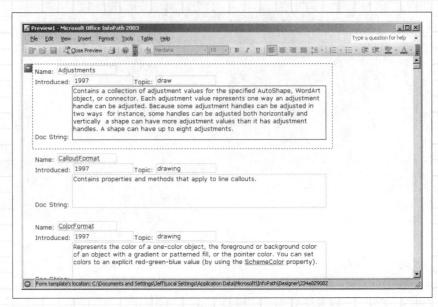

Figure 1-26. Previewing the XML data in InfoPath

The Preview mode displays what the form will look like for data entry; you can make edits, but you can't save data while previewing. One thing you'll notice right off is that InfoPath underlines words it thinks are misspelled, such as CalloutFormat. If you right-click that word and choose Spelling, you get help in the task pane (see Figure 1-27).

That's kind of a neat idea for a form tool, but you can do standard form tasks as well, such as specifying required fields, validating data, selecting values from a set of predefined entries, etc.

Figure 1-28 shows an improved form that filters the data to display one object at a time. The form uses a secondary data source to supply predefined values for the introduced and topic fields. This ensures that those entries are consistent.

I purposely skip steps in the design process here. Those steps are covered in Chapter 7.

If you save the template at this point, you can open it from Window Explorer to add or change records. When you save the changes, InfoPath writes a new XML file. That new file has the same structure as the original *ExcelObjectsList.xml* and, in fact, you can re-import it back in to Excel to load the changes made through InfoPath.

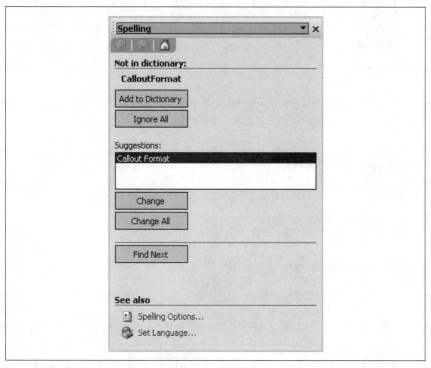

Figure 1-27. InfoPath displays spelling suggestions in the task pane

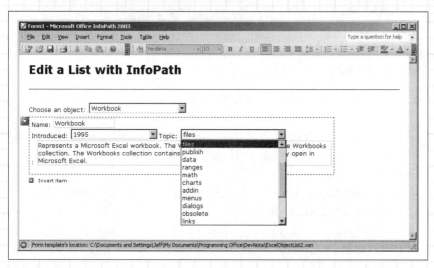

Figure 1-28. Improved form with filtering, drop-downs, and a secondary data source

Excel and InfoPath share Visual Basic .NET as a common programming language. That means you can automate the editing of a list in InfoPath, then reloading it in Excel through VSTO. To see how this works, close InfoPath and open the project created in "Kick-Start Security and .NET", then follow these steps:

In order to program InfoPath with .NET, you must install the InfoPath SPI and .NET Toolkit from http://www. microsoft.com/ downloads.

1. In VSTO, choose File → Add Project → New Project and select the Info-Path Form Template, as shown in Figure 1-29.

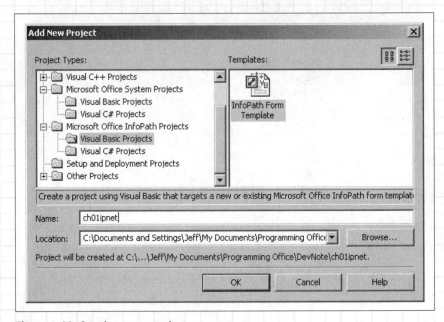

Figure 1-29. Creating a new project

2. VSTO starts the Project Wizard. Specify an existing template using the form template you just created, as shown in Figure 1-30.

3. When you click Finish, VSTO copies the template into a new project folder and creates .NET code-behind files for the InfoPath project, shown in Figure 1-31.

4. In the InfoPath project, add a reference to the COM object Microsoft Excel 11.0 Object Library.

5. In the Excel project, add a reference to the COM object Microsoft Info-Path 1.0 Type Library.

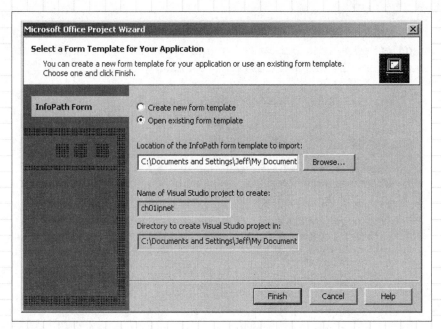

Figure 1-30. Selecting a template

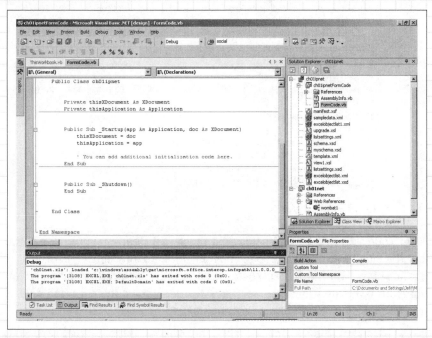

Figure 1-31. A VSTO solution containing Excel and InfoPath projects

You can now write Visual Basic .NET code that controls both the workbook and the InfoPath form. For example, you might want to add a command button next to the Excel list that opens the list in InfoPath for editing. The .NET code in the Excel project might look like this:

```
' Create object variable to get events from command button.
Friend WithEvents cmdEditList As MSForms.CommandButton

' Called when the workbook is opened.
Private Sub ThisWorkbook_Open() Handles ThisWorkbook.Open
    ' Initialize command button variable to hook in to events.
    cmdEditList = CType(FindControl("cmdEditList"), _
    MSForms.CommandButton)
End Sub

Private Sub cmdEditList_Click() Handles cmdEditList.Click
    ' Export list (to make sure data is current).
    Dim ws As Excel.Worksheet, pth As String, ippth As String, xmlObj = "",_
    xmlData As String
    pth = ThisWorkbook.Path
    ws = ThisWorkbook.Worksheets("Sheet1")
    ' Get XML data from list.
    ws.ListObjects("List1").XmlMap.ExportXml (xmlObj)
    ' Convert to a string (circumvents Excel COM bug).
    xmlData = CType(xmlObj, String)
    ' Edit the XML to add InfoPath's processing instructions.
    Dim ipinst As System.IO.StreamReader
    ipinst = System.IO.File.OpenText(pth & "\ipinst.txt")
    xmlData = xmlData.Replace("<application>", ipinst.ReadToEnd)
    ipinst.Close()
    ' Write the modified XML file to disk.
    Dim xmlFile As New System.IO.StreamWriter(pth & "\ExcelObjectsList.xml",_
    False)
    xmlFile.Write (xmlData)
    xmlFile.Close()
    ' Start InfoPath and import the data.
    Dim ip As New Microsoft.Office.Interop.InfoPath.ExternalApplication
    ' Open a new form from the template.
    ip.Open (pth & "\ExcelObjectsList.xml")
    ' Close this workbook
    ThisWorkbook.Close(True)
End Sub
```

That code is a little complicated, but most of it deals with changing the header of the exported XML to include InfoPath processing instructions (included in the file ipinst.txt) to associate the saved XML file with an InfoPath template. Once you've made those changes, the exported XML is recognized by InfoPath and so can be opened.

Now, if you run the project and click the Edit List button, Excel saves the list as an InfoPath form, then opens that form for editing (Figure 1-32).

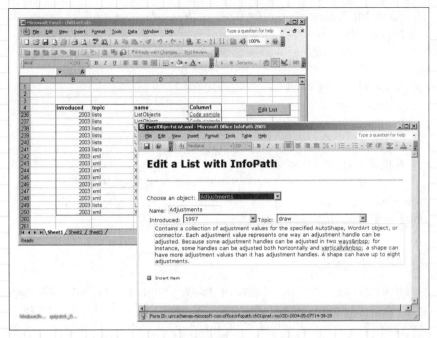

Figure 1-32. Edit Excel list using an InfoPath form

Once you're in InfoPath, you probably want to update the Excel list when the form closes. Since Excel can simply re-import data from the InfoPath form file, the .NET code to do that is pretty simple:

```
' In InfoPath project.
Public Sub _Shutdown()
    ' Start Excel.
    Dim xl As New Microsoft.Office.Interop.Excel.Application
    Dim wb As Microsoft.Office.Interop.Excel.Workbook
    Dim lo As Microsoft.Office.Interop.Excel.ListObject
    Dim pth As String
    ' Make Excel visible.
    xl.Visible = True
    ' Open the Excel workbook.
    pth = System.IO.Path.GetFullPath(".")
    wb = xl.Workbooks.Open(pth & "\ch01net.xls")
    ' Get the list and import the XML.
    lo = wb.Worksheets("Sheet1").ListObjects("List1")
    lo.XmlMap.ImportXml(thisXDocument.DOM.xml)
End Sub
```

However, InfoPath is very security-aware, so you need to take special steps to ensure that the form is permitted access to Excel and other resources on your computer. To do that you must:

1. Close InfoPath and edit the file *manifest.xsf* in the InfoPath project to remove the following attribute:

   ```
   publishUrl="C:\Documents and Settings\Jeff\My Documents\Programming
   Office\DevNote\ch01ipnet\manifest.xsf"
   ```

2. Replace the following attribute:

   ```
   trustSetting="automatic"
   ```

3. With this one:

   ```
   requireFullTrust="yes"
   ```

4. Run a script to register the form on your machine. I include the script *Register.vbs* with the sample project and explain it in Chapter 7.

When you run the project, the Excel list is updated after you finish your edits and close InfoPath.

What Next?

Using Excel and InfoPath together takes you full circle through lists, SharePoint, XML, web services, security, and .NET. I hope these examples gave you a good idea of what these features have in common, how they can be used together, and how they might be useful to you.

There are a couple of points I want you to take away from this experience:

- If you don't know XML, learning it will help your career as a programmer.
- Ditto for .NET.

There is still a great deal that can be done with VBA and non-XML approaches to sharing data in Excel, but XML and .NET are the next wave. Ignore it at your own risk.

I didn't give much detail on the how or why of any of these kick-start tutorials. Rest assured, I offer much more detail in the following chapters. My goal here is to help you decide if this approach is right for you, and (hopefully) get you a little excited about it.

CHAPTER 2

Share Workspaces and Lists

If you've ever tried to collaborate on a budget, project bid, or other team-oriented workbook in Excel, you know that just putting the .xls file up on a public server somewhere doesn't cut it. Only one person can edit the workbook at a time, and if somebody leaves the file open, the rest of the team is locked out till you find out who the culprit is and get him to close his session.

Earlier versions of Excel solved this problem with *shared workbooks*, which let more than one user have a single workbook open for editing. Changes are merged automatically, and conflicting changes can be resolved. That's great, but it's a file-based system, so there is no way to manage the document's users, notify teammates of changes, assign tasks, or do other team-oriented work.

Microsoft Excel 2003 finally solves these problems with *shared workspaces* and *shared lists*. This solution is server-based (Windows 2003 server-based, in fact) and integrated right into the Excel menus and object model.

Get SharePoint Services

If you don't have SharePoint Services, you need it. I don't care if you work alone from your home office (as I do). SharePoint is too useful to pass up and it's *free*...well, kind of. SharePoint Services are actually part of Windows 2003 so if you have Windows Server 2003 already, you can download the installation from Microsoft and install it fairly easily.

If you don't have Windows Server 2003, you can sign up for a free 30-day trial though one of the SharePoint hosting providers. These third parties are a lot like the web hosting services you can find on the Internet. You get an account with some space on their server. You can administer your site yourself through a web-based interface, and after the free trial period, they'll bill you monthly.

How to do it

I recommend you use the 30-day free trial of SharePoint before install-ing it on Windows 2003. There are several reasons for this:

- It's free
- It's painless
- It's quick

Then, if you like it, go ahead and put it on your server. To get a free SharePoint site:

1. Go to *http://www.sharepointtrial.com/default.aspx*.
2. Follow the sign up instructions.
3. Wait for email confirming your site has been created.

If everything goes correctly, you'll get a new SharePoint site that looks something like Figure 2-1.

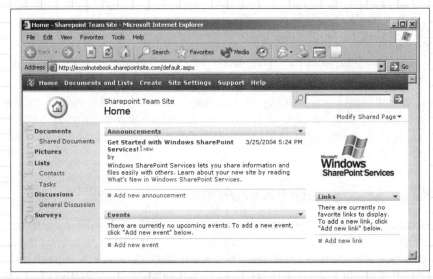

Figure 2-1. Voila! A free SharePoint site courtesy of Apptix

At this point, you can move on in the notebook to experiment with shar-ing workspaces and lists or you can just mess around with your new SharePoint site for a while, changing its main page (click Modify Shared

Page), adding users (click Site Settings → Manage Users), adding a welcome announcement (click Add new announcement), and posting your vacation pictures (click Pictures → Create Picture Library). Get a feel for what it can do. If you think it will be useful, come back here and read about installing it on your Windows Server 2003.

Hey, you're back! OK, to install SharePoint on Windows Server 2003:

1. Sign on to your server as a user with administrative privileges.

2. Download SharePoint Services installation from *http://www.microsoft.com/windowsserver2003/techinfo/sharepoint/wss.mspx* and save it to disk.

3. Run the installation (*STSV2.EXE*).

Once installation completes, your server will provide a default web site similar to what is shown in Figure 2-2.

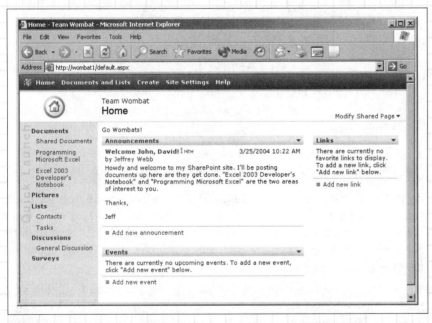

Figure 2-2. SharePoint creates a default site on your server (this is mine)

How it works

If you look on your server after installing SharePoint, you'll have a very hard time finding exactly where Default.aspx in Figure 2-2 is coming from. SharePoint installs that web site in the *C:\Program Files\Common Files\Microsoft Shared\Web Server Extensions\60\TEMPLATE\1033\STS* folder by default. If you look at Default.aspx in Notepad, you won't see any of the content (I won't even bother to show the HTML for that page here—it's not very informative).

Where's the content? SharePoint puts most of it in a SQL database. If you don't have SQL Server on your system when you install SharePoint, SharePoint installs the Microsoft SQL Data Engine (MSDE), which is a stripped-down version of the SQL runtime. MSDE lets applications, such as SharePoint, create and access SQL databases.

The web pages you see at your SharePoint site are Active Server .NET Pages (ASP.NET in Micro-speak). Those pages are little more than templates for the content retrieved from the SQL database. ASP.NET is part of the .NET Framework, and it runs under the Microsoft Internet Information Service, 6.0 (IIS 6.0). See Figure 2-3.

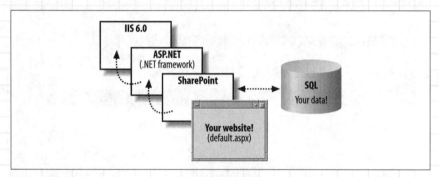

Figure 2-3. The many layers of a SharePoint web site

If your server was already hosting ASP.NET web sites, SharePoint takes over. You'll need to take special steps to host other web sites on your SharePoint Server. Web server administration and ASP.NET programming are enormous topics. If you're interested, I wrote an 850 page book on the subject last year.

The beauty of using SharePoint, is that you don't need to read that long book. SharePoint creates any new ASP.NET web pages you need and populates them with data from SQL. You create new pages, sub-webs, documents, etc., through SharePoint's web-based interface.

What about...

To	Look here
Try SharePoint free for 30 days	*http://www.sharepointtrial.com/ default.aspx*

To	Look here
Download SharePoint Services for Windows 2003	*http://www.microsoft.com/ windowsserver2003/techinfo/share-point/wss.mspx*
Compare SharePoint Portal and SharePoint Services	*http://www.microsoft.com/office/ sharepoint/prodinfo/relationship. mspx*
Have SharePoint coexist with other web applications (such as Exchange server)	*http://support.microsoft.com/default. aspx?scid=kb;en-us;823265&Prod-uct=winsps*

Create a Shared Workspace

Excel calls workbooks shared through SharePoint *shared workspaces* or sometimes *shared lists*. The Excel documentation isn't always careful about it, but there is a difference:

- *Shared workspaces* are entire documents stored on SharePoint.
- *Shared lists* are parts of documents stored on SharePoint.

How you share those two things is different, so, first-things-first, let's talk about shared workspaces.

How to do it

Once you've signed up for a trial SharePoint site or installed SharePoint on your own server, you'll have an address (also know as a URL) for your site. Write that down. My SharePoint URLs are:

//excelnotebook.sharepointsite.com
> For my trial site from Apptix. This is available to me over the Web from anywhere.

//wombat1
> For my local site on my local server. This is the URL I use for accessing the server from my local, home network.

//65.11.195.07 (not my real IP address for security reasons)
> For my local server over the Web. This is the IP address my Internet provider assigned me, and I haven't bothered to associate it with a domain name since I don't expose that server to the public very often.

I can use any of those URLs to share a workbook, though //wombat1/ is the quickest since it goes over a very fast local network connection. To share a workbook through your SharePoint site:

Shared workspaces are a big improvement over shared workbooks—Excel's earlier feature that allowed multiple users to share edits. For one thing, workspaces provide tools to manage a workbook's users or send out notices to those users.

Don't confuse
Tools → Share
Workspace with
File → Save
Workspace. Save
Workspace creates
an .xlw file that
stores your Excel
windows and
open documents.
Also don't confuse
it with Tools →
Share Workbook—
Share Workbook is
the old way of
allowing multiple
authors access.

1. If this is the first time you are using your SharePoint site, add its URL to your Trusted Sites list. From within Internet Explorer, select Tools → Internet Options → Security tab and add the URL to the Trusted Sites zone. You have to close and restart Excel for Excel to recognize new trusted sites.

2. Open the workbook to share in Excel and select Tools → Shared Workspace. Excel displays the Shared Workspace task pane.

3. Type the URL of your SharePoint site in the Locate for new workspace box and click Create.

4. The SharePoint site may ask you to sign in. If it's a trial site, sign in using the username and password provided by your provider. If it's your own server, use your Windows username and password for the server.

5. Once the workbook is shared, Excel changes the task pane. You can click on Open site in browser to view the new shared workspace.

Figures 2-4 through 2-7 illustrate these steps.

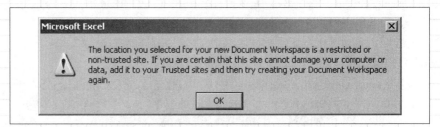

Figure 2-4. Step 1-you'll see this if you haven't added the SharePoint URL to your Trusted Sites in Internet Explorer

How it works

Excel connects to the SharePoint site and creates a new document workspace for each workbook you share from Excel. The workbook stored locally on your computer is now linked to the workbook stored on SharePoint. If you save the workbook, changes are saved locally and then sent to the server. If you close and then reopen the local workbook, Excel connects to SharePoint to get any changes from others.

Each new workspace has its own folder on the site. This relationship, one file per folder, may seem a little strange, but it has to do with the way ASP.NET controls access for other users. You'll learn more about that later. You can put additional documents in the workspace folder by clicking Add new document on the workspace page (Figure 2-7).

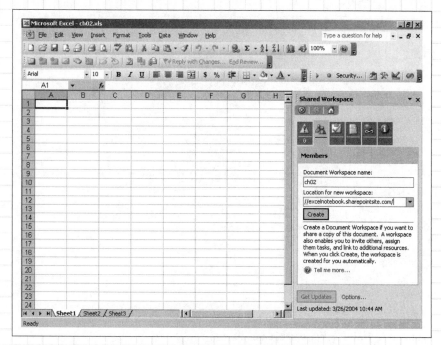

Figure 2-5. Steps 2 and 3—Create the shared workspace

Figure 2-6. Step 4—Sign on to the SharePoint site

You can control how the workbook displays the Shared Workspace task pane and how updates are handled by clicking Options on the task pane (Figure 2-8.)

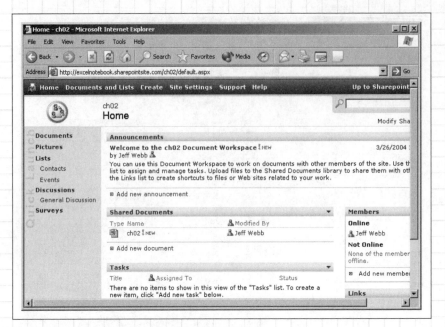

Figure 2-7. Finito!—The workbook is shared

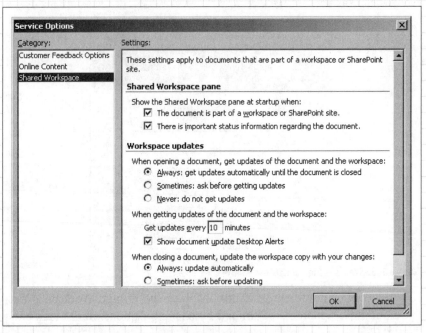

Figure 2-8. Shared Workspace options set how updates, alerts, and the task pane are handled

Share a Workbook

Anything you can do through the task pane, you can also do in code—actually, you can do more.

Use the Workbook object's `SharedWorkspace` property to work with shared workspaces in Excel. The `SharedWorkspace` property returns a SharedWorkspace object that you use to share the workbook, update the workbook, and navigate among other elements in the shared workspace.

How to do it

Use the SharedWorkspace object's `CreateNew` method to create a new shared workspace and add a workbook to it:

```
ThisWorkbook.Save
ThisWorkbook.SharedWorkspace.CreateNew _
"http://excelnotebook.sharepointsite.com", "ch02"
```

You must save the workbook before adding it to a shared workspace, otherwise the `CreateNew` method fails. The preceding code adds the current workbook to the SharePoint site on the excelnotebook.sharepointsite.com server. If you click on Open site in browser in the Excel Shared Workspace pane, Excel displays the new workspace created at *http://excelnotebook.sharepointsite.com/ch02* (Figure 2-7).

If you call CreateNew again, Excel will create another, new workspace and increment the site name to *http://excelnotebook.sharepointsite.com/ch02(1)*. Remember, Excel creates one workspace folder per document.

In some cases, you may want to add other documents to an existing workspace. To do that, follow these steps:

1. Open an existing document from the SharePoint site.
2. Get a reference to that document's SharedWorkspace object.
3. Add your workbook to the SharedWorkspace object's Files collection.
4. Close the document you opened in Step 1.
5. Close the workbook you just added and reopen it from the SharePoint site.

So if you're starting with a workbook that has already been shared, you can use that workbook's `SharedWorkspace` property to add other files to the same workspace:

You can do a lot with shared workspaces through the SharePoint site and the Excel task pane, but by understanding the object model you can customize sharing (almost) any way you like.

Use the
Connected
property to check
if a workbook is
part of a
workspace. The
SharedWork-
space property
always returns an
object, even if
the workbook has
not been shared.

```
Dim sw As SharedWorkspace, dlg As FileDialog, fil as String
If ThisWorkbook.SharedWorkspace.Connected Then
    Set sw = ThisWorkbook.SharedWorkspace
    ' Get a file to add.
    Set dlg = Application.FileDialog(msoFileDialogOpen)
    dlg.Title = "Add file to shared workspace."
    dlg.AllowMultiSelect = True
    dlg.Show
    For Each fil In dlg.SelectedItems
        sw.Files.Add fil, , , True
    Next
End If
```

How it works

The preceding code checks if the current workbook is shared
(ThisWorkbook.Connected) and if it is, it gets a reference to the workbook's shared workspace.

Next, it displays Excel's File Open dialog to get the list of files to add to
the workspace. If the user selects one or more files, the For Each loop
adds each file to the SharedWorkspace object's File collection. The last
argument of Add links the local file to the workspace.

Open a Shared Workbook

Use sharepointobj.
Files.Add to add
files to an existing
workspace.
CreateNew
always creates a
new workspace
(which isn't
always what you
want).

If the local file is linked to a shared workspace, opening that file automatically connects to the SharePoint site and updates the local file. The
user may have to sign on to the SharePoint site, and Excel displays the
update status (Figure 2-9).

If the local workbook is not linked, or if the workbook is not stored
locally, you can open the workbook from the SharePoint site. If you
double-click on a workbook in the SharePoint site, Excel opens the
workbook as Read-Only. To open the workbook for editing, select Edit
from the pop-up menu on the site (Figure 2-10).

How to do it

To open a workbook from a shared workspace in code, simply use the
Workbooks collection's Open method. For linked workbooks, use the local
address of the file:

```
Application.Workbooks.Open "ch02.xls"
```

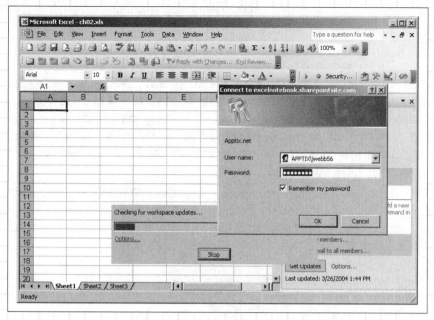

Figure 2-9. Opening a workbook linked to a shared workspace

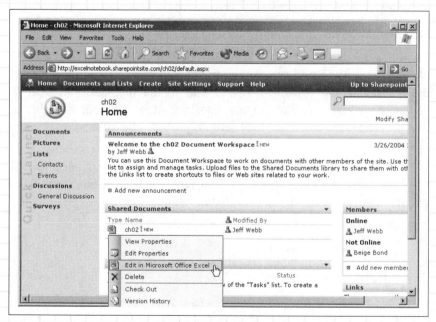

Figure 2-10. Opening a shared workbook from the SharePoint site

For workbooks that aren't stored locally, use the address of the workbook from the SharePoint site:

```
Application.Workbooks.Open "http://excelnotebook.sharepointsite.com/" & _
    "ch02/Shared Documents/ch02.xls"
```

Multiple users can have the same file open, and changes to the file are synchronized among users. If you want exclusive access to a file, you can choose Check Out in Figure 2-10 before opening the workbook for editing—*checking out* doesn't open the file, it just reserves it so other users can't make changes. You won't be able to check out the workbook if other users have the file open, however.

To check out a file from code, use the Workbooks collection's CanCheckOut property and the CheckOut method. For example, the following code attempts to check out a file, and if it is successful it opens the file in Excel:

```
fil = SPSITE & "/Shared Documents/ch02.xls"
If Application.Workbooks.CanCheckOut(fil) Then
    Application.Workbooks.CheckOut fil
    Set wb = Application.Workbooks.Open(fil)
    MsgBox wb.Name & " is checked out to you."
End If
```

How it works

You have to specify the full server path when checking out a file—SharePoint puts shared workbooks in the /Shared Documents folder of the workspace—so you have to add that to the filename you pass to CanCheckOut and CheckOut. Notice also that those methods are part of the Workbooks collection; they aren't part of the SharedWorkspace object.

The CheckOut method doesn't open the workbook, so you need to add the Open method, as shown above. However, checking a workbook back in automatically closes the file, as shown below:

```
Set wb = Application.Workbooks("ch02.xls")
If wb.CanCheckIn Then
    ' CheckIn closes the file.
    wb.CheckIn True, "Minor change"
    MsgBox "File was checked in."
Else
    MsgBox wb.Name & " could not be checked in."
End If
```

In some cases, a file may not be able to be checked in. For instance, you can't check in the current workbook from within its own code:

```
If ThisWorbook.CanCheckIn Then ' Always False!
```

The problem here is `ThisWorkbook`—you can only check the file back in from external code. In these cases, you can display the SharePoint site to provide a way to check the workbook back in. See the next topic for instructions.

Display a SharePoint Site

I have to admit that I wrote my own VBA procedure to do this at one point—but I didn't need to. The Workbook object's `FollowHyperlink` method provides a built-in way to display the SharePoint site or any web page using the default browser.

How to do it

The SharedWorkspace object provides a `URL` property that returns the address of the shared workspace. You can use this property or the SPSITE constant with the `FollowHyperlink` method to display the site:

```
ThisWorkbook.FollowHyperlink ThisWorkbook.SharedWorkspace.URL
```

Or:

```
ThisWorkbook.FollowHyperlink SPSITE
```

If you're going to perform an action on the current workbook, you may need to close the workbook as part of the process and display the Share-Point site. For example, you can't check a workbook back in from its own code. The following code warns the user that she can't check an open file in, and then it displays the SharePoint site:

```
Dim sw As SharedWorkspace, msg As String
Set sw = ThisWorkbook.SharedWorkspace
' Can't check ThisWorkbook in! Must close first.
If sw.Connected Then
    msg = "You must close this workbook before it can be checked in. " & _
      "OK to close? After closing you can check in from SharePoint."
    If MsgBox(msg, vbYesNo) = vbYes Then
        ThisWorkbook.Save
        ThisWorkbook.FollowHyperlink sw.URL
        ThisWorkbook.Close
    End If
End If
```

How it works

Because Excel doesn't wait for `FollowHyperlink` to finish, the preceding code works smoothly, saving and closing the workbook while the Share-Point site displays. `Close` has to be the last executable line, because after that, the code is unloaded (along with the workbook).

You might notice that you can't test CanCheckIn from the current workbook. It always returns False since Excel doesn't let you check it back in from code (this probably has something to do with CheckIn closing the workbook).

Perhaps a better solution to this problem is just to avoid it. If you're going to check workbooks in and out, don't write that code as part of a workbook. Make it part of an Addin instead.

What about...

Deleting files and managing the connection between a workbook and SharePoint are basic maintenance tasks. You need to understand the repercussions of those tasks as well as how to do them.

To learn about	Look here
The Workbook object	*C:\Program Files\Microsoft Office\OFFICE11\1033\ VBAXL10.CHM*

Remove Sharing

You can remove sharing from a workbook stored in a shared workspace at two levels:

- Delete the file from the SharePoint server. This breaks the connection for all users.
- Disconnect the local workbook from the shared workspace. This breaks the connection between the local copy of the workbook and the server.

How to do it

Use the RemoveDocument method to delete the current document from the shared workspace, as shown by the following code:

```
If ThisWorkbook.SharedWorkspace.Connected Then _
    ThisWorkbook.SharedWorkspace.RemoveDocument
```

The preceding code leaves local copies that users have downloaded from the shared workspace, but they become disconnected since the shared workbook no longer exists. Alternatively, you can leave the workbook in the shared workspace, but disconnect your local copy with this code:

```
If ThisWorkbook.SharedWorkspace.Connected Then _
    ThisWorkbook.SharedWorkspace.Disconnect
```

Now, the local copy can no longer be updated from, or send updates to, the shared workbook. If you want an updatable copy, you must reopen the workbook from the shared workspace. There's no way to reattach an existing local workbook to the server copy.

You can also use the Files collection to remove workbooks from a shared workspace. This technique works well if you want to remove a file other than the current workbook. For example, the following code removes *Security.xls* from the current workbook's shared workspace:

```
Dim file As Office.SharedWorkspaceFile
If ThisWorkbook.SharedWorkspace.Connected Then
    For Each file In ThisWorkbook.SharedWorkspace.Files
        If InStr(1, file.urlThisWorkbook, "security.xls") Then _
            file.Delete
    Next
End If
```

How it works

In the preceding code, you need to locate the file to remove using the Instr function—the Files collection doesn't provide an indexer to locate the file by name. Once you've located the file you want to remove, you can use the File object's Delete method to remove it.

After a shared workbook is removed from the server, any user who had a linked copy of the workbook is warned when he opens his local copy (Figure 2-11). The warning is only displayed the first time the file is opened.

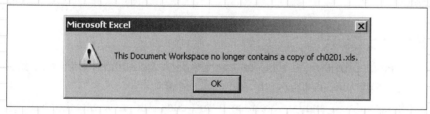

Figure 2-11. Users with linked copies see this warning when they open a file that has been removed

To avoid confusion, you may want to send email to team members before deleting files, as shown here:

```
Dim usr As SharedWorkspaceMember, tolist As String
' Get the email names of all members.
For Each usr In ThisWorkbook.SharedWorkspace.Members
    tolist = usr.Email & ";" & tolist
Next
' Send a notice.
ThisWorkbook.FollowHyperlink "mailto:" & tolist & _
    "?SUBJECT=Deleting " & ThisWorkbook.Name
```

The preceding code builds a list of email addresses from the workbook's Members collection, then starts the user's mail system by using the mailto protocol in a hyperlink. This is a quick-and-dirty way to send mail messages from inside Excel code. The mailto protocol has this form:

```
mailto:addresses?SUBJECT=subject;BODY=message
```

What about...

To learn about	Look here
The mailto protocol	*http://msdn.microsoft.com/workshop/ networking/predefined/mailto.asp*
The ShareWorkspace objects	*C:\Program Files\Microsoft Office\OFFICE11\ 1033\VBAOF11.CHM*

Add Users and Permissions

A workspace without members is a lonely place.

If you read the previous topic, you saw sample code using the Members collection, but so far we haven't added any members to the workspace. The user who creates the workspace is automatically a member, of course, but you can add other members and set their permissions either through the SharePoint site, through the Excel task pane, or through code.

How to do it

Adding members through Excel or through code does not send notification to those members, the way that adding members through the SharePoint site does.

SharePoint provides an easy-to-use interface for adding users and setting permissions, as shown in Figures 2-12 and 2-13.

Excel provides a similar interface if you click Add new member on the Shared Workspace task pane. To add users from code, use the Members collection's Add method:

```
Set sw = ThisWorkbook.SharedWorkspace
If sw.Connected Then
    sw.Members.Add "ExcelDemo@hotmail.com", "APPTIX\ExcelDemo", _
"Contributor"
End If
```

The last argument of the Add method sets the users' permissions, as shown in the following table.

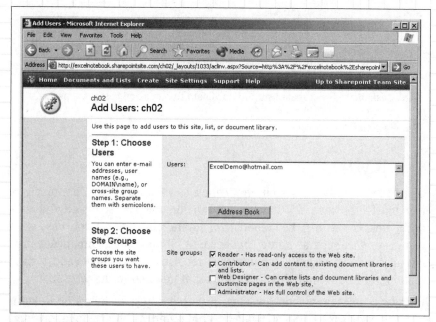

Figure 2-12. Click Add new member and SharePoint displays this form

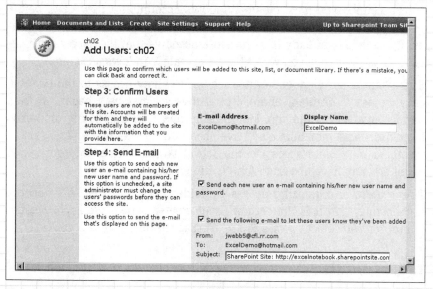

Figure 2-13. SharePoint creates accounts and notifies new members

Setting	Permission
Guest	No access by default, but can be granted access to specific items.
Reader	Read-only access to the site.
Contributor	Add content to existing document libraries and lists.
Web designer	Create lists and document libraries and customize pages in the site.
Administrator	Full control of the site.

How it works

SharePoint uses Windows authentication to validate users. That means a user must first have a Windows account on the server (or on the network) before she can be added to a SharePoint site. In the case of a hosted service, such as a free trial account, SharePoint automatically creates a Windows account whenever it receives a request to add a new member, then the SharePoint site adds that member to the workspace.

Automatic account creation is also available if you installed SharePoint on your own server, but it must be configured during installation, and you must be using Active Directory on your server. If you don't configure auto accounts, you must create Windows accounts for new user, before you can add those users as members to a site. In a corporate environment, users may already have network accounts that the server can validate—in those cases, you won't have to create Windows accounts.

SharePoint uses Windows authentication to allow access to the site, but once access is granted, SharePoint authorizes members based on their permissions within the site. Membership and permissions are organized by folder, so all members may have access to the site homepage, several members may have access to the /ch02 workspace, a different set of members may have access to /ch03, and so on.

This system of organizing access by folder is part of the .NET security architecture, and it is the reason Excel creates a new workspace folder whenever you select Tools → Share Workspace from a workbook.

What about...

To learn how to	Look here
Configure SharePoint Services to use Kerberos authentication	*http://support.microsoft.com/default. aspx?scid=kb;en-us;832769*

Allow Anonymous Users

Granting limited access to anonymous users makes your SharePoint site a public portal.

If your SharePoint site is used over the Internet, you may want to enable users who don't have Windows accounts on your server or network. This allows the general public access to some or all of your SharePoint site.

How to do it

SharePoint disables anonymous access when it is installed, so you must re-enable it in IIS and then authorize the anonymous user within the SharePoint site.

To enable anonymous access in IIS:

1. From your SharePoint server, start the IIS Services Manager. Select Start → All Programs → Administrative Tools → Internet Information Services (IIS) Manager.

2. Expand the treeview and select Default Web Site (Figure 2-14), then select Properties. IIS displays the web site's properties pages.

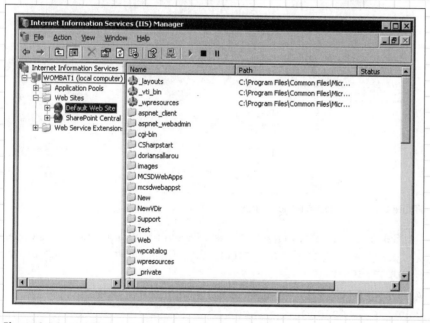

Figure 2-14. Use IIS to enable the default user

3. Select the Directory Security Tab, then click Edit in the Authentication and access control section. IIS displays the Authentication Methods dialog (Figure 2-15).

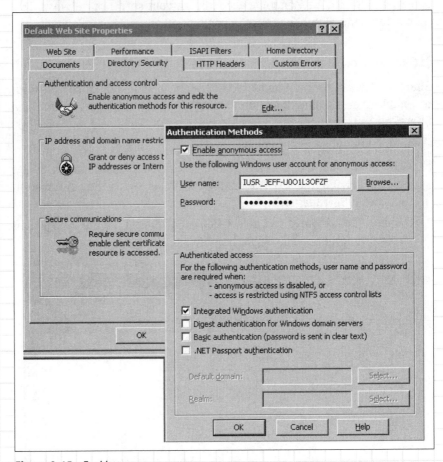

Figure 2-15. Enable anonymous access

4. Select Enable Anonymous Access. IIS maintains the anonymous user password, so don't worry about that. Click OK to close each of the open dialogs.

After enabling the default user in IIS, authorize that user for your Share-Point site. To do that:

1. From your SharePoint site, select Site Settings and click on Go to Site Administration. The Top-level Site Administration page diplays (Figure 2-16).

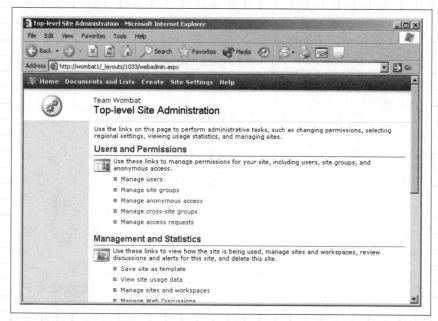

Figure 2-16. Use Site Administration to enable anonymous access

2. Click Manage anonymous access. The Anonymous Access page displays (Figure 2-17). Select the level of access to provide anonymous users, and click OK.

Enabling anonymous access for the entire web site allows unauthenticated users to view all of the folders in your site. Allowing access to lists and libraries restricts anonymous users to folders that have anonymous access specifically enabled. This is the most practical setting for most SharePoint sites since they usually contain a mix of public, and not-so-public, information.

To enable anonymous access to a specific list or workspace:

1. Follow the previous two procedures and select Lists and libraries (Figure 2-17).

2. Navigate to the workspace or list on the SharePoint site and select Modify settings and columns. The Customization page displays (Figure 2-18).

3. In General Settings, select Change permissions for this document library. The Change Permissions page displays (Figure 2-19).

4. Select Change Anonymous access. The Anonymous Access page displays (Figure 2-20).

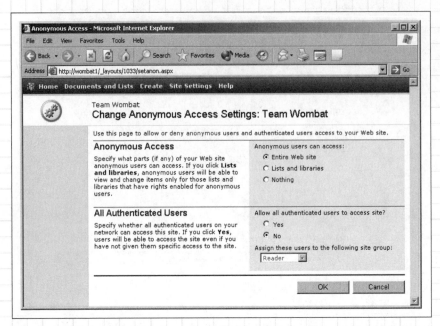

Figure 2-17. Select the level of access to allow for anonymous users

5. Select the permissions for anonymous access and click OK.

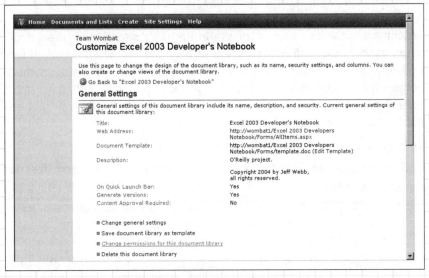

Figure 2-18. Customize a workspace to enable anonymous access

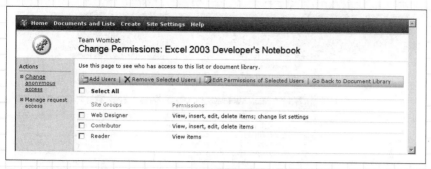

Figure 2-19. Select Change anonymous access

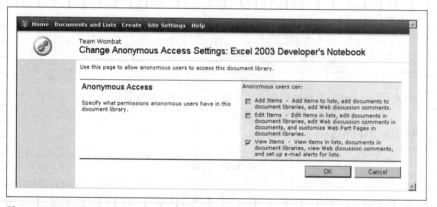

Figure 2-20. Choose the level of access for anonymous users

How it works

Allowing anonymous access lets users view SharePoint site pages without being prompted for a user name and password. When a user tries to open a workbook from the SharePoint site, SharePoint displays the Windows authentication dialog (Figure 2-9), whether or not anonymous access is enabled. Anonymous users may cancel that dialog and the workbook opens in read-only mode. Users with valid accounts may enter their usernames and passwords to get read/write access.

SharePoint disables the anonymous access account in IIS during installation as a security measure. You must deliberately re-enable that account in IIS before SharePoint allows any anonymous access or even displays the anonymous access options through the site administration pages.

Anonymous access to the SharePoint site is tracked through the IIS anonymous user account (shown in Figure 2-15). That username has the form IUSR_*xxx*. You can track access by that account to audit security using the Computer Management Console, as shown in Figure 2-21.

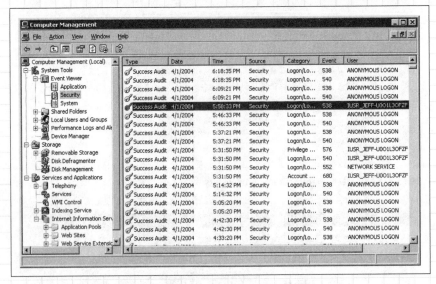

Figure 2-21. Track access by anonymous users to audit security

What about...

To learn how to	Look here
Administer a SharePoint site	Search *http://www.microsoft.com/downloads* for "SharePoint Administrator" and download *Windows SharePoint Services Administrator's Guide*

Create a List

In Microsoft Excel 2003, *lists* are ranges of cells that can easily be sorted, filtered, or shared. Lists are a little different from the AutoFilter feature available in earlier versions of Excel in that lists are treated as a single entity, rather than just a range of cells. This unity is illustrated by a blue border that Excel draws around the cells in a list (Figure 2-22).

There are other nice-to-have advantages to lists over AutoFilter ranges:

- Lists automatically add column headers to the range.
- Lists display a handy List Toolbar when selected.
- It is easy to total the items in a list by clicking the Toggle Total button.
- XML data can be imported directly into a list.

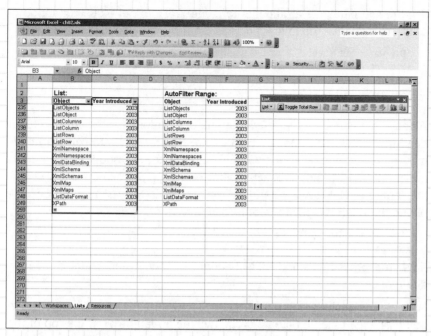

Figure 2-22. A list (left) and an AutoFilter range (right)

- Excel can automatically check the data type of list entries as they are made.
- Lists can be shared and synchronized with teammates via Microsoft SharePoint Services.

That last item is the key advantage of lists—really, lists are just a way to share information that fits into columns and rows.

How to do it

To create a list from Excel, select a range of cells and then choose Data → List → Create List. Excel converts the selected range into a list and displays the Lists toolbar (shown in Figure 2-22).

To create a list from code, use the Add method of the ListObjects collection. The ListObjects collection is exposed as a property of the Worksheet object. The following code creates a new list for all the contiguous data starting with the active cell:

```
ActiveWorksheet.ListObjects.Add
```

The word list is deceptively simple. A great many people use Excel to manage lists of data. By formalizing lists, Microsoft significantly enhanced one of the most-used features of the product.

Use the Add method's arguments to create a list out of a specific range of cells. For example, the following code creates a list from the range A1:C3:

```
Dim ws As Worksheet
Dim rng As Range
Set ws = ThisWorkbook.Sheets("Sheet1")
Set rng = ws.Range("A1:C3")
ws.ListObjects.Add xlSrcRange, rng
```

When Excel creates the preceding list, it automatically adds column headings to the list either by converting the first row into column headings or by adding a new row and shifting the subsequent data rows down. It's hard to know exactly what will happen because Excel evaluates how the first row is intended. You can avoid this assumption by supplying the HasHeaders argument, as shown here:

```
Set rng = ws.Range("A2:C4")
ws.ListObjects.Add xlSrcRange, rng, , xlNo
```

Now, the preceding code adds headers to row 2 and shifts the range down one row.

Lists always include column headers. To avoid shifting the range down one row each time you create a list, include a blank row at the top of the source range and specify xlYes for HasHeaders:

```
Set rng = ws.Range("A1:C4")
ws.ListObjects.Add xlSrcRange, rng, , xlYes
```

Since column headers and new rows added to a list cause the subsequent rows to shift down, it is a good idea to avoid placing data or other items in the rows below a list. If you do place items there, you receive a warning any time the list expands.

When creating lists in code, it is also a good idea to name the list so that subsequent references to the list can use the list's name rather than its index on the worksheet. To name a list, set the Name property of the ListObject:

```
Dim lst As ListObject
Set rng = ws.Range("A1:C4")
Set lst = ws.ListObjects.Add (xlSrcRange, rng, , xlYes)
lst.Name = "Test List"
```

You can get a reference to a named list using the Worksheet object's ListObjects property:

```
Set ws = ThisWorkbook.Worksheets("Test Sheet")
Set lst = ws.ListObjects("Test List")
```

How it works

If you omit the optional arguments with the ListObjects' Add method, Excel uses its own logic to determine the range of cells in the list and whether a list contains a header row. Basically, all contiguous cells containing data are assumed to be part of the list, and if the first row of data is text, that row is assumed to be a header row.

In general, it's not a good idea to deal with assumptions in code—it's better to be explicit so you know whether a new row was inserted for column headers and that inadvertent blank rows don't cause the list to omit subsequent data.

Another thing to remember is that sorting, filtering, and updating a list can shift or hide items on the worksheet that are not part of the list. It is not generally a good idea to place non-list items on the same rows as a list or below a list since those items may be moved, hidden, or overwritten in some situations.

Share a List

Excel calls sharing a list *publishing*. When a list is published, SharePoint Services creates a new item in the Lists folder that teammates can use to view or modify the list's data (Figure 2-23).

Publishing a list is a way to share a table of data— just like a database. But unlike databases, lists don't require any special knowledge to use.

How to do it

To publish a list in Excel, select the list and then choose Data → List → Publish List. Excel displays a series of steps that publish the list on the SharePoint server and display the address for the shared list (Figure 2-24).

To publish a list from code, use the ListObject's Publish method. The first argument of the Publish method is a three-element string array containing the address of the SharePoint server, a unique name for the list, and an optional description of the list. For example, the following code publishes a list created previously:

```
Set lst = ws.ListObjects("Excel Objects")
Dim str As String
Dim dest(2) As Variant
dest(0) = SPSITE
dest(1) = "Excel Objects"
dest(2) = "Excel objects listed by date introduced"
str = lst.Publish(dest, True)
MsgBox "Your list has been shared. You can view it at: " & str
```

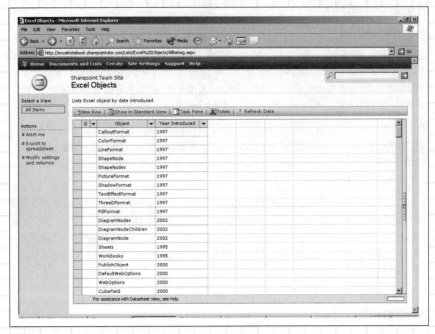

Figure 2-23. A published list

The Publish method returns a string containing the address of the published list. The preceding code displays that address in a message box, but you may want to navigate to that address or include a link to it somewhere on the sheet.

To add a hyperlink to the list on the SharePoint server, add a hyperlink to a range:

```
Dim lnk As Hyperlink
Set lnk = ws.Hyperlinks.Add(Range("C2"), str)
```

After adding the hyperlink, you can display the web page for the list by using the Follow method:

```
lnk.Follow
```

The ListObject's SharePointURL property returns the address of the list, so it is easy to get the address of the shared list after it has been created:

```
str = ws.ListObjects("Excel Objects").SharePointURL
Set lnk = ws.Hyperlinks.Add(Range("C2"), str, , _
  "Click to display list site.", "View")
```

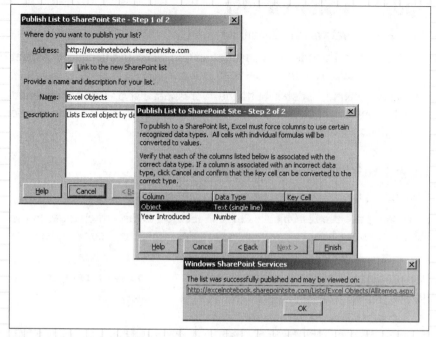

Figure 2-24. Steps in publishing a list

How it works

SharePoint Services stores lists as XML files. You can edit or link to a list through its SharePoint page, or you can use the SharePoint Lists web service to access the list directly through code.

Lists reflect a range of cells within a workbook, rather than the entire workbook file itself. By sharing only the germane range of cells, you avoid publishing the underlying data and macros, which lends to security and also to the utility of the shared data. The shared list can then be included in different workbooks used by others.

Access to lists is administered in the same way as for shared workspaces. If the list is shared at the root level of the site, all users of the site have access to the list. If the list is shared as part of a workspace, only workspace members have access.

The main limitation of lists is that they can be shared only through Windows Server 2003 running SharePoint Services. That's because the sharing and maintenance of lists is provided through the ASP.NET active server pages and web services that SharePoint provides. Other types of network shares are simply not supported.

Update a Shared List

There are several ways to update a shared list:

If you're not up-to-date, there's no point in sharing.

- *Refreshing* discards local changes and updates the (local) worksheet list with data from the SharePoint server.
- *Synchronizing* updates both the worksheet list and the SharePoint list. Conflicts between local edits and edits from other users can be resolved by the user who is synchronizing.

How to do it

From Excel, use the Data → List menu to refresh or synchronize a list.

From code, use the ListObject's `Refresh` method to discard changes to the list on the worksheet and refresh it with data from the SharePoint server:

```
lst.Refresh
```

Use the `UpdateChanges` method to synchronize the worksheet list with the SharePoint list:

```
lst.UpdateChanges xlListConflictDialog
```

If two authors modify the same item in a list, a conflict will occur when the second author updates his list. The `iConflictType` argument determines what happens when a conflict occurs. Possible settings are:

Setting	Description
xlListConflictDialog	Displays the Resolve Conflicts and Errors dialog box to resolve the conflict (this is the default).
xlListConflictRetryAllConflicts	Replaces conflicting data on the SharePoint server with data from the worksheet.
xlListConflictDiscardAllConflicts	Replaces conflicting data on the worksheet with updates from the SharePoint server.
xlListConflictError	Updates the items that do not conflict and generates an error—"Cannot update the list to Windows SharePoint Services"—leaving the conflicting items unchanged.

If the worksheet list is not shared, `UpdateChanges` causes an error.

The following code synchronizes a list and overwrites conflicting items with the worksheet version of the item (local version wins):

```
Set ws = ThisWorkbook.Worksheets("Lists")
Set lst = ws.ListObjects("Excel Objects")
lst.UpdateChanges xlListConflictRetryAllConflicts
```

The following code synchronizes a list and overwrites conflicting items with the SharePoint version of the item (server version wins):

```
Set ws = ThisWorkbook.Worksheets("Lists")
Set lst = ws.ListObjects("Excel Objects")
lst.UpdateChanges xlListConflictDiscardAllConflicts
```

How it works

Excel compares the data in the worksheet list with the change history in the SharePoint list and flags items that conflict when the worksheet list is synchronized. How the user responds (or how iConflictType is set) determines which changes become permanent.

Insert a Shared List

Once a list is published on a SharePoint site, team members can insert that list into existing worksheets or create new workbooks from the list. If they link their worksheet copy of the list to the SharePoint list, changes to their local copy can be synchronized across the team.

How to do it

To insert a shared list manually, navigate to the list on the SharePoint site, click Task Pane and then click Export and Link to Excel. SharePoint starts Excel and displays dialogs that let you create the list in a new workbook or insert the list into an existing one.

This is the trickiest part about programming with lists, in my opinion. You can't record this code to see how Excel does it and the Add method takes an array argument. It's hard to figure out on your own!

WARNING

Inserting a list *manually* from a SharePoint site into an existing workbook deletes all of the Visual Basic code contained in the workbook. Inserting a list from code does not delete a workbook's code, however.

To insert a shared list from code, use the ListObjects Add method and the SourceType argument xlSrcExternal:

```
Set ws = Workbooks.Add.Worksheets(1)
Dim src(1) As Variant
src(0) = SPSITE & "/_vti_bin"
src(1) = "Excel Objects"
ws.ListObjects.Add xlSrcExternal, src, True, xlYes, ws.Range("A1")
```

When `SourceType` is `xlSrcExternal`, the `Source` argument is a two-element array containing this information:

Element	Data
0	List address. This is the SharePoint address plus the folder name "/_vti_bin".
1	The name or GUID of the list. The GUID is a 32-digit numeric string that identifies the list on the server.

How it works

Notice that the first element of the Source array argument is the server address plus the folder name _vti_bin. SharePoint stores the Lists web service in that folder and Excel uses that web service to retrieve the list.

When you insert the list manually, SharePoint saves the target workbook as an XML spreadsheet as an intermediate step while importing the list data. That step removes any Visual Basic code from the workbook. As a rule, it is a good idea to create a new workbook when inserting a shared list manually.

Delete or Unlink a Shared List

As with workspaces, removing and unlinking lists from SharePoint is a basic management task. You need to know this stuff.

You can remove a list or remove the link between the worksheet list and the SharePoint list through Excel or through code. Deleting a list from the server is a little trickier, however.

How to do it

From Excel, use the List menu to unlink or convert a list to a range. To delete it from the worksheet, select the list and use Clear All.

From code, use these ListObject methods to unlink, unlist, or delete a list:

Method	Use to
Unlink	Remove the link between the worksheet list and the SharePoint list
Unlist	Convert the worksheet list to a range, preserving the list's data
Delete	Delete the worksheet list and all its data

Once you have unlinked a list, you can't relink it. To re-establish the link, you must delete the list and insert it back onto the worksheet from the SharePoint list.

All of these methods affect only the worksheet list. The SharePoint list can only be deleted using the SharePoint site or the Lists web service. To delete the SharePoint list from code, create a web reference to the Lists web service and use the following DeleteList method:

```
Dim lws As New clsws_Lists  ' Requires Web reference to
SharePoint Lists.asmx
lws.wsm_DeleteList ("Excel Objects")
```

If you delete a SharePoint list, but not the worksheet list that shares it, you get an error when you attempt to refresh or update the worksheet list. You can avoid this by unlinking the worksheet list.

How it works

The Lists web service provides a direct interface to lists stored on the SharePoint server. Excel actually wraps those web service method calls to provide its list-sharing features and objects.

What about...

The following section tells you more about the Lists web service.

Use the Lists Web Service

SharePoint Services includes the Lists web service for getting at shared lists and their data directly. The Lists web service lets you perform tasks on the server that you cannot otherwise perform through Excel objects. Specifically, you can use the Lists web service to:

- Add an attachment to a row in a list
- Retrieve an attachment from a row in a list
- Delete an attachment
- Delete a list from a SharePoint server
- Look up a list GUID
- Perform queries

I'm jumping ahead a bit here—web services are covered in Chapter 4. You need to know a bit about the Lists web service now because you can't delete a list from SharePoint or add attachments without it.

How to do it

To use a web service from Visual Basic:

1. Install the Web Services Toolkit from Microsoft at *www.microsoft. com/downloads*.

2. Close and restart Excel.

3. Open the Visual Basic Editor and select Web References from the Tools menu. Visual Basic displays the Microsoft Office 2003 Web Services Toolkit references dialog.

The SharePoint web services reside in the _vti_bin folder of the Share-Point site. To use the Lists web service:

1. Display the Microsoft Office 2003 Web Services Toolkit as described above.

2. Select the Web Service URL option button and type the address of the address using this form: *http://sharepointURL/_vti_bin/lists.asmx*.

3. Click Search. The Toolkit should find the Lists web service and display it in the Search Results list.

4. Select the checkbox beside Lists in Search Results and click Add.

5. The Toolkit generates a proxy class named `clsws_Lists` and adds it to the current project.

The SharePoint server must authenticate the Excel user before you can call any of the Lists web service methods. If the user has not been authenticated, a "Maximum retry on connection exceeded" error occurs. In Visual Basic .NET or C# .NET, you authenticate the user from code by creating a Credentials object for the user. For example, the following .NET code passes the user's default credentials to a web service:

```
wsAdapter.Credentials = System.Net.CredentialCache.DefaultCredentials
```

Unfortunately, you can't do that directly in Excel's Visual Basic. Instead, you must use one of the following techniques to connect to the Share-Point server through Excel:

- Update or refresh a worksheet list that is shared on the server
- Insert an existing SharePoint list on a worksheet; this can even be a dummy list placed on the server solely for the purpose of establishing connections
- Navigate to the SharePoint server in code, as shown in the section "Sharing Lists"

Any of these techniques displays the SharePoint authentication dialog box and establishes a user session for Excel. Afterward, you can call Lists methods and they will be authorized using the current session.

Debugging tip

One thing you will notice fairly quickly when using the Lists Web service is that the error reporting is minimal. When a method fails on the server side, you receive only a general error. To receive more detail, make the following modification to the clsws_Lists ListsErrorHander procedure:

```
Private Sub ListsErrorHandler(str_Function As String)
    If sc_Lists.FaultCode <> "" Then
        Err.Raise vbObjectError, str_Function, sc_Lists.FaultString & _
            vbCrLf & sc_Lists.Detail
    'Non SOAP Error
    Else
        Err.Raise Err.Number, str_Function, Err.Description
    End If
End Sub
```

Now errors will be reported with details from the server.

How to add attachments to a list

Excel does not directly support attachments to lists. However, you can use the Lists web service AddAttachment method to add a file attachment to a row in a list, then use GetAttachmentCollection to retrieve attachments from within Excel.

For example, the following code attaches the image file *joey.jpg* to the second row of a shared list:

```
' Requires web reference to SharePoint Lists.asmx
Dim lws As New clsws_Lists, str As String
src = ThisWorkbook.Path & "\joey.jpg"
dest = lws.wsm_AddAttachment("Excel Objects", "2", "joey.jpg",
FileToByte(src))
```

The AddAttachment method's last argument is an array of bytes containing the data to attach. To convert the image file to an array of bytes, the preceding code uses the following helper function:

```
Function FileToByte(fname As String) As Byte()
    Dim fnum As Integer
    fnum = FreeFile
    On Error GoTo FileErr
    Open fname For Binary Access Read As fnum
    On Error GoTo 0
    Dim byt() As Byte
    ReDim byt(LOF(fnum) - 1)
    byt = InputB(LOF(fnum), 1)
    Close fnum
    FileToByte = byt
    Exit Function
FileErr:
    MsgBox "File error: " & Err.Description
End Function
```

How to retrieve attachments

Use the Lists web service GetAttachmentCollection method to retrieve
an attachment from a list. The GetAttachmentCollection method returns
an XML node list that contains information about each attachment for the
row. The following code retrieves the location of the file attached in the
previous section:

```
Dim lws As New clsws_Lists  ' Requires web reference to
SharePoint Lists.asmx
Dim xn As IXMLDOMNodeList  ' Requires reference to Microsoft XML
Set xn = lws.wsm_GetAttachmentCollection("Excel Objects", "2")
ThisWorkbook.FollowHyperlink (xn.Item(0).Text)
```

Notice that the returned XML node list is a collection since rows can have
multiple attachments. Since the preceding example only attached one
file, this sample simply retrieves the first item from the node list. The
Text property of this item is the address of the attachment on the Share-
Point server.

How to delete attachments

Finally, it is very simple to delete an attachment using the
DeleteAttachment method:

```
Dim lws As New clsws_Lists  ' Requires Web reference to to SharePoint Lists.
asmx
lws.wsm_DeleteAttachment "Excel Objects", "2", _
SPSITE & "/Lists/Excel Objects/Attachments/2/joey.jpg"
```

Since DeleteAttachment requires the fully qualified address of the
attachment, it is useful to save the address of each attachment somewhere on the worksheet or to create a helper function to retrieve the
address from the SharePoint server:

```
Function GetAttachment(ListName As String, ID As String) As String
    Dim lws As New clsws_Lists ' Requires Web reference to to SharePoint
Lists.asmx
    Dim xn As IXMLDOMNodeList  ' Requires reference to Microsoft XML
    Set xn = lws.wsm_GetAttachmentCollection(ListName, ID)
    GetAttachment = xn.Item(0).Text
End Function
```

How to perform queries

In general, you don't need to perform queries through the Lists Web service. Most of the operations you want to perform on the list data are handled through the Excel interface or through the Excel list objects as described previously.

However, advanced applications—or especially ambitious programmers—may use the Lists Web service to exchange XML data directly with the SharePoint server. For instance, you may want to retrieve a limited number of rows from a very large shared list. In this case, you can perform a query directly on the SharePoint list using the GetListItems method. For example, the following code gets the first 100 rows from a shared list:

```
Dim lws As New clsws_Lists  ' Requires Web reference to to SharePoint Lists.
asmx
Dim xn As IXMLDOMNodeList   ' Requires reference to Microsoft XML
Dim query As IXMLDOMNodeList
Dim viewFields As IXMLDOMNodeList
Dim rowLimit As String
Dim queryOptions As IXMLDOMNodeList
rowLimit = "100"
Dim xdoc As New DOMDocument
xdoc.LoadXml ("<Document><Query /><ViewFields />" & _
  "<QueryOptions /></Document>")
Set query = xdoc.getElementsByTagName("Query")
Set viewFields = xdoc.getElementsByTagName("Fields")
Set queryOptions = xdoc.getElementsByTagName("QueryOptions")
Set xn = lws.wsm_GetListItems("Excel Objects", "", query, _
  viewFields, rowLimit, queryOptions)
```

The results are returned as XML. To see them you can simply display the root node of the returned object:

```
Debug.Print xn.Item(0).xml
```

The key to the preceding query is the XML supplied to the LoadXml method. You create conditional queries using the Query element and determine the columns included in the results using the ViewFields element. Perhaps the simplest way to create these queries is to write them as a text file in an XML editor (or Notepad), then load them from that file using the Load method:

```
xdoc.Load ("query.xml")
```

The query file takes this form:

```
<Document>
<Query>
   <OrderBy>
       <FieldRef Name="Column 1" Asending="FALSE"/>
    </OrderBy>
   <Where>
     <Gt>
        <FieldRef Name="_x0031_" />
        <Value Type="Value">6</Value>
     </Gt>
   </Where>
</Query>
<ViewFields>
       <FieldRef Name="ID" />
       <FieldRef Name="_x0031_" />
       <FieldRef Name="_x0032_" />
       <FieldRef Name="_x0033_" />
</ViewFields>
<QueryOptions>
   <DateInUtc>FALSE</DateInUtc>
   <Folder />
   <Paging />
   <IncludeMandatoryColumns>FALSE</IncludeMandatoryColumns>
   <MeetingInstanceId />
   <ViewAttributes Scope="Recursive" />
   <RecurrenceOrderBy />
   <RowLimit />
   <ViewAttributes />
   <ViewXml />
</QueryOptions>
</Document>
```

Notice that the FieldRef elements sometimes use the internal SharePoint names to identify columns—lists don't always use the titles displayed in the columns as column names. You can get the internal column names by examining the list's XML. To see the list's XML, use the GetList method, as shown here:

```
Dim lws As New clsws_Lists
Dim xn As IXMLDOMNodeList ' Requires reference to Microsoft XML
Set xn = lws.wsm_GetList ("Excel Objects")
Debug.Print xn(0).xml
```

What about...

To learn about	Look here
Installing the Web Services Toolkit	Navigate to *http://www.microsoft.com/downloads* and search for "Web Services Toolkit"
Lists web service	*http://msdn.microsoft.com/library/en-us/spptsdk/html/ soapcLists.asp*
DOMDocument	*http://msdn.microsoft.com/library/en-us/xmlsdk/htm/xml_ obj_overview_20ab.asp*
IXMLDOMNodeList	*http://msdn.microsoft.com/library/en-us/xmlsdk30/htm/ xmobjxmldomnodelist.asp*
Query element	*http://msdn.microsoft.com/library/en-us/spptsdk/html/ tscamlquery.asp*
ViewFields element	*http://msdn.microsoft.com/library/en-us/spptsdk/html/ tscamlviewfields.asp*
QueryOptions element	*http://msdn.microsoft.com/library/en-us/spptsdk/html/tsc-SPQuery.asp*
Batch element	*http://msdn.microsoft.com/library/default.asp?url=/library/ en-us/spsdk11/caml_schema/spxmlelbatch.asp*

Work with XML

As you may have realized from the previous chapter, lists are one of the ways Excel handles XML data. Shared lists are stored as XML, SharePoint exchanges updates via XML Web services, and lists can import and export XML.

I didn't address XML directly in the preceding chapter because lists are just one of the ways Excel handles XML. In this chapter I show the different ways you can work with XML in Excel. Specifically, I show you how to:

- Save a workbook as XML
- Transform XML from a workbook into other forms of output
- Transform a non-Excel XML file into an XML Spreadsheet
- Import XML to a list
- Export XML from a list
- Create templates for XML
- Respond to XML import and export events
- Program with the XML Map objects
- Bind lists and ranges to XML data sources

Speak XML

Simply put, XML is a way to store data as plain text. This useful because it allows all sorts of hardware and software to exchange data and, more importantly, understand that data. If Office 2003's goal is integration, then XML is the means to accomplish that goal.

Excel 2003 supports XML at two levels:

- The XML spreadsheet file format lets you save and open Excel workbooks stored as plain text in XML format.
- Lists and XML Maps let you import and export XML to a range of cells in a worksheet.

How it works

The concept behind XML has been around for a very long time. The core idea is that if you store content in plain text, add descriptive tags to that content, then describe those tags somewhere, you enable that content to be shared across applications, networks, and hardware devices in some very interesting ways.

XML is the standard for tagging content and navigating among those tags. XML has related standards for describing tags and transforming documents. All of these standards are maintained by W3C and are published at *http://www.w3.org*. There are quite a few acronyms associated with XML, and the following tables will help you understand them.

Code used in this chapter and additional samples are available in ch03.xls.

XML is a large and complex topic. You don't have to be an expert to use XML effectively in Excel, but you do need a basic understanding of the concepts and components.

Acronym	Full name	Use to
XML	Extensible Markup Language	Describe data as plain text documents.
XPath	XML Path Language	Define parts of an XML document and navigate between those parts.
DTD	Document Type Definition	Define the tags used to identify content in an XML document.
XSD	XML Schema Definition	An XML–based version of DTD. XSD is the successor to DTD.
XSL/XSLT	XML Style Sheet Language (Transformation)	Transform XML documents into other documents, such as HTML output.

In addition to the language standards cited above, there are a number of different ways to access XML data from code and to transmit XML across networks. The following table describes these key terms.

Acronym	Full Name	Description
DOM	Document Object Model	API for manipulating XML documents.
SAX	Simple XML API	Another API for manipulating XML documents.
SOAP	Simple Object Access Protocol	Defines the structure of XML data transmitted over a network and how to interpret that structure as it is received.
WSDL	Web Service Description Language	Describes services that can be invoked across a network through SOAP.

The last two items in the preceding table concern web services, which are a way to execute programs over the Internet and to receive responses from those programs.

I don't have space here to provide tutorials on how to use the items listed above, but fortunately there are some very good books and online information available about each.

What about...

To learn how to	Look here
Use XML/XSD/XSLT (tutorials)	*http://www.w3schools.com/*

XML Side-story

The Extensible Markup Language (XML) was developed in response to fears in the 1990s that software developers would run out of acronyms by the year 2010.

How it works

Acronyms are what separate us from the apes.

To solve the problem, XML provides a standard for *namespaces*, whereby the letters in an acronym could be arbitrarily assigned to any letter in a spelled-out word. Thus, Extensible Markup Language became "XML", not "EML", which was already trademarked by a gangsta rap artist.

Furthermore, namespaces allow hierarchical lists of acronyms to be built without collisions—XML includes XSLT (Extensible Style Sheet Transformation Language, or E-S-S-T-L, really), XSD (Extensible Markup Language Schema Definition Language, or E-M-L-S-D-L), XPath (Extensible Markup Language Path Language, or E-M-L-P-L), SAX (Simple Application Programming Interface for Extensible Markup Language Processing, or S-A-P-I-E-M-L-P), JAX (Java Application Programming Interface for Extensible Markup Language Processing, or J-A-P-I-E-M-L-P), and XHTML (Extensible Hypertext Markup Language, E-H-M-L which is easier to say than X-H-T-M-L).

Besides, everyone at the W3C agreed that adding "X" to anything makes it cool like Vin Diesel.

So what is XML really? All this hoo-ha is about two things: thing one is "<"; thing two is ">". By putting < > around everything, you make it vastly harder to type thereby raising the bar for programmers and decreasing the likelihood that our jobs will be exported to Kuala Lumpur. < See ^? > < how /> < much /> < harder /> < this /> < is /> < to /> < say /> </ See ^? >

Not only that, but XML makes *everything* case-sensitive. Studies at IBM in the 1970s showed that processors became constipated if they received too much uppercase text and that they developed the opposite problem if their input was exclusively lowercase. XML ensures the right mix of textual roughage and starch for smooth processing and regular output.

Does XML do anything else? No, XML is not about *doing* anything. It's a standard and, as such, it is a vehicle for other things—attending symposiums, for instance.

What about...

To learn how to	Look here
Drive like Vin Diesel	*http://www.toyota-supra.com/*
Read your rap sheet in XML after driving like Vin Diesel	*http://it.ojp.gov/jsr/public/viewDetail. jsp?sub_id=177*
Party like the W3C	*http://www.w3.org*

Save Workbooks as XML

In Excel 2003, you can now save a workbook as an XML spreadsheet or as XML data from the Save As dialog box (Figure 3-1).

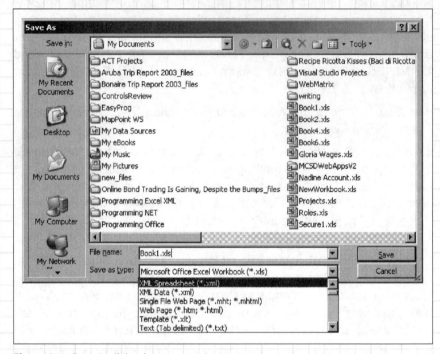

Figure 3-1. Save As dialog box

How to do it

Choosing the XML Spreadsheet file type saves the workbook in an XML file that uses the Microsoft Office schema. Choosing the XML Data file type saves the workbook file in an XML file that uses a schema you provide through an XML map. Since it's a good idea to start simply, I'll discuss the XML Spreadsheet format here and the XML Data format later in "Use XML Maps" later in this chapter.

If you save a workbook as an XML spreadsheet, you can open the file in Notepad, edit it, and still reopen/edit it in Excel later—provided you haven't broken any of the rules in the file's schema. A simple default workbook includes a lot of items that aren't required by the Office schema, and you can simply delete those items to see the simplified "core" of an XML spreadsheet, as shown in the following XML:

```
<?xml version="1.0"?>                            }- Processing instruction
<?mso-application progid="Excel.Sheet"?>
<Workbook xmlns="urn:schemas-microsoft-com:office:spreadsheet"  }
  xmlns:o="urn:schemas-microsoft-com:office:office"            }
  xmlns:x="urn:schemas-microsoft-com:office:excel"             }
  xmlns:dt="uuid:C2F41010-65B3-11d1-A29F-00AA00C14882"         }-Namespaces
  xmlns:ss="urn:schemas-microsoft-com:office:spreadsheet"      }
  xmlns:html="http://www.w3.org/TR/REC-html40"                 }
  xmlns:x2="http://schemas.microsoft.com/office/excel/2003/xml"> }
  <Worksheet ss:Name="Sheet1">                                        }
    <Table ss:ExpandedColumnCount="5" ss:ExpandedRowCount="2"          }
      x:FullColumns="1"                                               }
      x:FullRows="1">                                                 }
      <Column ss:Index="5" ss:AutoFitWidth="0" ss:Width="54.75"/>     }
      <Row>                                     }        }            }
        <Cell><Data ss:Type="Number">1</Data></Cell>     }        }            }
        <Cell><Data ss:Type="Number">2</Data></Cell> }- Cell  }-Row  }-Worksheet
        <Cell><Data ss:Type="Number">3</Data></Cell>     }        }            }
      </Row>                                    }        }            }
      <Row>                                                          }
        <Cell><Data ss:Type="Number">4</Data></Cell>                 }
        <Cell><Data ss:Type="Number">5</Data></Cell>                 }
        <Cell><Data ss:Type="Number">6</Data></Cell>                 }
      </Row>                                                         }
    </Table>                                                        }
  </Worksheet>                                                      }
</Workbook>
```

How it works

The preceding XML has these notable features:

- The mso-application processing instruction tells the Microsoft Office XML Editor (MsoXmlEd.Exe) to open the file with Excel.

- Office uses numerous namespace definitions to qualify the names used in its XML documents.

- The path to data on a spreadsheet is Workbook/Worksheet/Table/ Row/Cell/Data. The Cell node is used to contain formulas, formatting, and other information as attributes.

- The Column element is not a parent of the Row or Cell elements as you might expect. Instead, it is mainly used to set the width of the columns on the worksheet.

You can experiment with the XML spreadsheet by making changes in Notepad and seeing the results. For instance, if you change the mso-application processing instruction to:

```
<?mso-application progid="Word.Document"?>
```

Now, the spreadsheet will open in Word 2003 if you double-click on the file in Solution Explorer. Change the progid to "InternetExplorer.Application" or delete the processing instruction and Windows will open the file as XML rather than as an Excel spreadsheet in Internet Explorer.

The `mso-application` processing instruction is ignored if you don't have Office 2003 installed. So, if you post an XML spreadsheet on a network, clients that don't have Office 2003 will see that file as XML rather than as a spreadsheet.

What you lose and how to keep it

When Excel saves a workbook as XML, it omits these types of data:

- Charts, shapes, and OLE objects
- Macros

Other types of data (numbers, text, formulas, comments, validation, formatting, sheet layout, window and pane positioning, etc.) are preserved, however. It is best to think of XML spreadsheets as vehicles for data, rather than as full-featured workbooks.

To preserve charts, shapes, OLE objects, or macros, save the workbook file first in XML Spreadsheet format, then in Excel Workbook format:

```
ThisWorkbook.SaveAs , xlXMLSpreadsheet
ThisWorkbook.SaveAs , xlWorkbookNormal
```

By saving the file as a normal workbook last, you leave the current file type as .XLS, so if the user clicks Save the full version of the file is saved. Excel keeps the full workbook in memory even after you save it as an XML spreadsheet, so you don't lose data between the two saves. You are, however, prompted several times—first to overwrite existing files since you are using SaveAs, then to note that XML spreadsheets do not save contained objects. You can eliminate the first prompt by deleting the existing file before each step of the save, as shown below. You can only eliminate the second prompt by omitting non-saved items (such as macros) from the workbook:

```
' Requires reference to Microsoft Scripting Runtime
Dim fso As New FileSystemObject, xlsName As String, xmlName As String
xlsName = ThisWorkbook.fullname
base = fso.GetBaseName(xlsName)
xmlName = ThisWorkbook.path & "\" & base & ".xml"
If fso.FileExists(xmlName) Then _
    fso.DeleteFile (xmlName)
ThisWorkbook.SaveAs xmlName, xlXMLSpreadsheet
fso.DeleteFile (xlsName)
ThisWorkbook.SaveAs xlsName, xlWorkbookNormal
```

The preceding code saves two versions of the workbook: one full version with an .XLS file type, and one XML spreadsheet version with an .XML file type.

What about...

To learn about	Look here
Office 2003 XML (schema documentation)	*http://www.microsoft.com/office/ xml/default.mspx.*

Transform XML Spreadsheets

XML spreadsheets provide Excel data in a format that can be easily used by other applications or transformed into presentation documents, such as HTML web pages. For either task, you often need to modify the content of the XML spreadsheet, and the best way to do that is with XSLT.

You can use XSLT to perform a wide variety of transformations, such as:

- Extract specific items from a spreadsheet—such as retrieving only worksheets containing data
- Transform the spreadsheet into HTML
- Make global changes to the spreadsheet
- Highlight significant items, such as high or low outlier numbers

How to do it

To transform an XML spreadsheet, follow these general steps:

1. Create an XSLT file to perform the transformation, using Notepad or some other editor.
2. Perform the transformation in code, from the command line, or by including a processing instruction.
3. Save the result.

There are three different ways to perform the transformation. The following table compares each of those techniques, and the sections that follow describe each of the preceding steps in more detail.

Now that you've saved a workbook as XML, what can you do with it? XSLT lets you transform XML into other formats, extract or highlight information, or make other changes.

Transformation	Use to	Advantages	Disadvantages
Code	Automatically generate the result from within Visual Basic.	Can be performed with a single click by the user, or in response to an event.	Requires Excel to be running.
Command line	Perform batch transformations.	Transformed file is generally smaller than source file.	Uses command-line interface; utility must be downloaded.
Processing instruction	Dynamically transform the file when it is viewed in the browser.	Changes to the XSLT are reflected automatically, underlying source is preserved.	File is generally larger and displays more slowly, because it is transformed on the client. Doesn't work in all browsers.

How to create XSLT

XSLT is a simple language containing looping, decision-making, evaluation, branching, and functional statements. It follows the same conventions as XML and its sole purpose is to interpret and transform valid XML documents into some other text.

Excel qualifies the names of the XML nodes it creates with namespaces from the Microsoft Offices schemas. An Excel workbook defines the following namespaces:

```
<Workbook xmlns="urn:schemas-microsoft-com:office:spreadsheet"
  xmlns:o="urn:schemas-microsoft-com:office:office"
  xmlns:x="urn:schemas-microsoft-com:office:excel"
  xmlns:dt="uuid:C2F41010-65B3-11d1-A29F-00AA00C14882"
  xmlns:ss="urn:schemas-microsoft-com:office:spreadsheet"
  xmlns:html="http://www.w3.org/TR/REC-html40"
  xmlns:x2="http://schemas.microsoft.com/office/excel/2003/xml">
```

Notice that the default namespace (xmlns, highlighted in **bold**) is urn:schemas-microsoft-com:office:spreadsheet. This is the same as the namespace for the ss prefix (xmlns:ss, also in **bold**). You use this ss namespace prefix when referring to workbook nodes in your XSLT file.

Different nodes in the XML spreadsheet use different default namespaces. For instance, the DocumentProperties node uses the following default namespace:

```
<DocumentProperties xmlns="urn:schemas-microsoft-com:office:office">
```

Therefore, when referring to the DocumentProperties node or its children, define a prefix for the namespace urn:schemas-microsoft-com:office:office in your XSLT, and use that prefix to refer to those nodes. If you don't do this, your XSLT won't recognize the nodes in the XML spreadsheet. This is a very common problem, and it should be the first place you look if your XSLT outputs nothing.

It is convenient to copy the namespace definitions from the XML spreadsheet Worksheet node to your XSLT stylesheet. For instance, the following XSLT example uses the copied ss namespace to locate nodes in an XML spreadsheet:

```
<?xml version="1.0"?>
<!-- Strip.xslt transforms a XML Spreadsheet to its bare essentials -->
<xsl:stylesheet version="1.0"
    xmlns="urn:schemas-microsoft-com:office:spreadsheet"
    xmlns:xsl="http://www.w3.org/1999/XSL/Transform"
    xmlns:ss="urn:schemas-microsoft-com:office:spreadsheet">
  <xsl:output method="xml" indent="yes" />
  <xsl:template match="ss:Workbook">
  <xsl:processing-instruction name="mso-application">progid="Excel.Sheet"
</xsl:processing-instruction>
    <xsl:element name="ss:Workbook">
        <xsl:copy-of select="ss:Styles" />
        <xsl:for-each select="ss:Worksheet">
            <xsl:if test="count(ss:Table/ss:Row/ss:Cell/ss:Data) &gt; 0">
                <xsl:copy-of select="." />
            </xsl:if>
        </xsl:for-each>
    </xsl:element>
  </xsl:template>
</xsl:stylesheet>
```

The preceding transformation copies worksheets that contain data, and formatting styles used by cells in those worksheets, into a new XML spreadsheet file. Empty worksheets, document properties, and other items are simply omitted. Excel still recognizes the resulting output as an XML spreadsheet since it conforms to the Excel schema and contains the mso-application processing instruction.

To see how this transformation works:

1. Create a workbook in Excel and enter some data in its worksheets.

2. Save the workbook as an XML spreadsheet named *TestStrip.xml*.

3. Process the XML spreadsheet using the sample file XSLT. Ways to process the XML file are described in the following sections.

4. In Windows Explorer, double-click on the output file. Excel will display the transformed XML (Figure 3-2).

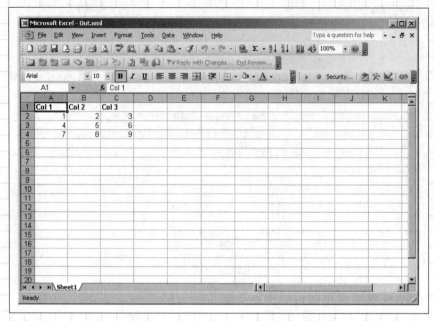

Figure 3-2. An XML spreadsheet with empty worksheets removed by a transformation

How to transform in code

As mentioned previously, there are several ways to transform XML. Transforming XML from Visual Basic code uses the Microsoft XML object library to call the Microsoft XML Parser (*msxml4.dll*). The Microsoft XML object library also provides a means to create new XML files; navigate between nodes; copy, delete, and add nodes; and more.

To perform a transformation in code, follow these steps:

1. In Visual Basic, add a reference to the Microsoft XML object library. The Microsoft XML object library provides the DOMDocument object, which is used to load, transform, and save XML documents.

2. In code, create two instances of DOMDocument objects from the Microsoft XML object library.

3. Load the XML spreadsheet in the first DOMDocument object.

4. Load the XSLT file in the second DOMDocument object.

5. Use the TransformNode method of the first DOMDocument object to perform the transformation.

For example, the following code loads the *TestStrip.xml* XML spreadsheet and Strip.xslt transformation, processes the transformation, and saves the result:

```
Sub Strip()
    ' Requires reference to Microsoft XML
    Dim xdoc As New DOMDocument, xstyle As New DOMDocument
    Dim xml As String
    xdoc.Load (ThisWorkbook.path & "\TestStrip.xml")
    xstyle.Load (ThisWorkbook.path & "\Strip.xslt")
    xml = xdoc.transformNode(xstyle)
    SaveFile xml, "Out.xml"
End Sub

Sub SaveFile(content As String, fileName As String)
    ' Requires reference to Microsoft Scripting Runtime
    Dim fso As New FileSystemObject, strm As TextStream
    fileName = ThisWorkbook.path & "\" & fileName
    If fso.FileExists(fileName) Then fso.DeleteFile(fileName)
    Set strm = fso.CreateTextFile(fileName)
    strm.Write (content)
    strm.Close
End Sub
```

The preceding SaveFile helper procedure is necessary because the
transformNode method returns a string containing the XML created by the
transformation. Once the XML is saved, you can open the file by double-
clicking on it in Windows Explorer, or by using the following code:

```
Application.Workbooks.Open ("out.xml")
```

How to transform from the command line

You can also perform transformations using the command-line transformation utility (msxsl.exe). *Msxsl.exe* is available from Microsoft for free in
the MSDN download area. It is a small shell executable that simply calls
the Microsoft XML Parser to perform the transformation.

For example, the following command line transforms the *TestStrip.xml*
file, using the Strip.xslt transformation shown previously, and writes the
output to Out.xml:

```
msxsl TestStrip.xml Strip.xslt -o Out.xml
```

The output is the same as that created by using the DOMDocument
object's TransformNode method shown in the preceding section. The
command-line utility allows you to automate transformations using batch
files rather than Visual Basic code.

How to transform in the browser

Another way to perform a transformation is to include an xml-stylesheet
processing instruction in the XML spreadsheet. The mso-application
instruction supersedes other instructions, so you must replace that pro-

cessing instruction in order to have a browser perform the translation. The following XML shows the changes you must make to the XML spreadsheet file: deletions are shown in strikethrough and additions are shown in **bold**:

```
<?xml version="1.0"?>
<?xml-stylesheet type="text/xsl" href="worksheet.xslt"?>
<?mso-application progid="Excel.Sheet"?>
<Workbook xmlns="urn:schemas-microsoft-com:office:spreadsheet"
 xmlns:o="urn:schemas-microsoft-com:office:office"

 ...
```

Now when a user opens the XML file, the browser transforms and displays the file (Figure 3-3).

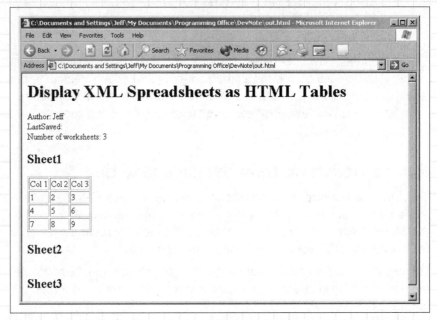

Figure 3-3. Transforming an XML spreadsheet in the browser

How it works

The transformation shown in Figure 3-3 converts cells in a worksheet to HTML table elements. It also displays document properties of the workbook. The transformation is performed by the following XSLT fragment:

```
<xsl:template match="ss:Workbook">
    <html>
        <body>
        <h1>Display XML Spreadsheets as HTML Tables</h1>
        Author:
```

Margin note:

> Not all browsers support this technique. Be sure to test your transformations in non-Microsoft browsers.

```
<xsl:value-of select="o:DocumentProperties/o:Author" />
<br />
        LastSaved:
<xsl:value-of select="o:DocumentProperties/o:LastSaved" />
<br />
        Number of worksheets:
          <xsl:value-of select="count(ss:Worksheet)" />
        <xsl:for-each select="ss:Worksheet">
            <h2><xsl:value-of select="@ss:Name" /></h2>
            <table border="1" frame="box">
            <xsl:for-each select="ss:Table/ss:Row">
            <tr>
                <xsl:for-each select="ss:Cell/ss:Data">
                    <td><xsl:value-of select="." /></td>
                </xsl:for-each>
            </tr>
            </xsl:for-each>
            </table>
        </xsl:for-each>
        </body>
    </html>
```

The advantage of using a processing instruction to perform the transformation is that you don't significantly alter the spreadsheet. You can switch the file back to an Excel XML spreadsheet simply by removing the xml-stylesheet instruction and replacing the mso-application instruction, as shown in the following XSLT fragment:

```
<xsl:template match="ss:Workbook">
    <xsl:processing-instruction name="xml-stylesheet">
type="text/xsl" href="Worksheet.xslt"</xsl:processing-instruction>
    <xsl:copy-of select="." />
</xsl:template>
```

To transform the file back into an XML spreadsheet, simply change the xsl:processing-instruction element:

```
<xsl:processing-instruction name="mso-application">
progid="Excel.Sheet"</xsl:processing-instruction>
```

When a user requests an XML file that includes an xml-stylesheet processing instruction, the file is downloaded and the transformation is processed on the user's machine. That takes more time than if the XML file had already been transformed, but any changes to the XSLT are automatically reflected, because the transformation is performed dynamically.

How to reset file associations

In order for the mso-application processing instruction to work correctly when the user opens the file from Windows Explorer, the XML file type must be associated with the Microsoft Office XML Editor (MsoXmlEd.Exe).

Some applications, such as Mozilla, can change this association and break the ability to easily open these files from Explorer.

If this happens, you can reset the XML file type by following these steps:

1. From Windows Explorer, right-click an XML file and choose Open With → Choose Program. Windows displays the Open With dialog box.

2. Select XML Editor and select Always use the selected program to open this type of file, then click OK. Windows updates the system registry to associate XML files with the Microsoft Office XML Editor.

What about...

To get	Look here
Free IE XML Validation/XSL Transformation viewer	Search for "Validating XSLT" at *http://www.microsoft.com/downloads/*
Free XML/XSL Editor	*http://xmlcooktop.com/*
XML/XSL Debugger (free trial of a good product)	*http://new.xmlspy.com/products_ide.html*

Transform XML into a Spreadsheet

XML is a two-way street. Getting XML into Excel is as important as knowing how to set it out.

You can also use XSLT or other tools to transform XML files created outside of Excel into XML spreadsheets. In this way, you can create native Excel documents from your own applications.

How to do it

For instance, the following abbreviated XML represents a customer order created outside of Excel:

```
<?xml version="1.0"?>
<!-- SimpleOrder.xml -->
<Orders>
<Order>
    <ID>1002</ID>
    <BillTo>
        <Address>
            <Name>Joe Magnus</Name>
            <Street1>1234 Made Up Place</Street1>
            <City>Somewhere</City>
            <State>FL</State>
```

```
            <Zip>33955</Zip>
        </Address>
    </BillTo>
    <ShipTo>
        <Address>...</Address>
    </ShipTo>
    <Line>
        <Number>20</Number>
        <Description>Mahogany Tiller</Description>
        <Quantity>1</Quantity>
        <UnitPrice>95.00</UnitPrice>
        <Taxable>Yes</Taxable>
        <Total>95.00</Total>
    </Line>
    <Line>...</Line>
    <Total>
        <SubTotal>540.00</SubTotal>
        <Tax>3.24</Tax>
        <Due>543.24</Due>
    </Total>
</Order>
</Orders>
```

To convert this XML into an XML spreadsheet, create XSLT that creates the following nodes and processing instruction:

1. The mso-application processing instruction that identifies this file as an XML spreadsheet.

2. A root Workbook node that defines the Microsoft Office namespaces.

3. A Styles node defining the cell formatting to display in the worksheet. Styles include number formats, such as Currency, Percentage, or General number.

4. A Worksheet node for each order.

5. Column nodes to set the width of the columns on the worksheet.

6. Row, Cell, and Data nodes for the order items you want to include in the worksheet.

Some of the preceding steps involve extensive XSLT, so it is convenient to break the steps into separate templates that are called or applied by a root template:

```
<!--OrderToExcel.xslt transform an Order XML file into an Excel XML
Spreadsheet--> <xsl:template match="/Orders">
    <xsl:processing-instruction name="mso-application">progid="Excel.Sheet"
</xsl:processing-instruction>
    <xsl:element name="Workbook"
namespace="urn:schemas-microsoft-com:office:spreadsheet" >
    <xsl:call-template name="AddStyles" />
        <xsl:for-each select="Order">
            <!-- Create a worksheet for each order -->
            <xsl:element name="Worksheet">
```

```
                    <!-- Name the worksheet -->
                    <xsl:attribute name="ss:Name">
                        <xsl:value-of select="BillTo/Address/Name" />
                        <xsl:value-of select="ID" />
                    </xsl:attribute>
                    <xsl:element name="Table">
                    <xsl:call-template name="AddColumns" />
                    <!-- Add bill to headings -->
                    <xsl:apply-templates select="BillTo" />
                    <!-- Add send to headings -->
                    <xsl:apply-templates select="ShipTo" />
                    <!-- Add column headings -->
                    <xsl:call-template name="AddColumnHeads" />
                        <xsl:for-each select="Line">
                            <xsl:apply-templates select="." />
                        </xsl:for-each>
                    <xsl:call-template name="AddTotals" />
                    </xsl:element>
                </xsl:element>
            </xsl:for-each>
        </xsl:element>
    </xsl:template>
```

The preceding template uses xsl:call-template to call named templates when the content output does not depend on a specific node. A
good example of this is the AddStyles template, which creates the cell
formats used in the worksheet:

```
    <xsl:template name="AddStyles">
      <Styles xmlns:ss="urn:schemas-microsoft-com:office:spreadsheet">
      <Style ss:ID="ColHead">
        <Alignment ss:Horizontal="Center" ss:Vertical="Bottom"/>
        <Borders>
        <Border ss:Position="Bottom" ss:LineStyle="Continuous" ss:
Weight="1"/>
        </Borders>
        <Font ss:Bold="1"/>
      </Style>
      <Style ss:ID="ItemHead">
        <Alignment ss:Horizontal="Right" ss:Vertical="Bottom"/>
        <Font ss:Bold="1"/>
      </Style>
      <Style ss:ID="Currency">
        <NumberFormat ss:Format="Currency"/>
      </Style>
      </Styles>
    </xsl:template>
```

The AddStyles template just inserts the Excel Style elements since they
are static and it is fairly easy to cut and paste the Style elements created
by Excel into this template. This is also true for the Columns element created by AddColumns template (not shown).

The main work is performed by the following template, which is applied to each Line in the order needed to create the rows in the worksheet:

```
<xsl:template match="Line">
    <xsl:element name="Row">
        <xsl:element name="Cell">
            <xsl:element name="Data">
                <xsl:attribute name="ss:Type">Number</xsl:attribute>
                <xsl:value-of select="Number" />
            </xsl:element>
        </xsl:element>
        <xsl:element name="Cell">
            <xsl:element name="Data">
                <xsl:attribute name="ss:Type">String</xsl:attribute>
                <xsl:value-of select="Description" />
            </xsl:element>
        </xsl:element>
        <xsl:element name="Cell">
            <xsl:element name="Data">
                <xsl:attribute name="ss:Type">Number</xsl:attribute>
                <xsl:value-of select="Quantity" />
            </xsl:element>
        </xsl:element>
        <xsl:element name="Cell">
            <xsl:attribute name="ss:StyleID">Currency</xsl:attribute>
            <xsl:element name="Data">
                <xsl:attribute name="ss:Type">Number</xsl:attribute>
                <xsl:value-of select="UnitPrice" />
            </xsl:element>
        </xsl:element>
        <xsl:element name="Cell">
            <xsl:attribute name="ss:StyleID">Currency</xsl:attribute>
            <xsl:attribute name="ss:Formula">=RC[-2]*RC[-1]
              </xsl:attribute>
            <xsl:element name="Data">
                <xsl:attribute name="ss:Type">Number</xsl:attribute>
                <xsl:value-of select="Total" />
            </xsl:element>
        </xsl:element>
    </xsl:element>
</xsl:template>
```

How it works

The preceding template transforms a Line node from an order into a Row node in a worksheet. Two important things to note are shown in **bold**:

- First, notice that you format cells using the StyleID attribute of the Cell node. This formatting includes aspects programmers sometimes consider data type, such as whether a number is currency, percentage, date, or time. It's easy to confuse this with the Type attribute of the Data node.

- Second, you include calculations using the `Formula` attribute of the `Cell` node. The formula shown here uses row/column notation, although you can use absolute or named ranges as well.

Other templates convert the `BillTo` and `ShipTo` nodes into rows, add column heads, and totals. Rather than reproduce those templates here, please refer to the OrderToExcel.xslt sample file. You can use that file as a starting point for converting your own XML files into XML spreadsheets.

Once processed, the transformed orders can be opened in Excel (Figure 3-4).

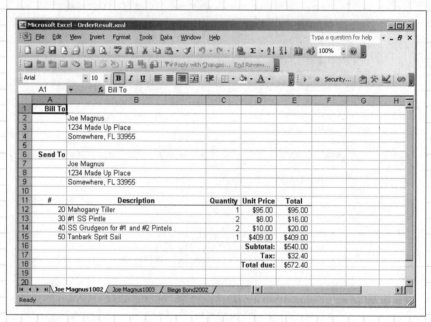

Figure 3-4. XML order information transformed into an XML spreadsheet

One of the beauties of creating your own transformations is that repeating items, such as multiple `Order` nodes, can be mapped to items other than rows. In this sample case, each order becomes a separate worksheet, which then receives a unique name (see the worksheet tabs in Figure 3-4).

What about...

To learn how to	Look here
Use the Office XML schemas	*http://www.microsoft.com/office/ xml/default.mspx*

Use XML Maps

If all of the XSLT in the preceding sections intimidated you, relax a bit. Excel also provides graphical tools for importing XML into workbooks through XML maps. *XML maps* are the way Excel represents XML schemas within a workbook. Excel can generate these maps from the structure of an imported XML file, or Excel can load an XML schema as an XML map.

Excel uses XML maps as a way to bind data from an XML file to cells and list columns on a worksheet. You create this binding by selecting items from an XML map displayed in the XML Source task pane and dragging them to locations on a worksheet.

You don't have to know XSLT to read or write XML from Excel. XML maps let you work with XML at a higher level and ignore some of the complexities.

How it works

To see how this works, follow these steps:

1. Open the sample file *SimpleOrder.xml* in Excel using the regular File Open menu. Excel displays the Open XML dialog box (Figure 3-5).

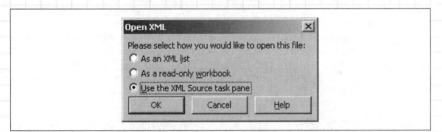

Figure 3-5. The Open XML dialog box

2. Select the Use the XML source task pane option and click OK. Excel creates a new, blank workbook and informs you that the file did not contain a schema (Figure 3-6), so Excel will infer one from the XML.

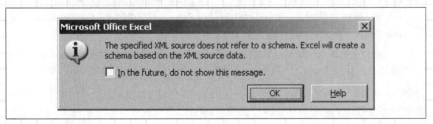

Figure 3-6. Excel inferring a schema for you

3. Click OK. Excel displays the XML map it created in the task pane (Figure 3-7).

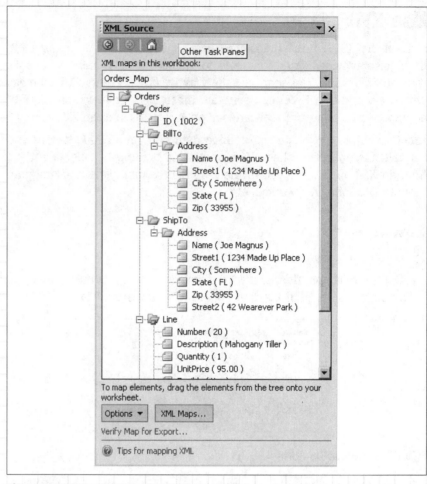

Figure 3-7. XML structure in the XML Source pane

4. Import XML nodes into a worksheet by selecting the nodes in the XML map and then dragging them onto a worksheet. Excel creates these new items as a list, so select multiple nodes to include multiple items in one list (Figure 3-8).

5. Choose Data → XML → Refresh XML Data to import the data from the XML file into the list (Figure 3-9).

This tutorial works well for the summary information imported above. The Order ID, Name, SubTotal, and Tax nodes occur once per Order. You can sort the list, filter it to see only a specific Order ID, and so on. However, if you want to include the detail lines of the order, the list can become hard to interpret, because non-repeating items are repeated (Figure 3-10).

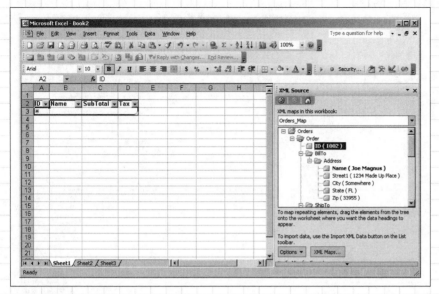

Figure 3-8. A list of nodes in Excel

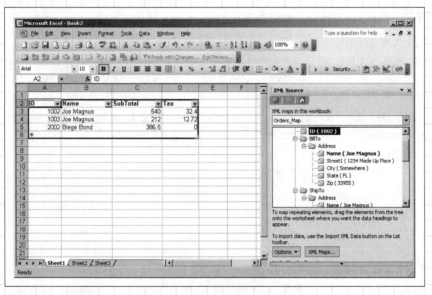

Figure 3-9. A list, populated with data from the XML document

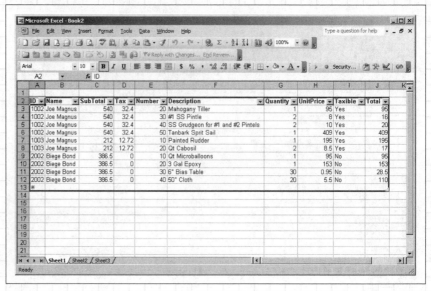

Figure 3-10. Mapped XML with summary and detail combined

What you lose and how to keep it

The preceding tutorial demonstrates a subtle limitation of XML maps—optional nodes, such as Street2 in *SimpleOrder.xml*, are sometimes not included in the XML map. This occurs because Excel generates the schema from the first instance of each node it encounters.

To correct this, add an empty `Street2` node to the first `Address` nodes, as shown below, and open the XML as a new workbook:

```
<Address>
    <Name>Joe Magnus</Name>
    <Street1>1234 Made Up Place</Street1>
    <Street2 />
    <City>Somewhere</City>
    <State>FL</State>
    <Zip>33955</Zip>
</Address>
```

You can't update an existing XML map, you can only create new ones and delete existing ones from within Excel. This means that lists created from XML maps must be recreated any time the source XML schema changes.

Since XML maps are row-based, you can't conditionally omit optional nodes as you can with XSLT. For example, the sample transformation *OrderToExcel.xslt* omits the optional `Street2` node if it is empty using the following `xsl:if` element:

```
<xsl:if test="./Address/Street2 != ''">
    <xsl:element name="Row">
        <xsl:element name="Cell" />
        <xsl:element name="Cell">
            <xsl:element name="Data">
                <xsl:attribute name="ss:Type">String</xsl:attribute>
                    <xsl:value-of select="Street2" />
            </xsl:element>
        </xsl:element>
    </xsl:element>
</xsl:if>
```

You can't do that type of conditional processing with XML maps.

Another limitation is that calculated elements, such as Total, import from XML as data values rather than as formulas. The sample *OrderToExcel.xslt* creates formulas to calculate line item totals:

```
<xsl:element name="Cell">
    <xsl:attribute name="ss:StyleID">Currency</xsl:attribute>
        <xsl:attribute name="ss:Formula">=RC[-2]*RC[-1]
    </xsl:attribute>
    <xsl:element name="Data">
        <xsl:attribute name="ss:Type">Number</xsl:attribute>
        <xsl:value-of select="Total" />
    </xsl:element>
</xsl:element>
```

Such calculations must be created manually on the worksheet when using XML maps.

How it works

When Excel imports an XML file that does not reference an XML schema, it *infers* a schema from the nodes in the XML file. The preceding section explains one of the limitations of inferring a schema—optional nodes are sometimes omitted from the resulting XML map.

Another solution to this problem is to include a schema with your XML file. For example, the following XML fragment references a schema for the *SimpleOrder.xml* file:

```
<Orders xmlns="http://www.mstrainingkits.com"
    xmlns:xsi="http://www.w3.org/2001/XMLSchema-instance"
    xsi:schemaLocation="http://www.mstrainingkits.com SimpleOrder.xsd">
```

The optional schemaLocation attribute identifies the namespace and location of a document's schema. It's supported by all XML parsers.

When Excel imports an XML file that references a schema, it copies that schema into the workbook. If the XML is valid according to that schema, you can drag nodes from the XML map onto the worksheet to create lists and import data, as shown previously.

If the XML is not valid for the schema, however, no data will appear in the lists you create. Excel does not automatically validate XML against schemas or display errors if the XML is invalid. To validate XML within Excel:

1. Choose the Data → XML → XML Map Properties. Excel displays the XML Map Properties dialog box (Figure 3-11).

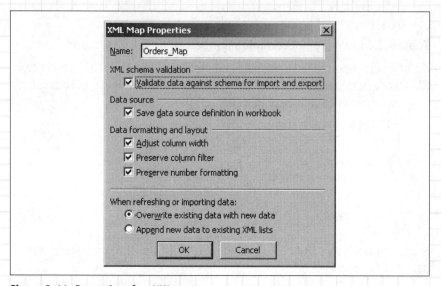

Figure 3-11. Properties of an XML map

2. Select Validate data against schema for import and export, and click OK to close the dialog box.

Now, Excel will display an error if the XML doesn't conform to the schema. Excel checks the XML against the schema whenever the XML data is imported, exported, or refreshed. You can get detailed information about validation errors by clicking Details on the XML Import Error dialog box (Figure 3-12).

Unfortunately, Excel copies the referenced XML schema into the XML map the first time it loads an XML file, rather than referencing the schema as an external file. Subsequent changes to the schema do not affect the XML map in the workbook. Again, you can only add or delete XML maps, you can't update them from Excel.

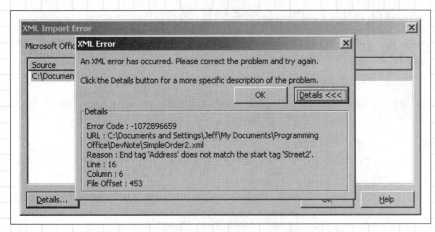

Figure 3-12. Detailed XML validation errors when refreshing a list

Manage XML Maps

Excel adds an XML map for each unique XML file you import into a workbook. If you import the same file twice, Excel simply reuses the XML map it already created for that file.

To view a list of the XML maps, click the drop-down listbox in the XML Source task pane. To add or delete XML maps, click the XML maps button at the bottom of the XML Source task pane.

Items in an XML map may or may not be bound to cells on a worksheet. Items that are bound (or *mapped*) to cells import data to those cells. Items that repeat in an XML map are bound to Excel lists (see Chapter 2 for information about using lists). Items that don't repeat may be bound to individual cells, however if a non-repeating item is placed adjacent to a list, Excel adds that item to the list and repeats the item on the worksheet even though the item is not repeated in the source XML file!

There are a couple of important points to note here:

- Items in an XML map can bind to only one location in a workbook.
- If an item in an XML map is not bound to a cell or list, its data won't be imported to, or exported from, the workbook.
- If you include a non-repeating item from an XML map in an Excel list, the data Excel saves on the worksheet becomes *denormalized* and can't be exported.

These points are spelled out in more detail in the next section.

Exporting through XML Maps is trickier than importing through them. You can't export all types of XML and Excel omits any items that don't appear on a worksheet. You should understand these limitations before you count on writing XML data from Excel.

Exporting Through XML Maps

Once you have created lists containing XML data, you can export that data to a new XML file from Excel two ways:

- By saving the workbook using the XML Data file type
- By clicking the Export XML toolbar button or selecting Export from the Data menu's XML submenu

In either case, you can only export data using one XML map at a time. If a workbook contains more than one XML map, you are prompted to choose the map to use (Figure 3-13).

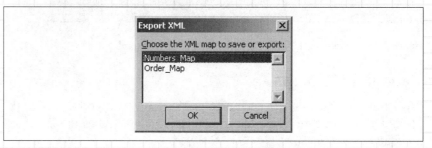

Figure 3-13. Exporting XML uses only one XML map at a time

How it works

When Excel exports a list as XML, it uses the schema stored in the workbook to generate XML that matches the XML source file that the list was created from. However, Excel omits the following items:

- Schema definitions
- Processing instructions
- XML nodes not included in the list

For example, if you create a list from *SimpleOrder.xml* containing only names and totals, only those elements are saved when you export the list as XML:

```
<Orders>
    <Order>
        <BillTo>
            <Address>
                <Name>Joe Magnus</Name>
            </Address>
        </BillTo>
        <Total>
            <Due>572.4</Due>
        </Total>
```

```
        </Order>
        <Order>...</Order
    </Orders>
```

In the preceding XML, the original address and order information is omitted because it wasn't included in the list. From Excel's point of view, the data doesn't exist if it doesn't reside on a worksheet somewhere.

What this means

The limitations that come with XML maps imply a set of approaches when using them with XML. You can't just assume that you will be able to successfully import, edit, and export arbitrary XML data using Excel. XML maps are best suited for XML structured a certain way.

For example, the preceding *SimpleOrder.xml* sample requires some changes if you want to be able to view and edit orders via XML maps. Specifically:

- Each order should be stored in a separate file. XML maps can't export lists of lists, so including multiple orders, each with multiple line items, prevents you from exporting the orders.

- Line items must be presented as a separate list. Simply importing an order as a single list results in denormalized data, which can't be exported from the list.

These changes and other recommendations are explained in the following sections.

Avoid lists of lists

Excel can import XML that contains lists more than one level deep, but it can't export those lists. In XML schema terminology, a list is an element with a maxOccurs attribute greater than one. Therefore, XML using the following schema can't be exported from an XML map:

```
<xsd:element minOccurs="0" maxOccurs="unbounded" nillable="true"
name="Order" form="qualified">
    <xsd:complexType>
        <xsd:sequence minOccurs="0"> ... </xsd:sequence>
        <xsd:element minOccurs="0" maxOccurs="unbounded" nillable="true"
        name="Line" form="qualified">
            <xsd:complexType>
                <xsd:sequence minOccurs="0"> ...</xsd:sequence>
            </xsd:complexType>
        </xsd:element>
    </xsd:complexType>
</xsd:element>
```

You can solve this problem by breaking the source XML into smaller pieces. In the case of *SimpleOrder.xml,* this means creating a separate file for each Order node. The XML map's root node then becomes Order (Figure 3-14).

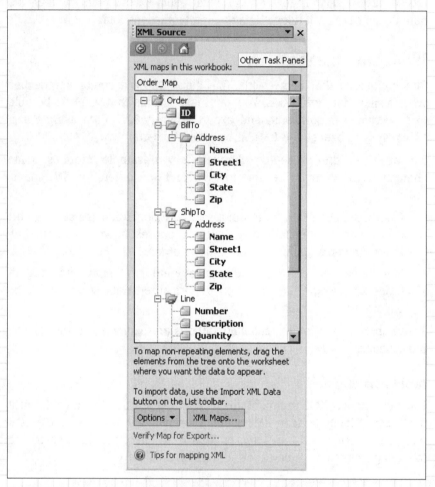

Figure 3-14. Break XML into smaller files to avoid lists of lists

You can organize the new, smaller files into a separate folder or by using a unique file extension, such as ".ord". For example, the following code allows the user to select an order file to open in Excel:

```
Sub cmdOpenOrder_Click()
    ' Get a file name to open. Use ".ord" extension for orders.
    Dim fname As String
    fname = Application.GetOpenFilename("Orders (*.ord),*.ord", 1, _
    "Open an Order", "Open", False)
```

```
        If fname <> "" Then
            ThisWorkbook.XmlMaps("Order_Map").Import (fname)
        End If
    End Sub
```

Using the unique .ord file extension organizes orders (Figure 3-15). Excel (and XML) don't care what file extension you use when importing or exporting files.

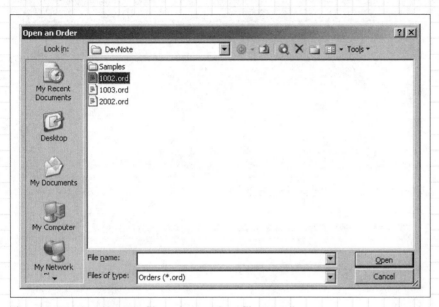

Figure 3-15. Organize XML files using a unique file extension

Avoid denormalized data

If you drag the Order node shown in Figure 3-14 onto a worksheet, you get a list containing denormalized data, as shown in Figure 3-16.

Denormalized means that non-repeating data elements appear multiple times on the worksheet. A user could change one of the non-repeating items, such as Name, on one row, making that item inconsistent with other rows that are supposed to show the same data. There is no way for Excel to reconcile this inconsistency, so the list can't be exported.

To avoid this, create non-repeating and repeating nodes in separate lists (Figure 3-17).

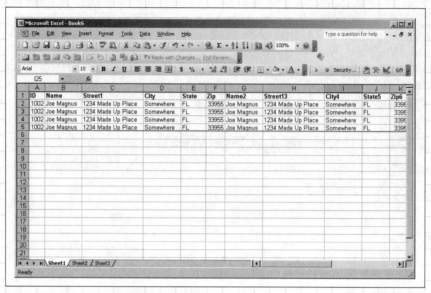

Figure 3-16. A list with denormalized data

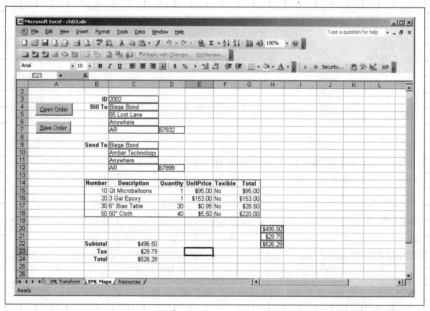

Figure 3-17. Put repeating and non-repeating data items in separate lists to avoid denormalized data

Create an XML schema

Allowing Excel to infer a schema for an XML map is fine if the nodes don't contain optional items or if the first occurrence of each node contains all of its possible children. Otherwise, Excel may omit items from the schema it creates and some nodes won't appear in the XML map.

You can solve this problem by creating an XML schema and referencing that schema in the XML file you import. Excel copies the referenced XML schema into the XML map when the XML map is created.

Having an external XML schema is also useful for making changes to the XML map. As mentioned earlier, you can't update an XML map inside of Excel; you can, however, modify the XML schema stored in the workbook by editing it *outside* of Excel. To edit an XML map schema:

1. In Excel, save the workbook as an XML spreadsheet.
2. Close the workbook in Excel.
3. Open the XML spreadsheet in an XML editor. It is a good idea to use a full-featured XML editor here because the schema generated by Excel does not include whitespace such as tabs and linefeeds.
4. Edit the items in the MapInfo/Schema node as needed, or simply replace the entire Schema node with the contents of your external schema definition file.
5. Save the file.
6. Open the workbook in Excel and click Refresh XML Data to verify that the schema is still valid.

The XML spreadsheet nodes for the schema appear as follows. The nodes to edit or replace are highlighted in **bold**.

```
<x2:MapInfo x2:HideInactiveListBorder="false"
x2:SelectionNamespaces="xmlns:ns1='http://www.mstrainingkits.com'">
<x2:Schema x2:ID="Schema1"
x2:Namespace="http://www.mstrainingkits.com">
        <xsd:schema xmlns:xsd="http://www.w3.org/2001/XMLSchema"
        targetNamespace="http://www.mstrainingkits.com"
        xmlns:ns0="http://www.mstrainingkits.com">
                <xsd:element nillable="true" name="Order">
                ...
                </xsd:element>
        </xsd:schema>
    </x2:Schema>
</x2:MapInfo>
```

Include all nodes if exporting

When you export XML, Excel takes the data found in mapped items on worksheets, applies the XML map, and generates XML nodes defined in the XML map's schema. If some of the XML map's data nodes are not mapped, that data is omitted from the exported XML.

In some cases, this is what you want. But if you are trying to read and write an XML file without losing content, you need to make sure that all elements from the XML map appear somewhere on the worksheet (even if they are hidden).

In cases where a node contains a calculated value, you will need to perform the calculation in a non-mapped cell, then copy that value to the mapped cell before exporting (see Figure 3-17).

The Save Order button in the sample copies the calculated subtotal, tax, and total values to cells created from the XML map before exporting the XML using the following code:

```
Sub cmdSaveOrder_Click()
    ' Update mapped cells with calculated values.
    Range("XmlSubTotal") = Range("SubTotal")
    Range("XmlTax") = Range("Tax")
    Range("XmlTotal") = Range("Total")
    ' Create file name to save.
    Dim fname As String
    fname = ThisWorkbook.path & "\" & Range("OrderID") & ".ord"
    ' Save the order.
    ThisWorkbook.XmlMaps("Order_Map").Export fname, True
End Sub
```

Other things to avoid

There are a number of other XML schema constructs that Excel does not support when importing XML, and a number of schema constructs that are not supported when exporting XML. These constructs are listed in Table 3-1 and Table 3-2.

Table 3-1. XML schema features not supported when importing XML

Feature	Description
any, anyAttribute	The any and anyAttribute elements allow you to include items that are not declared by the schema. Excel requires imported schemas to be explicit.
Recursive structures	Excel does not support recursive structures that are more than one level deep.

Table 3-1. XML schema features not supported when importing XML (continued)

Feature	Description
Abstract elements	Abstract elements are meant to be declared in the schema, but never used as elements. Abstract elements depend on other elements being substituted for the abstract element.
Substitution groups	Substitution groups allow an element to be swapped wherever another element is referenced. An element indicates that it's a member of another element's substitution group through the `substitutionGroup` attribute.
Mixed content	Mixed content is declared using mixed="true" on a complex type definition. Excel does not support the simple content of the complex type, but does support the child tags and attributes defined in that complex type.

Table 3-2. XML schema features not supported when exporting XML

Feature	Description
Lists of lists	Excel can only export repeating items that are one level deep. See the previous section "Avoid Lists of Lists".
Denormalized data	See the previous section "Avoid Denormalized Data".
Non-repeating siblings	If nonrepeating items are mapped to lists, they will result in denormalized data.
Repeating elements	If the repetition is not defined by an ancestor, the data relationships can't be preserved.
Child elements from different parents	If children from different XML maps are mapped to the same list, the relationship can't be preserved.
Choice	Elements that are part of an XML schema choice construct can't be exported.

Use Templates with XML

So far I've worked with XML maps in workbooks. I did this because that's the way I structured my samples for this book. Actually, XML maps become a lot more useful when stored in Excel templates (*.xlt*). That way, new workbooks based on those templates automatically contain the XML map and lists you need to display data.

How to do it

To see how this works, create a new workbook and add an XML map, as described previously. Drag items from the XML map onto worksheets as you want them displayed, and save the workbook as a template (*.xlt*). Figure 3-18 shows a template created for displaying the Order_Map.

Storing an XML map in a template makes a lot of sense once you have finished developing and debugging your Excel solution. Your template code doesn't have to create the XML map or bind items from the map to list columns—all that comes with the template.

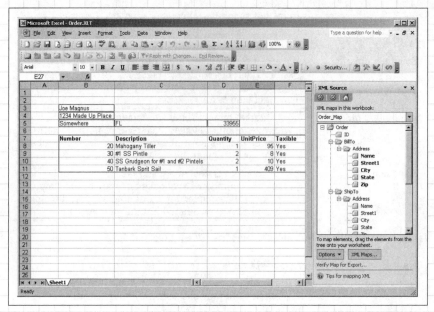

Figure 3-18. An Excel template for displaying orders

Now, you can use code to open specific file types using this template. For example, the following code displays a list of .ord files, creates a new Order template, and displays the selected file in the newly created workbook:

```
Private Sub cmdOpenOrder_Click()
    Dim wb As Workbook
    ' Get a file name to open. Use ".ord" extension for orders.
    Dim fname As String
    fname = Application.GetOpenFilename("Orders (*.ord),*.ord", 1, _
      "Open an Order", "Open", False)
    If fname <> "" Then
        ' Create a new workbook based on the Order template.
        Set wb = Workbooks.Add(ThisWorkbook.Path & "\Order.xlt")
        ' Import the XML data into the existing Map in the template.
        wb.XmlImport fname, wb.XMLMaps("Order_Map")
    End If
End Sub
```

Alternately, you could put the code inside of the template Workbook_ Open event procedure, so that whenever the user created a new document from the template, he would be prompted for the data file. For example, the following code uses a custom document property to tell whether or not an XML file has been loaded into the template—if XML-Source is False (as when a new workbook is created from the template), then the user is prompted for a file to load:

```
' Template code.
Private Sub Workbook_Open()
    Dim wb As Workbook
    Set wb = ThisWorkbook
    If wb.CustomDocumentProperties("XMLSource") = "False" Then
        ' Get a file name to open. Use ".ord" extension for orders.
        Dim fname As String
        fname = Application.GetOpenFilename("Orders (*.ord),*.ord", 1, _
          "Open an Order", "Open", False)
        If fname <> "False" Then
            ' Import the XML data into the existing Map in the template.
            wb.XmlImport fname, wb.XmlMaps("Order_Map")
            wb.CustomDocumentProperties("XMLSource") = fname
        End If
    End If
End Sub
```

How it works

Putting the XML map in a template avoids having to recreate the XML map every time you create a new workbook. The best part is that you can map elements to lists on a worksheet and get the layout and formatting set up the way you want it. Then, the template can prompt for the XML file to open whenever you create a new workbook.

This approach avoids a subtle problem: each XML map can only be used once. There's a one-to-one correspondence between the XML data source, the XML map, and the list object displaying the data. If you want to import multiple XML files through, you either have to use a different map for each file or clear the data binding used by the list object.

If you want to be able to display multiple Orders using the preceding template, you can address these problems by writing code to:

1. Make a copy of the existing worksheet. This copy saves the data that has already been loaded in the workbook. The new worksheet does not preserve the data bindings from the lists, so once this copy is made it is static.

2. Change the data bindings on the original worksheet to load new XML data.

The following code illustrates these steps:

```
Private Sub cmdOpen_Click()
    Dim wb As Workbook, ws As Worksheet, fname As String, xmap As XmlMap
    Set wb = ThisWorkbook
    Set ws = wb.Worksheets("Order")
    ' Keep a copy of the Order worksheet.
    ws.Copy ws
    ' Activate the Order worksheet.
```

```
        ws.Activate
        ' Change data bindings for Order worksheet.
        fname = Application.GetOpenFilename("Orders (*.ord),*.ord", 1, _
            "Open an Order", "Open", False)
        If fname <> "False" Then
            Set xmap = wb.XmlMaps("Order_Map")
            ' Update the databinding
            xmap.DataBinding.LoadSettings fname
            ' Refresh the data.
            xmap.DataBinding.Refresh
        End If
    End Sub
```

Figure 3-19 shows a workbook based on this template after several XML files have been loaded. Note that the copies are placed before the Order worksheet—this gives the user the impression that the new data is displaying a new worksheet, even though it is actually using the original (data-bound) worksheet.

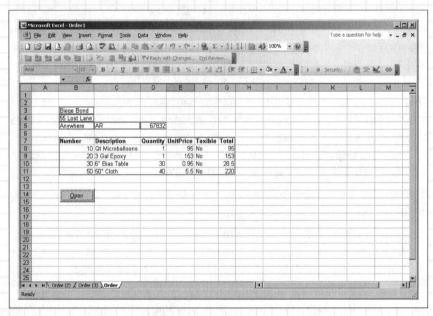

Figure 3-19. Loading multiple files in an XML template

What about...

To learn how to	Look here
Control XML data binding	"Get an XML Map from a List or Range"

Respond to XML Events

The Workbook object provides events that occur before and after data is imported or exported through an XML map. You can use these events to control how the import/export occurs, respond to errors, or cancel the operation.

XML events occur at the workbook level. They identify which map is being exported through the Map argument. If you're going to reformat data while importing or exporting, you'll need to check that argument to make sure you apply your changes to the right list.

How to do it

For example, the following event procedures display information about import and export actions as they occur:

```
Private Sub Workbook_BeforeXmlImport(ByVal Map As XmlMap, _
  ByVal Url As String, ByVal IsRefresh As Boolean, Cancel As Boolean)
    Debug.Print "BeforeImport", Map, Url, IsRefresh, Cancel
End Sub

Private Sub Workbook_BeforeXmlExport(ByVal Map As XmlMap, _
  ByVal Url As String, Cancel As Boolean)
    Debug.Print "BeforeExport", Map, Url, IsRefresh, Cancel
End Sub

Private Sub Workbook_AfterXmlImport(ByVal Map As XmlMap, _
  ByVal IsRefresh As Boolean, ByVal Result As XlXmlImportResult)
    Debug.Print "AfterImport", Map, Url, Result
End Sub

Private Sub Workbook_AfterXmlExport(ByVal Map As XmlMap, _
  ByVal Url As String, ByVal Result As XlXmlExportResult)
    Debug.Print "AfterExport", Map, Url, Result
End Sub
```

To cancel an import or export action, set the event's Cancel argument to True. The following code allows the user to cancel refreshing or importing data from the Orders_Map:

```
Private Sub Workbook_BeforeXmlImport(ByVal Map As XmlMap, _
  ByVal Url As String, ByVal IsRefresh As Boolean, Cancel As Boolean)
    If Map.name = "Orders_Map" And Not IsRefresh Then
        res = MsgBox("This action will replace all the data " & _
        "in this list. Do you want to continue?", vbYesNo, "Import XML")
        If res = vbNo Then Cancel = True
    End If
End Sub
```

How it works

If the import or export action is caused by code, setting Cancel to True causes an "Operation cancelled by user" error to occur. You should trap for this error if you allow Cancel to be set. For example, the following code handles the potential error when importing data:

```
' If user cancels, handle error.
On Error Resume Next
' Import data.
xmap.Import ThisWorkbook.path & "\SimpleOrder.xml"
If Err = 1004 Then Debug.Print "User cancelled import."
On Error GoTo 0
```

Program with XML Maps

The preceding sections explained how to use the new XML features found in Excel and provided code for saving, transforming, importing, and exporting XML with Excel. Those sections provide a context for Excel's XML features and explain programming tasks that surround those features. The rest of this chapter deals exclusively with the XML objects Excel provides and offers specific examples of programming tasks you can perform with those objects, properties, and methods.

Excel's XML object model deals exclusively with XML maps. Opening and saving XML spreadsheets is done through the Workbook object's Open and Save methods. Figure 3-20 illustrates the Excel XML objects hierarchically.

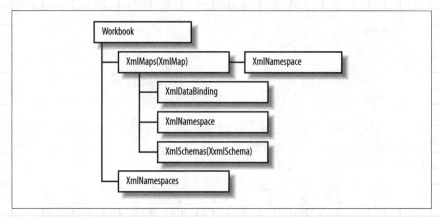

Figure 3-20. The XML object hierarchy

The XmlMap object allows you to perform the following tasks in code:

- Add XML maps to a workbook
- Delete XML maps from a workbook
- Export XML data through an XML map
- Import XML data through an XML map

- Bind an XML map to an XML data source
- Refresh mapped lists and ranges from an XML data source
- View the XML schema used by an XML map

The following sections explain these tasks in greater detail.

The XML Source task pane only gets you so far. By using code, you can create ways to update XML maps, change data bindings, and automate any other tasks that need automating.

How to add or delete XML maps

Use the XmlMaps collection to add or delete XML maps in a workbook. The Add method takes the location of an XML schema as its first argument, and when Excel adds an XML map to a workbook, it copies the contents of that schema into the workbook. For example, the following line creates a new XML map using the *SimpleOrder.xsd* schema file:

```
ThisWorkbook.XmlMaps.Add (ThisWorkbook.path & "\SimpleOrder.xsd")
```

If you substitute an XML source file for the XML schema, the Add method will infer a schema from the XML source. As noted earlier, inferring a schema can omit some nodes from the resulting XML map.

When Excel creates a new XML map, it names the map using the name of the root node and appending _Map. A number is added to the name if a map with that name already exists. For example, the preceding line of code creates a map named "Orders_Map" the first time it runs, "Orders_Map2" the second time, and so on.

Use the XmlMap object's Delete method to remove a map from a workbook. The following code deletes the map named "Orders_Map":

```
ThisWorkbook.XmlMaps("Orders_Map").Delete
```

If you use the Delete method on a map that is currently used to import data to a list, Excel simply deletes the map and disables the Refresh XML Data task for that list. Excel does not warn you as it does when you delete a map through the user interface.

How to export/import XML

Use the XmlMap object to import or export XML from code. For example, the following line imports an XML file through an existing XML map into a workbook:

```
ThisWorkbook.XmlMaps("Order_Map").Import (ThisWorkbook.Path & "\1002.ord")
```

Similarly, the XmlMap object's Export method exports XML data from a workbook. The following code exports data through an existing XML map:

```
ThisWorkbook.XmlMaps("Order_Map").Export ThisWorkbook.Path & "\1002.ord"
```

Use the ImportXml and ExportXml methods to import or export XML as a string variable rather than as a file. For example, the following code displays the contents of a list mapped using the Order_Map as XML in the Debug window:

```
Dim xmap As XmlMap, xml As String, res As XlXmlExportResult
Set xmap = ThisWorkbook.XmlMaps("Order_Map")
res = xmap.ExportXml(xml)
Debug.Print xml
```

How to refresh/change/clear data

Use the Databinding object's Refresh method to refresh a list that was linked to XML data through an XML map. The Refresh method is equivalent to clicking the Refresh XML Data button on the List toolbar.

You can use the Databinding object's LoadSettings method to change the data source used by the XML map. When combined, the LoadSettings and Refresh methods are equivalent to calling the XmlMap object's Import method. The advantage of combining LoadSettings and Refresh is that changing the data source and refreshing the list are handled in separate steps:

```
Dim xmap As XmlMap, res As XlXmlExportResult
Set xmap = ThisWorkbook.XmlMaps("Order_Map")
' Change the data source.
xmap.DataBinding.LoadSettings (ThisWorkbook.path & "\2002.ord")
' Refresh the list from the data source.
res = xmap.DataBinding.Refresh
```

How to view the schema

You can get the schema used by an XML map through the Schemas collection. Each XML map has one schema. You can't add or delete schemas through the Schemas collection.

Use the Schema object's Xml method to return the schema used by an XML map. The Xml method returns the schema without whitespace, so you will want to use a formatting helper function, such as PrettyPrint, when displaying the schema:

```
Dim xmap As XmlMap, xsd As String
Set xmap = ThisWorkbook.XmlMaps("Order_Map")
xsd = xmap.Schemas(1).xml
Debug.Print PrettyPrint(xsd)
```

PrettyPrint is shown here for your reference:

```
Function PrettyPrint(xml As String) As String
    ' Requires reference to the Microsoft Office SOAP type library
    Dim rdr As New SAXXMLReader, wrt As New MXXMLWriter
    Set rdr.contentHandler = wrt
    wrt.indent = True
    rdr.Parse (xml)
    PrettyPrint = wrt.output
End Function
```

Get an XML Map from a List or Range

Use the XPath object to get or set the data binding used by a list column or a range. Figure 3-21 shows the relationship between these objects.

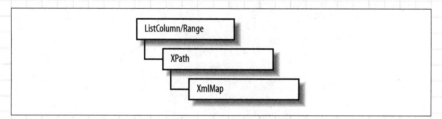

Figure 3-21. Getting an XML map from a list column or range

You can use the XPath object to add or remove bindings to list columns or ranges as described in the following sections.

How to bind XML to a list column

Use the XPath object's SetValue method to bind data from an XML map to a list column or range. SetValue allows you to dynamically create lists from an XML map. For example, the following code creates a new list, adds three columns to that list, and binds each column to a different node in an XML map:

An XML map is just a description of your XML. What data is imported or exported is determined by the data bindings you apply to cells and list columns.

```
Set ws = ThisWorkbook.Sheets("Mapped List")
Set xmap = ThisWorkbook.XmlMaps("Numbers_Map")
' Create a list object.
Set lo = ws.ListObjects.Add(xlSrcRange, [A3])
' Add a column to the list.
Set lc = lo.ListColumns.Add
' Map the column to an element in an XML map.
lc.XPath.SetValue xmap, "/Numbers/Number/One", , True
' Repeat for two more columns.
Set lc = lo.ListColumns.Add
lc.XPath.SetValue xmap, "/Numbers/Number/Two", , True
Set lc = lo.ListColumns.Add
lc.XPath.SetValue xmap, "/Numbers/Number/Three", , True
```

How to remove a binding

Use the XPath object's `Clear` method to remove a binding from a list column or range. For example, the following code removes the bindings from the list created in the preceding section:

```
Set ws = ThisWorkbook.Sheets("Mapped List")
Set lo = ws.ListObjects(1)
For Each lc In lo.ListColumns
    lc.XPath.Clear
Next
```

CHAPTER 4

Get Data from the Web

Today it is hard to remember a time when the Web didn't matter, but it wasn't that long ago that it didn't even exist. Because Excel was created long before the Web, it has adapted as the Web evolved. There are now three main approaches to retrieving data from the Web:

- *Web queries* retrieve data directly from a web page and import that data into a query table on an Excel spreadsheet. Although this was one of the first web access features added to Excel (introduced in 1997), it is still very useful.

- *Web services* execute applications remotely over the Web to return results in XML format. The number of services available over the web is growing quickly as this standard is becoming broadly adopted. Web services provide a standardized way of exchanging parameters and retrieving results over the Web—something that is missing from web queries.

- *Database access over the web* is now available through most database software. This technique depends on the database provider and is not covered here.

This chapter describes how to use web queries and web services to retrieve data from the Web and import it into Excel. The samples in this chapter demonstrate a variety of programming tasks with these two approaches, including:

- Passing parameters
- Formatting results
- Getting data asynchronously
- Displaying results through XML Maps

In this chapter:
- *Perform Web Queries*
- *Modify a Web Query*
- *Perform Periodic Updates*
- *Manage Web Queries*
- *Use Web Services*
- *Use the Web Services Toolkit*
- *Use Web Services Through XML*
- *Call a Web Service Asynchronously*
- *Reformat XML Results for Excel*

Code used in this chapter and additional samples are available in ch04.xls.

Perform Web Queries

Web queries are a quick way to import data from a web page into a worksheet using a QueryTable object.

How to do it

To perform a web query:

1. Choose Data → Import External Data → New Web Query. Excel displays the New Web Query dialog (Figure 4-1).

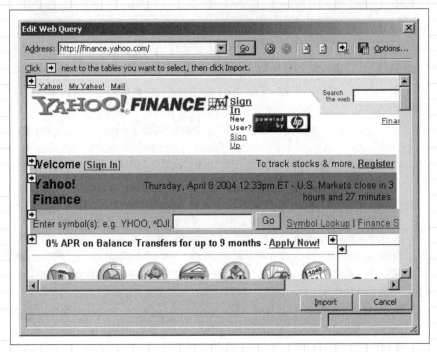

Figure 4-1. Use web queries to import data directly from a web page

2. Type the address of the web page you want to import data from in the Address bar and click Go to navigate to that page. It is usually easiest to find the page you want in your browser, then cut and paste that address into the New Web Query dialog box.

3. Excel places small yellow boxes next to the items you can import from the page. Click on the item or items you want to import and Excel changes the yellow box to a green check mark.

4. Click the Options button to set how Excel formats imported items. Formatting options are shown in Figure 4-2.

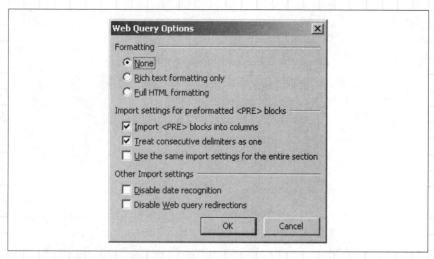

Figure 4-2. Set formatting options for the query

5. Close the Options dialog box and click Import. Excel displays the Import Data dialog box, as shown in Figure 4-3.

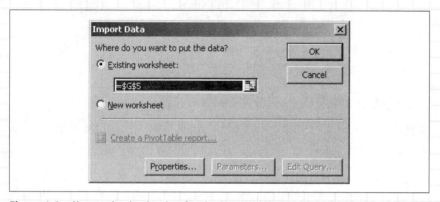

Figure 4-3. Choose the destination for the imported data

6. Click Properties to determine how the query is performed, such as how the data is refreshed. Figure 4-4 shows the query property settings.

7. Close the Properties dialog and click OK to import the data.

Figure 4-5 shows a real-time stock quote and quote history imported from the Yahoo! web site. Yahoo! is a good source for this type of web query because it is a free service and doesn't require you to register or sign in.

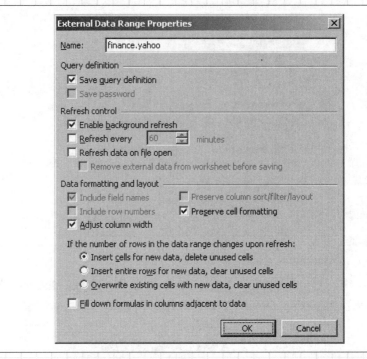

Figure 4-4. Use Query properties to name the query, set how data is refreshed, and how cells are inserted

How it works

If you choose Tools → Macro → Record New Macro, then perform the preceding web query, you'll get code that looks something like this:

```
With ActiveSheet.QueryTables.Add(Connection:= _
    "URL;http://finance.yahoo.com/q/ecn?s=SNDK", _
    Destination:=Range("C2"))
    .Name = "Real-Time Quote"
    .FieldNames = True
    .RowNumbers = False
    .FillAdjacentFormulas = False
    .PreserveFormatting = True
    .RefreshOnFileOpen = False
    .BackgroundQuery = True
    .RefreshStyle = xlOverwriteCells
    .SavePassword = False
    .SaveData = True
    .AdjustColumnWidth = True
    .RefreshPeriod = 0
    .WebSelectionType = xlSpecifiedTables
    .WebFormatting = xlWebFormattingNone
    .WebTables = "22"
```

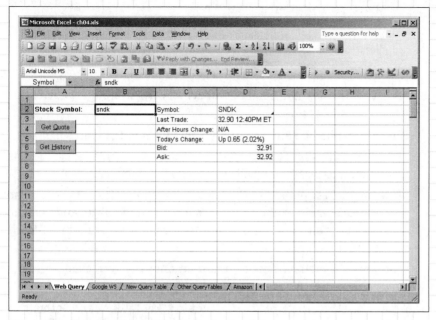

Figure 4-5. Using a web query to get stock price data

```
        .WebPreFormattedTextToColumns = True
        .WebConsecutiveDelimitersAsOne = True
        .WebSingleBlockTextImport = False
        .WebDisableDateRecognition = False
        .WebDisableRedirections = False
        .Refresh BackgroundQuery:=False
    End With

    With ActiveSheet.QueryTables.Add(Connection:= _
        "URL;http://finance.yahoo.com/q/hp?a=01&b=5&c=2003" &_
        "&d=01&e=5&f=2004&g=d&s=sndk", _
        Destination:=Range("A9"))
        .Name = "Price History"
        .FieldNames = True
        .RowNumbers = False
        .FillAdjacentFormulas = False
        .PreserveFormatting = True
        .RefreshOnFileOpen = False
        .BackgroundQuery = True
        .RefreshStyle = xlOverwriteCells
        .SavePassword = False
        .SaveData = True
        .AdjustColumnWidth = True
        .RefreshPeriod = 0
        .WebSelectionType = xlSpecifiedTables
        .WebFormatting = xlWebFormattingNone
        .WebTables = "30"
        .WebPreFormattedTextToColumns = True
```

```
                .WebConsecutiveDelimitersAsOne = True
                .WebSingleBlockTextImport = False
                .WebDisableDateRecognition = False
                .WebDisableRedirections = False
                .Refresh BackgroundQuery:=False
            End With
```

Some key properties and methods above shown in **bold** bear mention here:

- The `Add` method creates the query and adds it to the worksheet.
- The `RefreshStyle` property tells Excel to overwrite existing data rather than to insert new cells each time the query is refreshed.
- The `WebTables` property identifies which item from the page to import. Excel assigns an index to each item on the page, and you can import one or more items or the entire page if `WebSelectionType` is set to `xlEntirePage`.
- The `Refresh` method imports the data onto the worksheet. Without this method, the query results are not displayed.

The query itself consists of the `Connection`, `WebTables`, and formatting properties. If you save the web query to a query file (.iqy), the data looks like this:

```
WEB
1
http://finance.yahoo.com/q/hp?a=01&b=5&c=2003&d=01&e=5&f=2004&g=d&s=sndk

Selection=30
Formatting=None
PreFormattedTextToColumns=True
ConsecutiveDelimitersAsOne=True
SingleBlockTextImport=False
DisableDateRecognition=False
DisableRedirections=False
```

When Excel updates a web query, a small green globe is displayed in the status bar at the bottom of the screen (Figure 4-6). This symbol indicates that the query is being refreshed from the Internet.

Figure 4-6. Excel is refreshing the query from the Internet

Modify a Web Query

You can modify a web query by right-clicking on the query and select-ing Edit Query. In many cases, however, you'll want a more automated approach. For example, you may want to let the user change the stock symbol in the previous sample. To do that, use code to:

1. Change the Connection property of the query.
2. Refresh the query.

How to do it

The following code allows the user to enter a stock symbol in a named range on the worksheet to get current and historical price data for that stock:

```
Dim ws As Worksheet, qt As QueryTable
Set ws = ThisWorkbook.Sheets("Web Query")
Set qt = ws.QueryTables("Real-Time Quote")
qt.Connection = "URL;http://finance.yahoo.com/q/ecn?s=" & _
  ws.Range("Symbol").Value
qt.Refresh
Set qt = ws.QueryTables("Price History")
qt.Connection = "URL;http://finance.yahoo.com/q/
hp?a=01&b=5&c=2003&d=01&e=5&f=2004&g=d&s=" & _
  ws.Range("Symbol").Value
qt.Refresh
```

Recording code is a great way to learn how Excel does things, but it only takes you so far. You can modify recorded queries to change the query string dynamically based on user input.

How it works

If you run the preceding code, you may notice that the query is not updated right away. By default, web queries are done in the background asynchronously. This avoids tying up Excel while the web site responds to the query, but it can cause an error if you refresh the query again before the first request has had a chance to respond. You can avoid this by not performing the query in the background. For example, the follow-ing code turns off asynchronous queries, waiting for a response before executing the next line:

```
qt.BackgroundQuery = False
qt.Refresh
```

Or, more simply:

```
qt.Refresh False
```

This causes Excel to wait while the query completes. During this time, the user can't edit cells or perform other tasks. If this is too much of a burden, use the QueryTable object's Refreshing property to avoid asynchronous collisions:

```
Set qt = ws.QueryTables("Real-Time Quote")
If Not qt.Refreshing Then
    qt.Connection = "URL;http://finance.yahoo.com/q/ecn?s=" & _
        ws.[Symbol].Value
    qt.Refresh
Else
    MsgBox "Similar query is pending, please wait a second and try again."
End If
```

The preceding code checks if the web query is already executing before calling Refresh. If a previous query is still executing, the user is told to try again later. Notice that this code checks the status of a query performed by a single query table. Other, different query tables may have pending results without causing a collision—you only need to check the Refreshing property of the target query table before attempting to change or refresh a query.

Perform Periodic Updates

If the data in a web query changes frequently, you may want to have Excel automatically update the information periodically. Since web queries already run asynchronously in the background, getting them to update periodically is a simple matter of setting a property:

```
Set qt = ws.QueryTables("Real-Time Quote")
qt.RefreshPeriod = 1
```

Now, the query will update every minute. To turn off the background query, set the RefreshPeriod to 0:

```
qt.RefreshPeriod = 0
```

Interestingly, the BackgroundQuery property can be False and you can still perform periodic queries. In that case, the Excel user interface pauses periodically whenever the query is being refreshed.

Performing web queries in the background can seem a little strange—particularly if they are set to refresh periodically. Most Excel actions are synchronous, and it might surprise a user to see Excel pause for a second, update some cells, and then continue on as if nothing happened. This can become a big problem if the source of the web query changes and causes the web query to fail—the user will see an error message periodically and may not know what to do or how to fix it (Figure 4-7).

Events are a big deal any time you use an object asynchronously. Query tables don't automatically add their events to the worksheet's event list the way command buttons and other controls do. You need to take special steps to hook up query table events.

Figure 4-7. Failed web queries may display errors asynchronously

How to do it

To handle errors from asynchronous web queries, you must hook into the QueryTable events. You have to declare a QueryTable object variable using the WithEvents qualifier in order to trap its events. WithEvents can only be used in a class module or an Excel object module (such as the code module for a worksheet or workbook).

For example, to handle asynchronous events for a QueryTable in the wsWebQuery worksheet module, follow these steps:

1. Display the code window for the worksheet by double-clicking on wsWebQuery in the Visual Studio Project Explorer.

2. Add the following declaration to the worksheet's code module at the class level (outside of a procedure definition):

   ```
   Dim WithEvents qt As QueryTable
   ```

3. Select the qt object in the object list at the top of the code window, and then select AfterRefresh from the event list to create empty event procedures.

4. Add the following code to disable/enable the command buttons and to get feedback from the user if an error occurs:

   ```
   Private Sub qt_BeforeRefresh(Cancel As Boolean)
       ' Disable command button.
       cmdQuote.Enabled = False
   End Sub

   Private Sub qt_AfterRefresh(ByVal Success As Boolean)
       ' If update failed, get feedback.
       If Not Success Then
           If MsgBox("An error occurred getting web data. " & _
           "Cancel future updates?", vbYesNo, "Web Query") = vbYes Then _
           qt.RefreshPeriod = 0
       End If
       ' Re-enable command button.
       cmdQuote.Enabled = True
   End Sub
   ```

5. Write code to initialize the QueryTable object and to begin updates. For example, the following procedure hooks an existing QueryTable up to the event handlers defined above and sets the stock symbol the query uses:

```
Private Sub cmdQuote_Click()
    ' Get the QueryTable and hook it to the event handler object.
    Set qt = ActiveSheet.QueryTables("Real-Time Quote")
    ' Set the query.
    qt.Connection = "URL;http://finance.yahoo.com/q/ecn?s=" & [Symbol].Value
    ' Set the refresh period and make sure it's done asynchronously.
    qt.RefreshPeriod = 1
    qt.BackgroundQuery = True
    ' Refresh the data now.
    qt.Refresh
End Sub
```

Now, the user can stop the automatic updates if the query fails.

Strange but true

When working with asynchronous events in Excel, the event may run while you are editing it in Visual Basic. Often this will result in a runtime error because you haven't completed the code you were in the process of writing. It is a good idea to stop periodic updates while working on query table event code. You can do this by setting the query table's `RefreshPeriod` property to 0 in the Immediate window.

How it works

Anticipating potential asynchronous collisions can be a little tricky. One general way to deal with these is to lock out other operations in the BeforeRefresh event and re-enable operations in the AfterRefresh event by enabling and disabling the command button as shown in Step 4. That prevents the user from changing a query while it is pending. Another way is to check the `Refreshing` property (shown earlier). A final solution is not to use asynchronous queries at all.

For example, the following code gets the price history for a stock. Since price history data isn't very volatile, the code performs the query synchronously and waits for the result:

```
' Displays one year of the current symbol's price history.
Private Sub cmdHistory_Click()
    Dim ws As Worksheet, qt2 As QueryTable, conn As String
```

```
       Set ws = ThisWorkbook.ActiveSheet
       ' Build query string.
       conn = "URL;http://chart.yahoo.com/d?" &_
       YahooDates(Date - 365, Date) & ws.[Symbol].Value
       ' Get query
       Set qt2 = ws.QueryTables("Price History_1")
       ' Clear old history
       qt2.ResultRange.Clear
       ' Set connection property
       qt2.Connection = conn
       ' Make sure background queries are off.
       qt2.BackgroundQuery = False
       ' Refresh data
       qt2.Refresh
   End Sub

   ' Converts start and end dates to Yahoo query string for
   ' stock history.
   Function YahooDates(dtstart As Date, dtend As Date) As String
       ' Query sample string from Yahoo has this form:
       ' a=10&b=4&c=2003&d=1&e=5&f=2004&g=d&s=sndk
       Dim str As String
       str = "a=" & Month(dtstart) - 1 & "&b=" & Day(dtstart) & _
       "&c=" & Year(dtstart) & "&d=" & Month(dtend) - 1 & _
       "&e=" & Day(dtend) & "&f=" & Year(dtend) & "&g=d&s="
       Debug.Print str
       YahooDates = str
   End Function
```

When you run the preceding code, Excel changes the mouse pointer to the wait symbol and won't accept user actions till the query returns. This provides a much simpler logical path for programming.

Manage Web Queries

Most of the preceding samples get an existing QueryTable, modify its properties, and then call Refresh. I could have used the QueryTables collection's Add method to create these queries on the fly. However, I would need to remember to delete previously created QueryTables.

Getting rid of unneeded query tables on a worksheet can seem like an unimportant housekeeping chore, but it is very important to avoid having redundant or unneeded queries running in the background. Background queries degrade performance, spontaneously connect to the Internet, and can generate asynchronous errors, as mentioned earlier. This can really confuse users!

How to do it

The following code creates three new query tables on the active worksheet:

```
Dim ws As Worksheet, qt As QueryTable, i As Integer
Set ws = ActiveSheet
For i = 1 To 3
    Set qt = ws.QueryTables.Add("URL;http://finance.yahoo.com/q/ecn? _ &
    s=yhoo", [A12])
    qt.Name = "Temp Query"
    qt.WebTables = "22"
    qt.WebSelectionType = xlSpecifiedTables
    qt.WebFormatting = xlWebFormattingNone
    qt.BackgroundQuery = False
    qt.RefreshStyle = xlOverwriteCells
    qt.Refresh
Next
```

When this code runs it creates three query tables on the worksheet named Temp_Query, Temp_Query_1, and Temp_Query_2 respectively. There's no easy way to manage query tables through the Excel user interface, however, if you press Ctrl+G you'll see the names for the new query tables listed in the Go To dialog box (Figure 4-8).

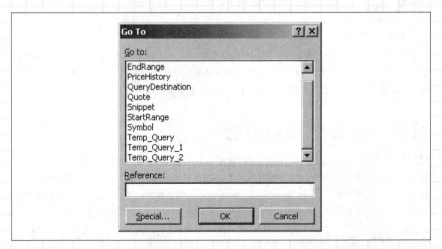

Figure 4-8. Excel automatically numbers query tables with those that have the same base name

It's possible to manually delete query tables by going to the named range and selecting Clear All, but that leaves the name in the worksheet, and subsequent names will be indexed _4, _5, etc. The easiest way to clean up mistaken or trial query tables is to write some code to help you remove them. For example, the following procedure lists each query table on a worksheet and lets you remove or keep it:

```
Sub RemoveOldQueries()
    Dim ws As Worksheet, qt As QueryTable, nm As Name
    Set ws = ActiveSheet
    For Each qt In ws.QueryTables
        If MsgBox("OK to delete " & qt.Name & "?", vbYesNo, _
        "Web Queries") = vbYes Then
            qt.Delete
        End If
    Next
    For Each nm In ws.Names
        If MsgBox("OK to delete " & nm.Name & "?", vbYesNo, _
        "Names") = vbYes Then
            nm.Delete
        End If
    Next
End Sub
```

Use Web Services

From an Excel perspective, web services are primarily useful for retrieving variable data over the Internet, but you can also use them to send data, to manipulate remote data, or to run other code on remote computers. Web services are designed to work just like procedure calls from code, so it is possible to use a web service without even knowing that it is running remote code.

That's possible, but it's not likely since web service methods often rely heavily on their underlying foundation: XML. That means Excel programmers must become familiar with the Microsoft XML type library before they can effectively use web services. The good news is that once you're comfortable working with XML, you can blast web service results directly into spreadsheet lists using Excel XML maps (which is *very* cool).

Queries versus services

Web queries are great for the ad hoc import of data onto a worksheet, but they rely on the position of elements on the page. If the structure of the source web page changes, the query may break. This means that web queries aren't well-suited for deployed solutions because you are likely to get a great number of support calls if the source web page changes or moves.

Also, you've got to compose complicated site-specific Connection properties (query strings) if you want to perform customized queries. Each web site has its own system of sending and receiving data through query strings, and it can be difficult to reverse-engineer those query strings correctly.

Web services do not have these limitations and generally provide a better interface for getting data from the Web. However, web services are not available for all data on the Internet so there are many, many cases where web queries are still very useful.

How it works

When Excel calls a web service, it sends a request across the Internet to the address of the web service and then waits for a response. The request is usually packaged as XML; the response is XML.

Web services, like many Internet-related things, are part of evolving standards. These standards have broad support by many companies, so web services are not likely to lose support in the future. However, since the standards are still evolving, there are different approaches to implementing, locating, and accessing web services. Of specific interest to Excel developers are the facts that:

- There are several ways to locate web services on the Internet. One way is through a directory service such as *http://uddi.microsoft.com/*, but a much more common way is just by browsing the business's own site or through a cross-listing site such as *http://www. xmethods.net/*.

- There are several ways to describe web services over the Internet. With Excel, you only really need to worry about one: WSDL.

- There are several ways to call web services. Some web services only support SOAP, while others, such as Amazon, also support access directly through their URLs.

The samples in this chapter focus on two widely used web services provided by Google and Amazon.com respectively. These services are nearly ideal for a chapter such as this because they are freely available, useful, well-documented, and demonstrate both SOAP and URL access.

Where to get it

Before you continue, however, you should download the following toolkits:

Toolkit	Location
Microsoft Office Web Services Toolkit	Search *http://www.microsoft.com/downloads* for "Web Services Toolkit"
Google web Service	*http://www.google.com/apis/*
Amazon web Service	Click on Web Services link at *http://www.amazon. com/*

Both of the preceding web services require you to register to get a developer ID to pass with method calls. I provide my developer ID with the code samples shown here, but you will want your own ID if you use these web services in your own code.

Use the Web Services Toolkit

The Web Services Toolkit provides a way to find and reference web services from Visual Basic. Once you create a reference to a web service, the Toolkit generates classes that give you a familiar interface to the XML expected by the web service. The Toolkit-generated classes also handle responses from the web service, converting those into objects, properties, and methods, rather than raw XML.

Depending on the web service you are using, the Web Services Toolkit may generate many or just a few new classes (Figure 4-9).

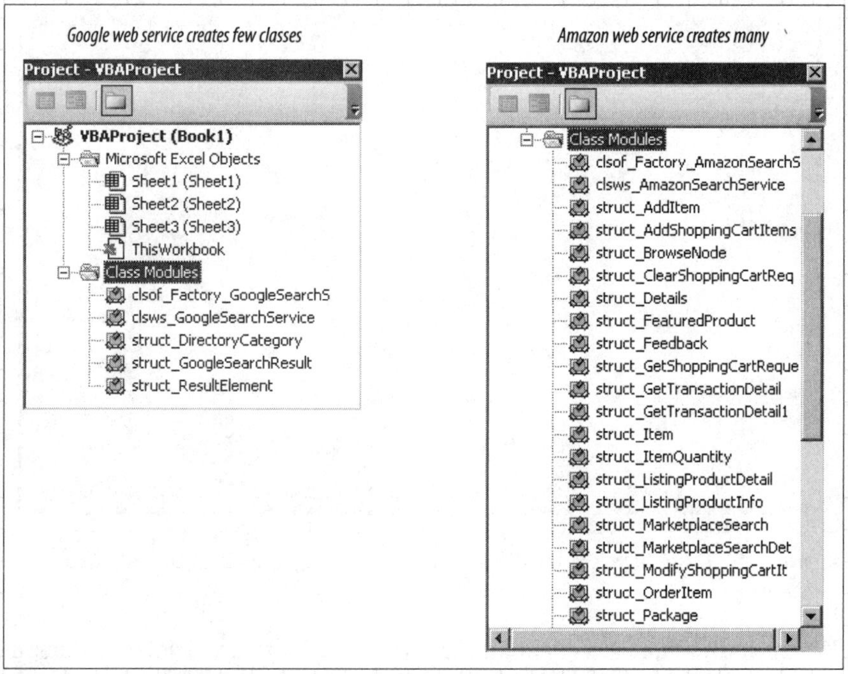

Office 2003 doesn't come with the Web Services Toolkit installed. You need to download and install that tool from Microsoft before proceeding.

Figure 4-9. Office Web Services Toolkit creates proxy classes for the referenced web service

How to do it

In order to use web services from Visual Basic, you must first follow these steps:

1. Find the Microsoft Office Web Services Toolkit from Microsoft by searching for "Web Services Toolkit" at *http://www.microsoft.com/downloads*.

2. Download the Web Services Toolkit installation program (*setup.exe*).

The Web Services Toolkit makes using web services easier by generating classes from the web service description. Those classes can then be used with a standard object-oriented approach to create an instance of the web service and invoke the web services properties and methods.

3. Run the downloaded installation program and follow the steps provided by the Setup Wizard.

4. Start Excel and open the Visual Basic editor.

5. In Visual Basic, select Web References from the Tools menu. Visual Basic displays the Microsoft Office 2003 Web Services Toolkit references dialog (Figure 4-10).

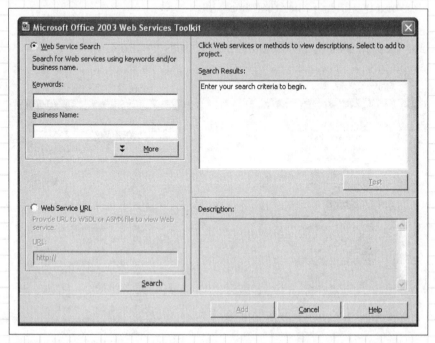

Figure 4-10. Use the Microsoft Office 2003 Web Services Toolkit to create a Web Reference

When you create a Web Reference, the Web Services Toolkit automatically adds references to Microsoft Office SOAP type library and the Microsoft XML library. Then, the toolkit generates proxy classes for the web service.

To see how this works, follow these steps:

1. From the Visual Basic Tools menu, select Web References.

2. Select Web Service URL and type the following line in the text box below that option:

```
http://api.google.com/GoogleSearch.wsdl
```

3. Click Search. The Web Services Toolkit displays the web services available from Google (Figure 4-11).

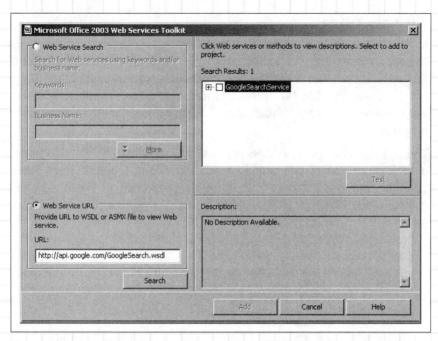

Figure 4-11. Creating a reference to the Google web service

4. Select the GoogleSearchService and click Add. The Web Service Toolkit adds references to the SOAP and XML libraries and creates proxy classes for each of the services (Figure 4-12).

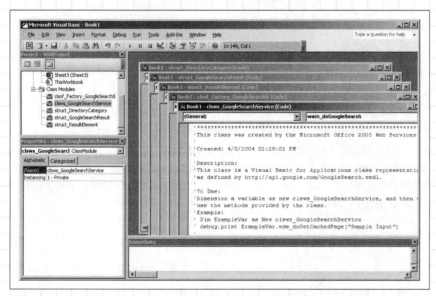

Figure 4-12. The Web Service Toolkit creates Google web service proxy classes

How it works

Proxy classes are modules of code that stand-in for the code that runs on the server providing the web service. You have to have a local copy of this code so you can compile your application against something. These proxy classes provide the properties and methods you call on the web service—they package those calls, send them, and receive their responses.

The code in these proxy classes is not simple. Fortunately, you don't have to understand much of it, just create an instance of the main class (identified by the prefix "clsws") and use its properties and methods. For example, the following code uses the generated classes to search Google for work I've done on Excel:

```
Dim i As Integer, wsGoogle As New clsws_GoogleSearchService
Dim wsResult As struct_GoogleSearchResult, wsElement As struct_ResultElement
Dim devKey As String, searchStr As String
' This key is from Google, used to identify developer.
devKey = "ekN14fFQFHK7lXIW3Znm+VXrXI7Focrl"
' Items to search for.
searchStr = "Jeff Webb Excel"
' Call the search web service.
Set wsResult = wsGoogle.wsm_doGoogleSearch(devKey, _
   searchStr, 0, 10, False, "", False, "", "", "")
' For each of the results
For i = 0 To wsResult.endIndex - 1
    ' Get the individual result.
    Set wsElement = wsResult.resultElements(i)
    ' Display the result.
    Debug.Print wsElement.title, wsElement.URL
Next
```

OK, that's not simple either. Most of the complication here comes from the web service itself. Google requires a license key to use their service, I include my key in the devKey variable. Google allows 1,000 search requests per day for this free license key, so you'll want to get your own key from Google eventually. But for now, it's OK to use my key.

Next, the wsm_doGoogleSearch method submits the search to Google. That method takes a lot of arguments and returns a structure, which is defined in another proxy class so you need to use Set to perform assignment. Similarly, you need to use Set to get elements from the result.

What about...

Table 4-1 lists the web service description addresses for the Google and Amazon web services. These are the addresses you enter in the Web Services Toolkits' Web Service URL field to create a reference to these services.

Table 4-1. Web service description addresses

Web Service	Web Service URL
Amazon	*http://soap.amazon.com/schemas3/AmazonWebServices.wsdl*
Google	*http://api.google.com/GoogleSearch.wsdl*

Use Web Services Through XML

Web services from different companies define their interfaces differently. For example, the Google web service provides methods that take simple string arguments, whereas the Amazon web service provides methods that take complex XMLNodeList arguments.

It's difficult to construct and debug XMLNodeList arguments for the Amazon web service. It's much easier to invoke this web service directly through its URL and receive the XML response directly.

How to do it

The following code performs a keyword search for books about wombats on Amazon:

```
Dim SearchUrl As String
' Create a new DOMDocument and set its options
Dim xdoc As New DOMDocument
xdoc.async = True
xdoc.preserveWhiteSpace = True
xdoc.validateOnParse = True
xdoc.resolveExternals = False

' Create the search request
SearchUrl = "http://xml.amazon.com/onca/xml2" & _
        "?t=" & "webservices-20" & _
        "&dev-t=" & "D1UCRO4XBIF4A6" & _
        "&page=1" & _
        "&f=xml" & _
```

You don't have to use the Web Services Toolkit to use web services. In some cases, it's actually easier to call a web service directly without using the generated proxy classes.

```
            "&mode=books" & _
            "&type=lite" & _
            "&KeywordSearch=wombat"

    ' Issue the request and wait for it to be honored
    Loaded = xdoc.Load(SearchUrl)
    ' Display the results
    Debug.Print xdoc.XML
```

Because the results are returned as XML, you can create XML map from
the result and import the results into a list created from that XML map as
shown here:

```
    Set wb = ThisWorkbook
    wb.XmlImportXml xdoc.XML, wb.XmlMaps("ProductInfo_Map"), True
```

Figure 4-13 displays the result of importing an Amazon search for
wombats into a list on a worksheet.

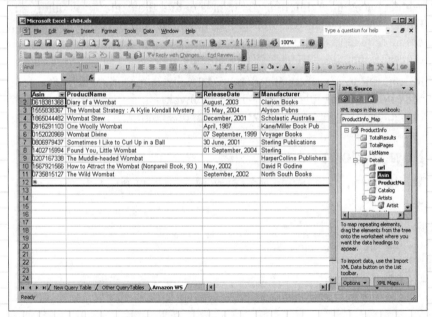

Figure 4-13. Displaying XML results from a web service through an XML map and list

How it works

The documentation for the Amazon web service is structured to show you
how to call its methods using its URL rather than using proxy classes and
SOAP. This means that you don't have to use the Web Services Toolkit to
create proxies for the Amazon web service, just add a reference to the
Microsoft XML type library.

This method of accessing a web service is sometimes called Representational State Transfer (REST). That acronym is useful as a search term when looking for this type of interface for a given web service. For instance, type "REST Google API" in a Google search to see an active debate on the relative features of REST and SOAP.

The Google web service doesn't support direct access through its URL, but you can avoid the proxies and call it directly through SOAP. For example, the following code performs a search for wombats and imports the result through an XML map directly into a list:

```
Dim soap As New SoapClient30, xn As IXMLDOMNodeList, strXML As String
soap.MSSoapInit "http://api.google.com/GoogleSearch.wsdl"
Set xn = soap.doGoogleSearch("ekN14fFQFHK7lXIW3Znm+VXrXI7Focrl", _
    "wombats", 0, 10, False, "", False, "", "", "")
' Build a string containing the results from the search in XML.
strXML = "<GoogleSearchResults>"
For i = 1 To xn.Length - 1
    strXML = strXML & xn(i).XML
Next
strXML = strXML & "</GoogleSearchResults>"
' Import the results through an XML Map into a list.
Set wb = ThisWorkbook
wb.XmlImportXml strXML, wb.XmlMaps("GoogleSearchResults_Map"), True
```

What about...

To learn about	Look here
Representational State Transfer (REST)	http://internet.conveyor.com/RESTwiki/moin.cgi/FrontPage
MSXML Documentation	http://msdn.microsoft.com/library/en-us/xmlsdk/htm/sdk_intro_6g53.asp
DOMDocument	http://msdn.microsoft.com/library/en-us/xmlsdk/htm/xml_obj_overview_20ab.asp
IXMLDOMNodeList	http://msdn.microsoft.com/library/en-us/xmlsdk30/htm/xmobjxmldomnodelist.asp

Call a Web Service Asynchronously

One advantage of calling a web service directly, rather than through proxies, is that it is very easy to handle the response asynchronously. The DOMDocument object provides an ondataavailable event that occurs when the object is finished loading XML from a source. This means that you can launch a web service request, release control to the user, and display results when a request is complete. Being able to handle a response asynchronously is especially important when the web service is returning a large amount of data.

How to do it

To use the DOMDocument object to respond to a web service asynchronously, follow these steps:

1. Declare a DOMDocument object at the module of a class. The class can be a workbook, worksheet, or code class module. For example, the following variable is declared in the wsAmazon worksheet class:

```
Dim WithEvents xdoc As DOMDocument
```

2. Select the xdoc object from the object list at the top of the code window, and then select ondataavailable from the event list to create an empty event procedure as shown here:

```
Private Sub xdoc_ondataavailable()

End Sub
```

3. In other code, initialize the xdoc object, set its async property to True, and then call the web service using the xdoc object's Load method. For example, the following event procedure searches Amazon.com for a keyword when the user clicks the Get Titles button on the wsAmazon worksheet:

```
Sub cmdTitles_Click()
    Dim SearchUrl As String
    ' Create a new DOMDocument and set its options
    Set xdoc = New DOMDocument
    xdoc.async = True

    ' Create the search request
    SearchUrl = "http://xml.amazon.com/onca/xml2" & _
            "?t=" & "webservices-20" & _
            "&dev-t=" & "D1UCRO4XBIF4A6" & _
            "&page=1" & _
            "&f=xml" & _
            "&mode=books" & _
            "&type=lite" & _
            "&KeywordSearch=" & txtSearch.Text

    ' Issue the request and wait for it to be honored
    Loaded = xdoc.Load(SearchUrl)
End Sub
```

4. Add code to the ondataavailable event procedure to respond to the web service data once it is returned. For example, the following code imports the result through an XML map and displays it in a list:

```
Private Sub xdoc_ondataavailable()
  Dim wb As Workbook
  ' Import the results through an XML Map into a list.
  Set wb = ThisWorkbook
  wb.XmlImportXml xdoc.XML, wb.XmlMaps("ProductInfo_Map"), True
End Sub
```

How it works

When you run the preceding code by clicking on the Get Titles button, Excel returns control to the user as soon as the click is done. The list is updated once the web service responds.

The Microsoft SOAP type library does not support asynchronous calls, so you can't use web services that only provide a SOAP interface asynchronously from Excel. The SOAP tools available with .NET do support asynchronous calls, however, so if you are programming with Visual Basic .NET outside of Excel, you can make asynchronous SOAP calls.

What about...

To learn about	Look here
The SOAP Toolkit	Search *http://www.microsoft.com/downloads* (for "SOAP Toolkit 3.0")
Creating .NET components for use in Excel	Chapter 5, *"Programming Excel with .NET"*

Reformat XML Results for Excel

One thing you may notice when you return web service results directly to Excel through an XML Map is that mixed content is not automatically formatted. HTML/XML formatting tags such as < b > and < i > appear as "< b >" and "< i >" rather than as bold and italic (Figure 4-14).

This might be the biggest gotcha for using web services from Excel. If the results returned by a web service are formatted in any way, that formatting is usually indicated by tags that Excel doesn't automatically interpret. You need to use a little trick to set formatting to look right.

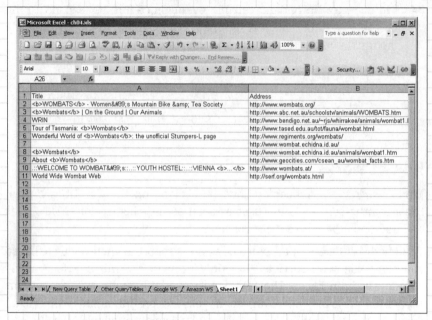

Figure 4-14. Excel does not automatically interpret HTML formatting

How to do it

There's no simple way to prevent this problem, but you can fix it using the automatic text formatting features of Excel. Excel automatically reformats HTML text pasted from the Clipboard, so all you have to do is place the data in the Clipboard as HTML, then paste that data back into cells on the spreadsheet.

In Excel, you access the Clipboard using the DataObject object, so the following code puts the data from each cell of a worksheet into the Clipboard as HTML, then pastes that data back, causing Excel to correctly interpret HTML formatting:

```
Sub TestReformat()
    ' Call Helper function to interpret HTML formatting codes.
    ReformatHTML ActiveSheet.UsedRange
End Sub

Sub ReformatHTML(rng As Range)
    Dim clip As New DataObject, cell As Range
    For Each cell In rng
        clip.SetText "<html>" & cell.Value & "<html>"
        clip.PutInClipboard
        cell.PasteSpecial
    Next
End Sub
```

How it works

After you run TestReformat on a worksheet, Excel interprets the HTML formatting codes as if you cut/pasted them from a web page (Figure 4-15).

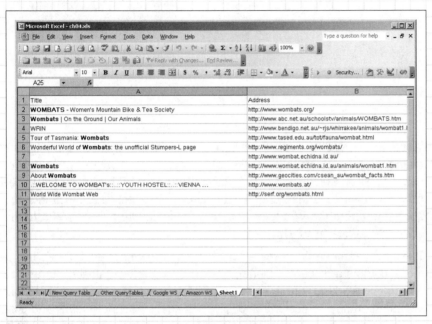

Figure 4-15. HTML formatting after running ReformatHTML

CHAPTER 5

Program Excel with .NET

Visual Basic .NET (VB.NET) is Microsoft's next generation of the Basic language. The name change marks another milestone in the evolution of Basic: BASICA, QuickBasic, Visual Basic (VBA), and VB.NET each mark distinct changes in underlying technology. This latest change marks the graduation from the Windows Common Object Model (COM) in VBA to the .NET Framework in VB.NET.

The .NET Framework solves a lot of the shortcomings in COM—it has a more complete security model; provides a well-organized library of objects for working with HTTP, XML, SOAP, encryption, and other things; is fundamentally object-oriented; protects against memory leaks and corruption; promotes self-describing code—gosh, I'm starting to sound like a commercial—in short, .NET is the future for programming Windows.

Now the bad news: Excel is (and probably always will be) a COM application. This means that you have to take special steps if you want to use .NET components from Excel or if you want to program Excel from VB.NET.

But back to the good news: Microsoft provides many tools for making the transition between COM and .NET as easy as possible. In this chapter you will learn how to use those tools both to take advantage of .NET from Excel and vice versa.

Work with .NET

There are three main approaches to using .NET with Excel. You can use .NET to create:

- Components that can be used from Excel macros. This approach works with all Excel versions and is much the same as creating COM components for use with Excel using Visual Basic 6.0. The .NET tools automatically generate the type libraries needed to use .NET objects from COM applications such as Excel.

- Standalone applications that use Excel as a component. This approach works best with Excel XP and 2003, since those versions provide the files needed to use Excel from .NET applications smoothly. In this scenario, the user starts a stand-alone application to create or modify Excel workbooks.

- Workbook-based applications that run all of their code as .NET. This approach works for Excel 2003 only. In this scenario, the user opens the workbook which automatically loads the .NET assembly containing the application code. The workbook contains a link to this assembly, so the workbook file (*.xls*) can be distributed to many different users and locations, while the assembly (*.dll*) resides in a single location (for example at a network address).

Code used in this chapter and additional samples are available in ch05.xls.

.NET isn't important just because it's new. It is much more consistent than VBA, includes a lot of great built-in classes, has a more complete security model, and supports inheritance. There's a lot to digest, so lets get started!

What you need

From the user's standpoint, the main differences between these approaches are how you start the application and what versions of Excel are supported. From a developer's standpoint, the differences affect how you develop, debug, and deploy the applications. Even the development tools you need vary somewhat between these approaches as described in Table 5-1.

Table 5-1. Software requirements for developing between Excel and .NET

To create	You need
.NET components for use in Excel	Visual Studio .NET standard edition or higher.
Standalone .NET applications that use Excel	Visual Studio .NET standard edition or higher Microsoft Office XP or 2003 Primary Interop Assemblies (PIAs).
Excel .NET Applications	Visual Studio .NET Tools for Office (includes above plus project templates)

Where to get it

To get	Look here
Visual Studio .NET editions	*http://msdn.microsoft.com/vstudio/howtobuy/*
Office XP PIAs	Search *http://www.microsoft.com/downloads* for "Office XP PIAs"

To get	Look here
Office 2003 PIAs	Install Professional Edition with the .NET programmability option selected for each application.
Visual Studio .NET Tools for Office	*http://msdn.microsoft.com/vstudio/howtobuy/office-tools/*

Create .NET Components

You can use .NET components from any VBA application. There are no version restrictions and no prerequisites other than the .NET Framework.

If you are an experienced VBA programmer, this is a great way to start learning .NET because you can take advantage of features built in to the .NET Framework in small, incremental steps.

How to do it

To create a .NET component for use in Excel:

1. From within Visual Studio .NET, create a new Class Library project using VB.NET or C#. Visual Studio creates a folder and template files for the project as shown in Figure 5-1.

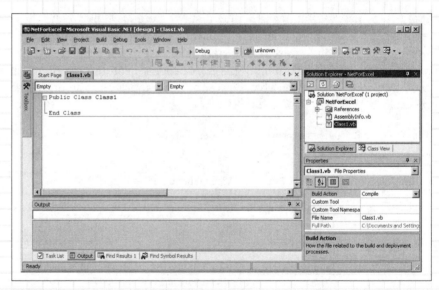

Figure 5-1. A new, empty .NET class library project

2. From the Project menu, choose Add Class. Visual Studio displays the Add Project Item dialog box, as shown in Figure 5-2.

3. Give the new class a descriptive name and click OK. Visual Studio registers the project to interoperate with COM (the Register for COM

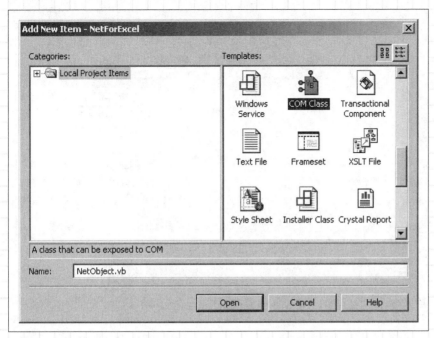

Figure 5-2. Create a new COM class to contain components for use from Excel

Interop selection on the Project Options, Build dialog box) and creates a new, empty code template for your class, as shown in
Figure 5-3.

4. Add code to the class library for the objects, properties, and methods
you want to use from Excel.

5. Compile the project by selecting Build Solution from the Build menu.
Visual Studio builds the class library as a .NET assembly (.dll) and
creates a type library file (.tlb) that allows Excel and other COM
applications to use that assembly. Both of these files are placed in a
/bin folder within the project folder created in Step 1.

For example, the NetForExcel project (*NetForExcel.sln*) includes a simple
class that provides a single method, which displays a message passed in
as an argument:

```
' .NET code.
Public Class NetObject
    Public Sub Test(ByVal arg As String)
        MsgBox(arg)
    End Sub
End Class
```

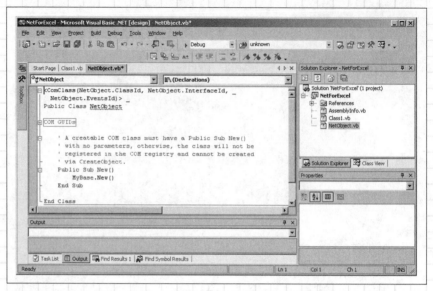

Figure 5-3. The COM class code template contains the basic elements you need for a component

What about...

The next section shows you how to use this sample .NET component from within Excel.

Use .NET Components

.NET components that contain COM classes show up in the References dialog box in VBA. You can add a reference and use those components much as you would any other component.

Visual Studio .NET projects that contain COM classes can be used from Excel VBA, or any other COM-based programming language even though they are .NET executables.

How to do it

Once you compile a .NET component with Register for COM Interop enabled, using that component from Excel is simply a matter of following these steps:

1. From within the VBA editor, select References from the Tools menu. VBA displays the References dialog box.

2. Click Browse and navigate to the /bin folder for the .NET component you wish to use. Select the type library (*.tlb*) for the component as shown in Figure 5-4, and click OK to add a reference to that component.

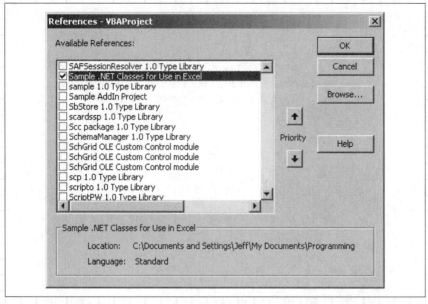

Figure 5-4. Use the .NET component's type library to create a reference to the component in VBA

3. Click OK to close the Reference dialog box.

4. Declare an object variable for the .NET class using the New keyword, then call the members of the class.

The components you create using VB.NET are named using their project name (.NET calls that the *namespace* of the component), so you would use the following code to call the NetForExcel project's NetObject created in the preceding section:

```
' Excel code
Sub TestNetObj()
    Dim x As New NetForExcel.NetObject
    x.Test "I worked!"
End Sub
```

Now, if you run the preceding code, Excel uses the type library to start the .NET assembly and invoke the Test method with a string argument. The .NET component, in turn, displays a message box saying "I worked!"

Though that demonstration isn't very impressive, what you can do with .NET components becomes exciting once you've learned more about the classes that come with the .NET Framework. For example, you can do some pretty useful things with even the basic .NET String and Array classes as shown here:

```
' .NET code
Public Class NetString

    + COM GUIDS

    ' A creatable COM class must have a Public Sub New( )
    ' with no parameters, otherwise, the class will not be
    ' registered in the COM registry and cannot be created
    ' via CreateObject.
    Public Sub New( )
        MyBase.New( )
    End Sub

    Public Function Split(ByVal arg As String, _
      Optional ByVal sep As String = " ") As String( )
        If Len(sep) <> 1 Then _
          Throw New Exception("Separator must be one character long")
        Return arg.Split(CType(sep, Char))
    End Function

    Public Function Join(ByVal arg( ) As String, _
      Optional ByVal sep As String = " ") As String
        If IsArray(arg) Then
            If arg.Rank <> 1 Then _
                Throw New Exception("Array must have one dimension")
        Else
            Throw New Exception("First argument must be an array")
        End If
        Return String.Join(sep, arg)
    End Function

    Public Function Sort(ByVal arg As String, _
      Optional ByVal ascending As Boolean = True) As String
        ' Declare an array.
        Dim ar( ) As String
        ' Break the string up and put it in the array.
        ar = arg.Split(" "c)
        ' Sort the array.
        ar.Sort(ar)
        ' Reverse the order if requested.
        If Not ascending Then ar.Reverse(ar)
        ' Convert the array back to a string and return it.
        Return String.Join(" ", ar)
    End Function
End Class
```

To use the preceding .NET class in code, compile the project and establish a reference to that project in the VBA Editor, then write code similar to the following:

```
' Excel code
Sub TestNetString()
    Dim str As String, ar() As String, i As Integer
    Dim NetStr As New NetForExcel.NetString
    str = "Some random text that you'd want to sort."
    Debug.Print NetStr.Sort(str)
    ar = NetStr.Split(str)
    For i = 0 To UBound(ar)
        Debug.Print ar(i)
    Next
End Sub
```

How it works

The preceding code displays the sorted string in the Immediate window, then splits the string in to an array and displays it one word at a time. Since Visual Studio .NET generates a type library for the component and registers it with your system, you automatically get Intellisense and auto-complete features when you work with .NET objects in VBA as shown in Figure 5-5.

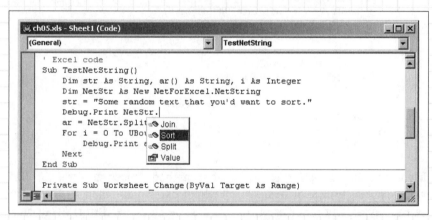

Figure 5-5. .NET objects registered for COM automatically get Intellisense and autocomplete in VBA

Respond to Errors and Events from .NET

The .NET code in the preceding section included a couple lines that may be unfamiliar to you:

```
If Len(sep) <> 1 Then _
    Throw New Exception("Separator must be one character long")
```

And:

```
If IsArray(arg) Then
    If arg.Rank <> 1 Then Throw New Exception("Array must have one
dimension")
Else
    Throw New Exception("First argument must be an array")
End If
```

VB.NET and VBA use different error-handling constructs and terminology. You need to understand these differences to translate between the two.

These lines demonstrate VB.NET's new error-handling constructs: Throw raises an error (.NET calls these *exceptions*), the error is created as a New Exception object, and would be handled by a Try...Catch structure (not shown) if the method was called from .NET.

How to do it

Since this code is called from Excel, however, you handle it using the VBA On Error statement. For example:

```
' Excel code.
Sub TestNetError()
    Dim ar(1, 1) As String
    Dim NetStr As New NetForExcel.NetString
    ar(0, 0) = "causes": ar(0, 1) = "an": ar(1, 0) = "error"
    On Error Resume Next
    ' Cause error.
    Debug.Print NetStr.Join(ar)
    ' Catch and report error
    If Err Then
        Debug.Print "Error:", Err.Description
        Err.Clear
    End If
    On Error GoTo 0
End Sub
```

If you run the preceding code, the Join method causes an error (in .NET you'd say it *throws an exception*) which can be handled in Excel the same way as any other error. In this case, a message "Error: Array must have one dimension" is displayed in the Immediate window.

Handling events from .NET components in VBA is much the same as handling events from Excel objects: declare the object variable WithEvents at the module level of an Excel class, initialize the object, and respond to the event in an event-hander procedure. For example, the following code defines and raises an event in the .NET NetString class:

```
' .NET code
Public Class NetString
    ' Declare event.
    Public Event Sorted As EventHandler
    Private m_value As String
```

```
' Other code omitted.

Public Function Sort(ByVal arg As String, _
    Optional ByVal ascending As Boolean = True) As String
        ' Declare an array.
        Dim ar() As String, res As String
        ' Break the string up and put it in the array.
        ar = arg.Split(" "c)
        ' Sort the array.
        ar.Sort(ar)
        ' Reverse the order if requested.
        If Not ascending Then ar.Reverse(ar)
        ' Convert the array back to a string and set value property
        m_value = String.Join(" ", ar)
        ' Raise event.
        OnSorted()
        ' Return result
        Return m_value
End Function

' By convention, events are raised from OnXxx procedures in .NET
Friend Sub OnSorted()
    RaiseEvent Sorted(Me, System.EventArgs.Empty)
End Sub

' Property that returns Sort result (added to illustrate event).
Public ReadOnly Property Value() As String
    Get
        Return m_value
    End Get
End Property
End Class
```

The preceding event occurs any time the Sort method completes a sort.
This actually occurs very quickly, so this isn't the greatest use for an
event but it's clearer to build on this previous example than to start a
completely new one. To handle this event in Excel, add the following
code to the class for a worksheet:

```
' Excel code in a worksheet class.
Dim WithEvents NetStr As NetForExcel.NetString

Private Sub Worksheet_Change(ByVal Target As Range)
    If Target.Address = "$A$2" Then
        ' Create object if it hasn't been initialized.
        If TypeName(NetStr) = "Nothing" Then _
            Set NetStr = New NetForExcel.NetString
        ' Sort text in range A2.
        NetStr.Sort [a2].Text
    End If
End Sub
```

```
Private Sub NetStr_Sorted(ByVal sender As Variant, _
    ByVal e As mscorlib.EventArgs)
        ' When sort is complete, display result in range B2.
        [b2].Value = NetStr.Value
End Sub
```

How it works

Now, you can change the text in cell A2 and the Sorted event displays the result in cell B2 once the sort is complete. There are a couple of points to note here:

- VBA can only respond to events from within classes—that includes workbook and worksheet classes, as well as custom classes (.NET calls these *instance classes*). You can't use events from modules (.NET calls these *static classes* or *code modules*).

- Once you declare a .NET object WithEvents, that component's events appear in the listbox at the top of the VBA editor code window.

- You can't combine New and WithEvents, so you must initialize the object somewhere in a procedure (as shown previously in the Worksheet_Change procedure).

Debug .NET Components

If you've been following along with the preceding example by writing code in Excel and Visual Studio .NET, you've probably noticed that you can't build the .NET project while Excel has a reference to that project's type library. You need to close Excel or remove the reference each time you make a change in the .NET project. That's because Visual Studio .NET can't overwrite the type library while another application is using it.

This makes debugging .NET components from Excel difficult. In fact, it's not a very good practice. It is a much better practice to add a second test project to your .NET component solution and make that project the start-up project.

Building tests into your development projects is a good practice. In fact, there's a school of thought (called extreme programming) that says you should write tests first, before you implement any feature.

How to do it

To add a test project to the NetForExcel sample, follow these steps:

1. From Visual Studio .NET, choose File → Add Project → New Project. Visual Studio .NET displays the Add New Project dialog box.

2. Select the Console Application template from the VBA project types, give the project a descriptive name, and click OK. Visual Studio .NET

creates a folder and template files for the new Windows console application.

3. Right-click on the new project title in the Solution Explorer and select Set As Startup Project from the pop-up menu, as shown in Figure 5-6. Visual Studio .NET makes the project name bold, indicating it is the startup project.

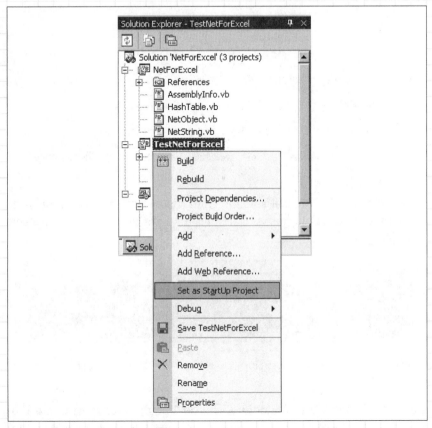

Figure 5-6. Make the test project the startup project for the solution

4. Add code to the test project's Main procedure to test the .NET component.

For example, the following code tests the NetString class from the NetForExcel component created earlier:

```
' .NET test code
Module Module1
    Dim WithEvents NetStr As New NetForExcel.NetString
```

```
Sub Main()
    Dim ar() As String = {"This", "That", "Other"}
    Dim ar2(1, 1) As String, str As String = "Some more text"
    ar2(0, 0) = "This" : ar2(0, 1) = "That" : ar2(1, 0) = "Other"
    Console.WriteLine(NetStr.Join(ar, ", "))
    Console.WriteLine(NetStr.Sort(str, False))
    ' Cause error.
    Try
        'NetStr.Join("Test, That, Other")
        'NetStr.Join(ar2)
        NetStr.Split(str, " r")
    Catch ex As Exception
        Console.WriteLine("Error: " & ex.Message)
    End Try
    ' Wait for Enter keypress to end.
    Console.Read()
End Sub

Private Sub NetStr_Sorted(ByVal sender As Object, _
    ByVal e As System.EventArgs) Handles NetStr.Sorted
        Console.WriteLine("Sort event complete. Result: " & NetStr.Value)
End Sub
End Module
```

If you run the NetForExcel solution from Visual Studio .NET by pressing
F5, Windows starts the test project and displays the results in a console
window as shown in Figure 5-7.

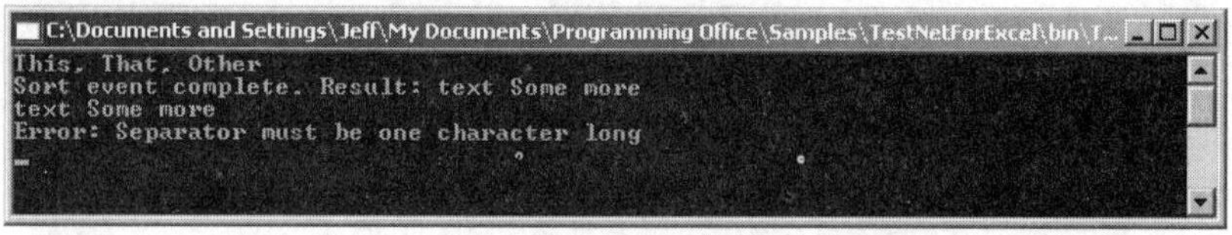

Figure 5-7. Using a console test project to debug a .NET component before using it
from Excel

Now, you can use Visual Studio .NET's debugging tools to step into procedures, set breakpoints and watches, and perform other typical debugging and testing tasks.

Distribute .NET Components

Visual Studio .NET uses Setup and Deployment projects to create the
installation applications you use to distribute .NET components or any
other type of application. These tools are greatly improved over the
Visual Basic 6.0 setup wizards and there are a number of paths you can
take to create an installation program for your .NET components.

*.NET Setup and
Deployment
projects create
Windows installer
files (.msi) that
can be installed
as standalone
components or
made part of a
chained installa-
tion involving other
applications—
including installa-
tions created
using the Office
Custom Installa-
tion Wizard
(CIW).*

How to do it

The following steps outline one of the possible paths:

1. From Visual Studio .NET, choose File → Add Project → New Project. Visual Studio .NET displays the Add New Project dialog box.

2. Select the Setup and Deployment project type, then select the Setup Wizard from the Templates list. Name the setup project descriptively and click OK. Visual Studio .NET starts the Setup Wizard to walk you through creating the project.

3. Follow the steps in the Setup Wizard to install a Windows application and select the Primary output for NetForExcel project group in Step 3 of the Wizard as shown in Figure 5-8.

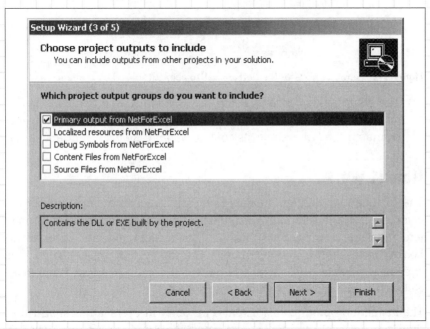

Figure 5-8. Select the primary output for the project to install

4. When you click Finish in the Setup Wizard, Visual Studio .NET creates a folder for the setup project, determines the dependencies for NetForExcel, and creates a setup project as shown in Figure 5-9.

5. From the Build menu, select Build Solution or Build setup project to package *NetForExcel.dll* and *NetForExcel.tlb* and build an installation program to install and register those files on a client's machine.

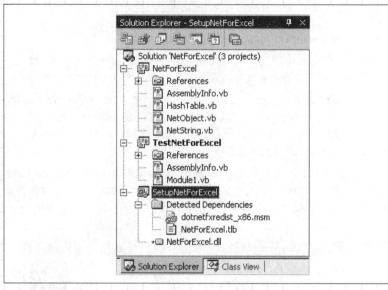

Figure 5-9. Setup project for the NetForExcel component

6. The setup project creates *Setup.exe*, *Setup.msi*, and *Setup.ini* files in its /Debug folder by default. Use those files to test deployment before changing the Setup project's configuration to Release and rebuilding.

How it works

The installation program created using the preceding steps installs the component in the /Program Files folder on the user's machine and registers the component's type library in the system registry. Excel workbooks that reference this type library use the system registry to find the component by its GUID (which is part of the code generated automatically when you create the COM class in .NET).

The installation program also creates an entry in users' application list so they can uninstall the application using the Windows Control Panel. In short, it does everything you need it to!

Use Excel as a Component in .NET

Another way for Excel to interact with the .NET world is to program with Excel objects directly in VB.NET. In this case, Excel becomes a component for use in a .NET application—the reverse of the case just shown.

Using Excel as a component in a .NET application is handy when you want to present application output using the Excel interface—as a spreadsheet or chart, for instance.

Excel works as a component, too. It's a big one, though, and you need to be careful when using it from .NET applications.

How to do it

To create a .NET application that uses Excel as a component:

1. Create a new Windows application project in Visual Studio .NET.

2. Choose Project → Add Reference. Visual Studio .NET displays the Add Reference dialog box, click the COM tab. Visual Studio .NET displays the COM objects registered on your system as shown in Figure 5-10.

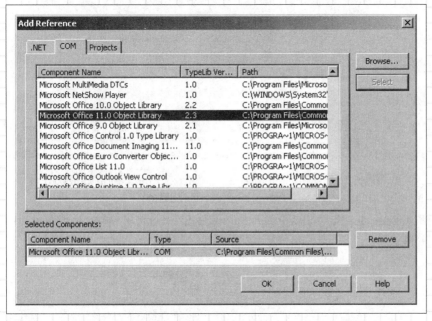

Figure 5-10. Adding a reference to the Microsoft Excel object library

3. Select the Microsoft Excel 11.0 Object Library and click Select, then OK to add the reference to your project. Visual Studio .NET automatically references the PIA for the Excel object library if it is installed on your system.

4. If the PIA is not installed, Visual Studio .NET creates a new interop assembly and adds it to your project (this is not what you want—the PIA is much more reliable). To make sure you are using the PIA, check the Name and Path properties of the Excel reference. They should appear as shown in Figure 5-11.

Look here

Use the COM page of the References dialog to add a reference to the Excel PIAs. Even though those are actually .NET assemblies, you won't find them on the .NET page.

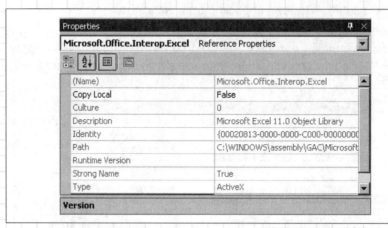

Figure 5-11. Check the reference properties to make sure you are using the Excel PIA

5. In code, create an instance of the Excel Application object and use that object's member to perform tasks in Excel.

For example, the following code starts Excel and creates a new workbook:

```
' .NET Windows form code
Dim WithEvents As Microsoft.Office.Interop.Excel.Application

Private Sub cmdStartExcel_Click(ByVal sender As System.Object, _
    ByVal e As System.EventArgs) Handles cmdStartExcel.Click
    ' If not initialized, create a new instance of the object.
    If IsNothing(m_xl) Then _
        m_xl = New Microsoft.Office.Interop.Excel.Application
    ' Make Excel visible.
    m_xl.Visible = True
    ' Create a new workbook.
    m_xl.Workbooks.Add()
End Sub
```

The m_xl variable is declared WithEvents so VB.NET can respond to events that occur in the application. The cmdStartExcel_Click procedure initializes the Excel Application object if it was not already initialized, and then it calls the Workbook collection's Add method to create a new workbook. It is important to note that if Visible is not set to True, all this happens invisibly in the background and, while that is kind of interesting, it is not usually what you want.

Use the following code to close the Excel application when you are done:

```
Private Sub cmdQuitExcel_Click(ByVal sender As System.Object, _
    ByVal e As System.EventArgs) Handles cmdQuitExcel.Click
    ' Close the Excel application.
    m_xl.Quit()
    ' Set object reference to Nothing.
    m_xl = Nothing
    ' Force .NET to perform garbage collection.
    System.GC.Collect()
End Sub
```

How it works

The preceding code illustrates a couple precautions you should take when working with Excel from .NET.

First, you should set the object variable to Nothing after you call Quit. Calling Quit doesn't set m_xl to Nothing, which can keep the application alive, running in the background.

Second, force .NET to get rid of unused resources by calling System.GC. Collect. .NET manages memory using a process called *garbage collection* and you need to force it to take out the garbage after you've thrown away Excel. Otherwise, .NET will leave Excel in memory until resources run low and automatic garbage collection takes place (I think of this as waiting for my son to take out the garbage, rather than doing it myself). You don't want to call GC.Collect frequently because it is an expensive operation, but it is great when you want to free very large objects like Excel.

Work with Excel Objects in .NET

Once you've got an instance of the Excel Application object, you can use it to get at any of the other objects in the Excel object library.

How to do it

VB.NET has an Imports declaration that you can use to create a shortcut for referring to objects from a particular library. For example, the following class-level declaration:

```
Imports Microsoft.Office.Interop
```

Using Excel objects from .NET is a little different from using them from VBA. There are no Set or default members in .NET.

shortens the Excel application declaration to:

```
Dim WithEvents m_xl As Excel.Application
```

which is easier to type and read. Notice that you don't use Set to get object references in VB.NET. For example, the following code gets a reference to Workbook and Range objects to display powers of 2 on a worksheet:

```
' .NET code.
Dim wb As Excel.Workbook, rng As Excel.Range
' Create a new workbook.
wb = m_xl.Workbooks.Add( )
' Add some data
For i As Integer = 1 To 10
    rng = wb.Worksheets(1).Cells(1, i)
    rng.Value = 2 ^ i
Next
```

VB.NET could get rid of Set because it also got rid of default members. In VBA, you can assign a value to a Range object because the Value property is the *default member* of the Range object. This is a clearer approach to a language—default members were never a very good idea.

This change can take some getting used to, especially if you don't explicitly declare a type for a variable. For example, the following .NET code gets a reference to a Range object, but then replaces that reference with an integer:

```
Dim obj
' Gets a reference to the A1 range object.
obj = wb.Worksheets(1).Cells(1, 1)
' Assigns a number to obj (does not set [A1].Value!)
obj = 42
```

Because of this, it is a good idea to declare variables with explicit data types when programming in VB.NET. Using explicit types also enables the Intellisense and autocomplete features when working with variables—so there are a lot of good reasons to be explicit!

Help!

You can't get help on Excel objects from within Visual Studio. It's a good idea to create a shortcut to the Excel VBA help files and open those files manually when you need reference information on Excel objects.

What about...

To get help on Excel objects	Open
For Excel 2003	*C:\Program Files\Microsoft Office\OFFICE11\1033\VBAXL10.CHM*
For Office 2003 (includes some objects used in Excel)	*C:\Program Files\Microsoft Office\OFFICE11\1033\VBAOF11.CHM*
For Excel XP	*C:\Program Files\Microsoft Office\OFFICE10\1033\VBAXL10.CHM*
For Office XP	*C:\Program Files\Microsoft Office\OFFICE10\1033\VBAOF10.CHM*

TIP

Excel VBA Help kept the same filename between the XP and 2003 versions, but there are differences between the two help files.

Respond to Excel Events in .NET

Responding to Excel events in .NET code is done much the same way as in VBA with one difference: in .NET, event procedures are associated with objects using the Handles clause. Excel uses the procedure name to associate an event with an object. The .NET approach means that a single procedure can handle multiple events.

Renaming an event procedure in .NET doesn't change its connection to an event. Changing the Handles clause does that.

How to do it

To respond to Excel events in .NET:

1. Declare a WithEvents variable for the Excel object providing the events at the class level. For example, the following code declares a worksheet with events:

    ```
    Dim WithEvents m_ws As Excel.Workbook
    ```

2. Assign the variable an instance of the object for which to handle events. For example, the following code hooks up the events for the first worksheet in a workbook (created in earlier examples):

    ```
    m_ws = wb.Worksheets(1)
    ```

3. Select the m_ws object from the object list at the top of the code window and then select an event from the event list. Visual Studio creates a new, empty event procedure.

4. Write code to respond to the event.

For example, the following code sorts any string entered in cell A2 and displays the result in B2. It may look familiar, since it uses the NetString class created earlier to perform the sort.

```
Private Sub m_wb_SheetChange(ByVal Sh As Object, _
    ByVal Target As Microsoft.Office.Interop.Excel.Range) _
    Handles m_wb.SheetChange
      If Target.Address = "$A$2" Then
          Dim NetStr As New NetForExcel.NetString
          m_wb.Worksheets(1).Range("B2").Value = NetStr.Sort(Target.Value)
      End If
End Sub
```

Respond to Excel Errors in .NET

In .NET, errors are reported as exception objects. You handle errors using the VB.NET Try...Catch...End Try construct. When .NET receives an error from a COM component, such as Excel, it checks the COM error code (COM identifies errors as *HRESULTs* which are 32-bit numbers) and tries to map that error to one of the .NET exception classes, such as DivideByZeroException.

If .NET can't map an HRESULT to a .NET exception class, it reports that error as a COMException. A COMException includes Source and Message properties that are filled in if they are available, plus it includes the HRESULT as an ErrorCode property.

How it works

The error codes that Excel reports are one of the weak spots in Excel VBA and that's no different when working with Excel from .NET. You need to know where to look when trying to handle Excel errors from .NET.

When working with Excel from .NET, you will find that most errors are reported as COMExceptions and that the Source and Message properties are sometimes, but not always, helpful. For example, referring to a worksheet that doesn't exist causes an COMException with Source equal to "Microsoft.Office.Interop.Excel" and a Message property "Invalid index." But setting a cell to an invalid value is reported as a COMException with an empty Source property and a Message property set to "Exception from HRESULT: 0x800A03EC."

The following code illustrates causing, catching, and reporting different types of Excel errors in .NET:

```
Private Sub cmdCauseErrors_Click(ByVal sender As System.Object, _
  ByVal e As System.EventArgs) Handles cmdCauseError.Click
    Try
      ' This worksheet (9) doesn't exist.
      m_xl.ActiveWorkbook.Sheets(9).Range("B2").value = 42
    Catch ex As System.Runtime.InteropServices.COMException
      Debug.WriteLine(ex.Source & " " & ex.Message & " " & _
        Hex(ex.errorcode))
    End Try
    Try
      ' This is an invalid value for a cell.
      m_ws.Range("A3").Value = "=This won't work."
    Catch ex As System.Runtime.InteropServices.COMException
      Debug.WriteLine(ex.Source & " " & ex.Message & " " & _
        Hex(ex.errorcode))
    End Try
    Try
      ' Set breakpoint here and edit a cell in Excel to see error.
      m_xl.ActiveWorkbook.Sheets(1).Range("B3").select()
      ' Can't change a cell while Excel is editing a range.
      m_xl.ActiveWorkbook.Sheets(1).Range("B2").value = 42
    Catch ex As System.Runtime.InteropServices.COMException
      Debug.WriteLine(ex.Source & " " & ex.Message & " " & _
        Hex(ex.errorcode))
    End Try
  End Sub
```

The preceding code catches the COMException that occurs for each deliberately caused error. If you run the code, the following report will display in the Visual Studio .NET Output window:

```
Microsoft.Office.Interop.Excel Invalid index. 8002000B
  Exception from HRESULT: 0x800A03EC. 800A03EC
mscorlib Call was rejected by callee. 80010001
```

As you can see, the Source and Message properties are not always helpful (or even present). In many cases, it is better to use the ErrorCode, which contains the original COM HRESULT.

HRESULTS consist of several parts, but the last 16 bits are the most useful when programming with Excel from .NET; those 16 bits contain the Excel error code for the error. The following helper function parses an HRESULT and returns the Excel error code:

```
' Returns the last 16 bits of HRESULT (which is Err code).
Function GetErrCode(ByVal hresult As Integer) As Integer
    Return hresult And &HFFFF
End Function
```

That said, Excel assigns the error code 1004 (application error) to most of the errors it returns. All of this means that it is pretty hard to find out what specific error occurred within Excel—usually you just know that the operation failed.

What this means

The best strategy for handling Excel errors in .NET is to:

- *Unitize* Excel operations—that is, try to group operations that use Excel into a single procedure that performs some atomic operation such as creating, populating, and saving a workbook.
- Call these unitized operations from within a Try...Catch structure.
- Notify users of a general problem if operation fails.
- Avoid user-interactive modes. Operations such as changing spreadsheet cell values can fail if the user is editing a cell when the programmatic operation occurs. Use the Excel Application objects Interactive property to turn user-interactive mode on and off.

The following code illustrates the preceding approaches in the context of making some changes to cells on a worksheet. The Excel operations are unitized in a single procedure and those operations all run within a Try...Catch block. User interaction is turned off at the start of the procedure then re-enabled at the end.

```
Private Sub cmdChangeCells_Click(ByVal sender As System.Object, _
    ByVal e As System.EventArgs) Handles cmdChangeCells.Click
    If Not SquareCells() Then _
        MsgBox("Excel operation failed.")
End Sub

Private Function SquareCells() As Boolean
    Try
        ' Try to turn off interactive mode.
        m_xl.Interactive = False
        ' For each cell in the active sheet's used range...
        For Each cel As Excel.Range In m_xl.ActiveSheet.UsedRange
            ' Square the value.
            cel.Value = cel.Value ^ 2
        Next
    Catch ex As System.Runtime.InteropServices.COMException
        ' Something happened in Excel.
        Debug.Fail(ex.Source & " " & Hex(ex.errorcode), ex.Message)
        Return False
    Catch ex As Exception
        ' Something happened in .NET (display error while debugging)
        Debug.Fail(ex.Source, ex.Message)
        Return False
    Finally
        Try
            ' Try to turn interactive mode back on.
            m_xl.Interactive = True
        Catch ex As Exception
            ' No need to do anything here.
        End Try
```

```
      End Try
      ' Success.
      Return True
   End Function
```

There are a couple of important details to point out here: first you must turn interactivity back on inside its own `Try...Catch` block. This protects against an unhandled exception if `m_xl` is not a valid object (perhaps because the user has closed Excel). Second, if the worksheet contains cells with text, an error will occur, but it will be handled. This may or may not be what you want to occur—that decision is up to you.

TIP

Be careful when using `For...Each` with the Excel UsedCells collection. VB.NET doesn't always recognize UsedCells as a proper collection. In those cases you will encounter a Member Not Found COM error. UsedCells seems to work only when called directly from the Application.ActiveSheet or Application.Worksheets(*index*) objects, rather than from variables referencing those objects.

What about...

To learn about	Look here
Structure of COM HRESULTs	Search *http://msdn.microsoft.com* for "Structure of COM Error Codes"
Problems using Excel collections from .NET	*http://support.microsoft.com/?kbid=328347*

Distribute .NET Applications That Use Excel

Use the Visual Studio .NET Setup and Deployment project to create an installation program for applications that use Excel as a component. (See "Distribute .NET Components" for a walk-through of using the Setup Wizard.)

How to do it

The .NET setup tools detect the .NET Frameworks and Excel PIAs as dependencies of any application that uses Excel as a component and includes those files with the installation. However, the setup tools do not automatically check for the installation of Microsoft Excel or any other Microsoft Office product.

Improperly installing a .NET application that uses Excel may overwrite Excel component files and possibly violate the user's license agreement. You need to know what you're doing!

To verify that Excel is installed before installing your .NET application, add a launch condition to your installation project. To do this, create an installation project in Visual Studio .NET and follow these steps:

1. Select the installation project, then click the Launch Conditions Editor in the Solutions Explorer (Figure 5-12).

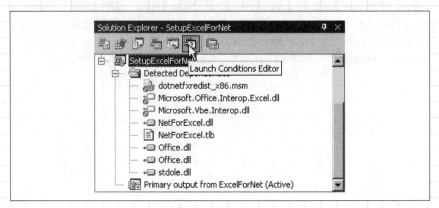

Figure 5-12. Adding a launch condition to an installation project

2. In the Launch Condition window, right-click Search the Target Machine and select Add File Search. Visual Studio .NET creates a file search item and displays its properties (Figure 5-13).

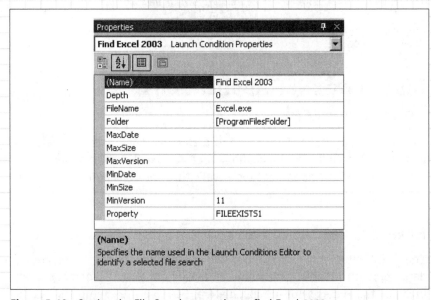

Figure 5-13. Setting the File Search properties to find Excel 2003

3. Set the FileName, Folder, and MinVersion properties, as shown in Figure 5-13.

If your application uses Excel 2003, you should exclude the Office PIAs from the automatically detected dependencies in your installation project. According to Microsoft, you should not distribute the Office 2003 PIAs as part of your application. Those files are a part of the Office System. If you include the PIAs as part of your installation, you could violate the user's license and uninstalling your application could remove the PIAs breaking Office features. Instead, you should use the Office 2003 Setup to install the PIAs.

To exclude the Office 2003 PIAs from your installation project, select the dependency in the Solution Explorer and set its Exclude property to True (Figure 5-14).

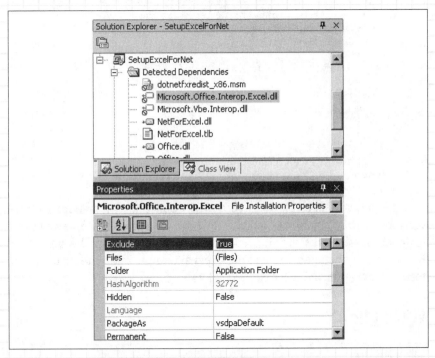

Figure 5-14. For Excel 2003, exclude the Office PIAs

There are PIAs available for both Excel XP and Excel 2003. According to Microsoft, it is OK to distribute the Excel XP PIAs with your application, since they aren't considered part of the Office XP system.

You can also use Visual Studio .NET type library import tools to create interop assemblies for earlier versions of Excel (they won't work as well as the PIAs, but they *will* work). All interop assemblies are tied to a specific version of Excel, so you should check that the required version of Excel is installed on the user's computer before installing your application and each time your application starts. You can use the following code to detect which version of Excel is installed:

```
' Uses the following Imports statement for RegistryKey classes:
Imports Microsoft.Win32
Function GetExcelVer() As String
    ' Define the RegistryKey objects.
    Dim regRoot As RegistryKey, regExcel As RegistryKey, ver As String
    ' Get root registry entry.
    regRoot = Microsoft.Win32.Registry.ClassesRoot
    ' Get the Excel current version registry entry.
    regExcel = regRoot.OpenSubKey("Excel.Application\CurVer")
    ' If regExcel is Nothing, then Excel is not installed.
    If IsNothing(regExcel) Then
        ' Close Registry key.
        regExcel.Close()
        ' Return 0, no version is installed
        ver = "0"
    Else
        ver = regExcel.GetValue("")
    End If
    ' Close registry.
    regExcel.Close()
    ' Return the Excel version.
    Return ver
End Function
```

It is theoretically possible to have a .NET application work with multiple versions of Excel, however you would have to install interop assemblies for each version, restrict the features you use based on the version of Excel that is installed, and expend considerable effort debugging and testing your application for each Excel version.

What about...

To learn how to	Look here
Create interop assemblies for earlier versions of Office	Search Visual Studio .NET Help to find the topic "Importing a Type Library as an Assembly"
Use the Launch Condition editor	Search Visual Studio .NET Help Index for "Launch conditions"

Create Excel .NET Applications

A third and final way for Excel and .NET to interact is through the Visual Studio .NET Tools for Office. This set of tools includes Visual Studio .NET project templates for Excel and Word. These project templates allow you to link a specific document to a .NET assembly that loads whenever the user opens that document. The .NET code in the assembly can control Excel and respond to Excel events as described in the preceding sections.

Excel .NET applications provide a document-centric interface. The user opens a workbook and the code loads invisibly behind the scenes.

How to do it

To create an Excel application in Visual Studio .NET:

1. From the Project menu, choose New, Project. Visual Studio .NET displays the New Project dialog box.
2. Select the Microsoft Office System Projects, Visual Basic Projects project type and Excel Workbook template, give the project a descriptive name and click OK. Visual Studio .NET starts the Microsoft Office Project Wizard to walk you through.
3. Click Finish to create the project folder and empty workbook and code template files.
4. Visual Studio .NET doesn't automatically add the workbook to the project, so it is a good idea to add it at this point. From the Project menu, choose Add Existing Item and then select the .xls file found in the application folder.
5. Once the workbook is added to the project, select the workbook in the Solution Explorer and set its Build Action property to Content. This will ensure that the workbook is distributed with your application if you create an installation program.

How it works

When Visual Studio .NET creates an Excel project, it adds references to the Microsoft Office and Excel 2003 PIAs, adds Imports statements to provide short cuts to the Office and Excel classes, and generates code to ThisApplication and ThisWorkbook objects as shown in Figure 5-15.

Visual Studio .NET links the workbook to the project's assembly through two custom document properties: _AssemblyLocation0 and _AssemblyName0. The _AssemblyLocation0 property corresponds to the Visual Studio .NET project's Assembly Link Location property as shown in Figure 5-16.

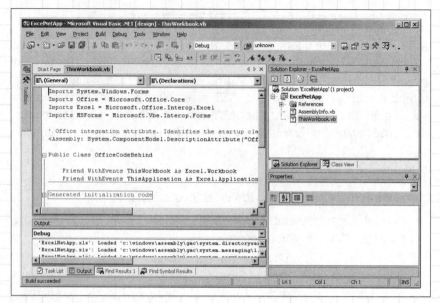

Figure 5-15. A newly created Excel project in Visual Studio .NET

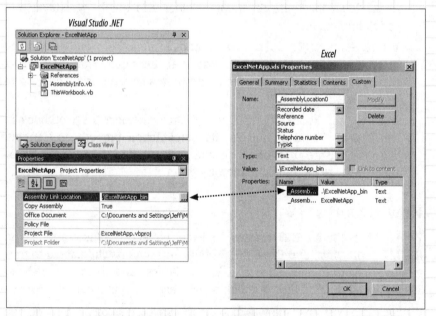

Figure 5-16. Setting Assembly Link Location changes the _AssemblyLocation0 custom document property in the Excel workbook

Chapter 5: Program Excel with .NET

You might notice that an Excel project has both a \bin and a *projectname*_bin folder. Excel projects write assembly output first to the \bin folder, then copy that file to the secondary folder. This allows the project to compile even if the Excel workbook has the assembly open in the secondary folder, plus it allows the project to be automatically deployed to a public location every time you build it—a process Microsoft calls *no touch deployment*.

When you open an Excel workbook that has _AssemblyLocation0 and _AssemblyName0 custom properties, Excel automatically starts the Office Toolkit Loader addin (*Otkloadr.dll*). The Office Toolkit Loader addin then starts the .NET assembly specified in the _AssemblyLocation0 and _AssemblyName0 properties.

TIP

Visual Studio .NET Tools for Office are built for use with the .NET Framework, Version 1.1. Applications built with these tools work with later versions of the .NET Framework, but the security configuration and debugging portions of the tools do not. If you have a later version of .NET installed, you must set the .NET security policy for the project manually and attach the debugger to the process manually.

What about...

To learn how to	Look here
Create Excel .NET Applications	Search *http://msdn.microsoft.com* for "Creating Office Solutions"

Set .NET Security Policies

In order for the Office Toolkit Loader to start the assembly, that assembly must have Full Trust permission on the user's machine. The Microsoft Office Project Wizard automatically sets this permission on your machine, but if you move the project or deploy it, you will need to set the permission using the .NET Configuration Tool.

The .NET and VBA security models are different. You don't need to sign your code in .NET, instead you set a security policy to grant Full Trust to your code. Without Full Trust, your code won't load.

How to do it

To set Full Trust permissions for the Excel project's assembly on your machine:

1. From the Control Panel, choose Administrative Tools and run the .NET Framework Wizards utility for the most recent version of the .NET Framework installed on your machine.

2. Select the Trust an Assembly Wizard. The Trust an Assembly Wizard starts and displays Step 1. Click Next.

3. Enter the address of the assembly (.dll) as shown in Figure 5-17 and click Next.

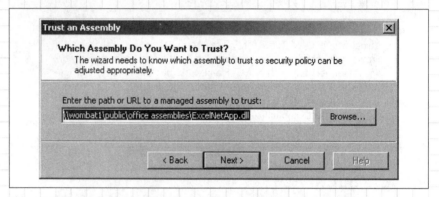

Figure 5-17. Set the location and name of the Excel application assembly

4. Set the level of trust to Full Trust (Figure 5-18), and click Next, then Finish to update your .NET security configuration.

You can view the .NET Framework security settings for .NET Office projects by starting the .NET Configuration Administrative Tool and expanding the My Computer, Runtime Security Policy, User, Code Groups, All_Code, Office_Projects treeview items, as shown in Figure 5-19.

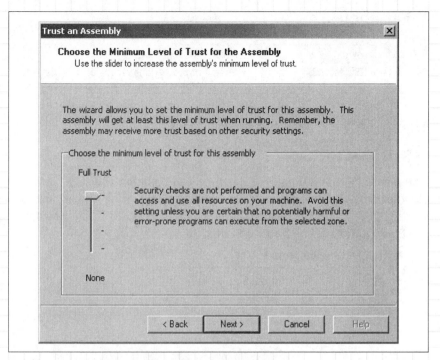

Figure 5-18. Set Full Trust for the Excel application assembly

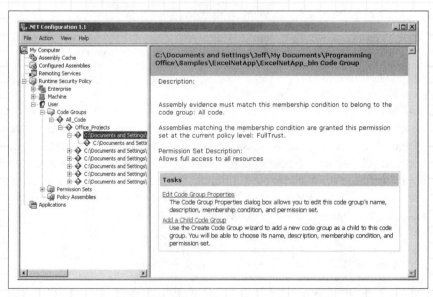

Figure 5-19. Viewing the .NET security policies for Excel .NET applications

What about...

To learn how to	Look here
Configure .NET assembly security	Search *http://msdn.microsoft.com* for "How to: Grant Permissions to Folders and Assemblies"

Respond to Events in .NET Applications

The default Visual Studio .NET Excel project contains object declarations for the Excel Application and Workbook objects using the WithEvents clause. That, plus the initialization code in the _Startup procedure, enables event handling for those two objects.

```
Public Class OfficeCodeBehind

    Friend WithEvents ThisWorkbook As Excel.Workbook
    Friend WithEvents ThisApplication As Excel.Application

#Region "Generated initialization code"
    ' Default constructor.
    Public Sub New()
    End Sub

    ' Required procedure. Do not modify.
    Public Sub _Startup(ByVal application As Object, _
      ByVal workbook As Object)
        ThisApplication = CType(application, Excel.Application)
        ThisWorkbook = CType(workbook, Excel.Workbook)
    End Sub
' Remaining class definition omitted here...
```

You can use events that occur for the Application and Workbook objects by selecting the object and event from the list boxes at the top of the Visual Studio .NET code window as you did in previous sections. If you want to add an Excel object to the objects and events lists, declare an object variable WithEvents and initialize the object somewhere in code. For example, the following additions (in **bold**) create an ActiveWorksheet object that responds to events:

```
Friend WithEvents ThisWorkbook As Excel.Workbook
Friend WithEvents ThisApplication As Excel.Application
Friend WithEvents ActiveWorksheet As Excel.Worksheet

' Called when the workbook is opened.
Private Sub ThisWorkbook_Open() Handles ThisWorkbook.Open
    ' Activate a worksheet.
    ThisApplication.Sheets("Sheet1").activate()
    ' Set the ActiveSheet object
```

.NET projects declare the Application and Workbook objects WithEvents. To add events for other Excel objects, you need to declare and initialize those objects.

```
        If ThisApplication.ActiveSheet.Type = _
            Excel.XlSheetType.xlWorksheet Then _
        ActiveWorksheet = CType(ThisApplication.ActiveSheet, _
            Excel.Worksheet)
End Sub

Private Sub ThisWorkbook_SheetActivate(ByVal Sh As Object) _
    Handles ThisWorkbook.SheetActivate
        ' Change active worksheet
        If Sh.Type = Excel.XlSheetType.xlWorksheet Then _
            ActiveWorksheet = CType(Sh, Excel.Worksheet)
End Sub
```

The preceding code creates an ActiveWorksheet object and hooks the active worksheet in Excel to that object's events. Whenever the active worksheet changes, the SheetActivate event updates the ActiveWorksheet object, ensuring that it is always current. If you add the following event procedure, any value entered in cell A1 is automatically squared and displayed in cell A2:

```
Private Sub ActiveWorksheet_Change(ByVal Target As Excel.Range) _
    Handles ActiveWorksheet.Change
        ' Square value entered in range A1 and display in A2.
        If Target.Address = "$A$1" Then
            ActiveWorksheet.Range("A2").Value = Target.Value ^ 2
        End If
End Sub
```

This approach works well for built-in Excel objects such as Worksheets and Charts, but when you add controls to a worksheet, you must use the code template's FindControl method to get the control so you can hook up its events. The FindControl method is *overloaded*—meaning it comes in two versions:

```
' Returns the control with the specified name
' on ThisWorkbook's active worksheet.
Overloads Function FindControl(ByVal name As String) As Object
    Return FindControl(name, CType(ThisWorkbook.ActiveSheet,_
        Excel.Worksheet))
End Function
' Returns the control with the specified name
' on the specified worksheet.
Overloads Function FindControl(ByVal name As String, _
    ByVal sheet As Excel.Worksheet) As Object
    Dim theObject As Excel.OLEObject
    Try
        theObject = CType(sheet.OLEObjects(name), Excel.OLEObject)
        Return theObject.Object
    Catch Ex As Exception
        ' Returns Nothing if the control is not found.
    End Try
    Return Nothing
End Function
```

Because `FindControl` is overloaded, you can call the method with one or two arguments. If you provide only the object name, `FindControl` assumes that the control is on the active worksheet. Overloading is VB.NET's way of dealing with optional arguments. The following code (in **bold**) hooks up events for the cmdReformat button found on Sheet1:

```
Friend WithEvents cmdReformat As MSForms.CommandButton

' Called when the workbook is opened.
Private Sub ThisWorkbook_Open() Handles ThisWorkbook.Open
    ' Activate the worksheet the control is found on.
    ThisApplication.Sheets("Sheet1").activate()
    ' Set the ActiveSheet object
    If ThisApplication.ActiveSheet.Type = _
        Excel.XlSheetType.xlWorksheet Then _
        ActiveWorksheet = CType(ThisApplication.ActiveSheet, _
        Excel.Worksheet)
    ' Find the control on the sheet and hook up its events.
    cmdReformat = CType(FindControl("cmdReformat"), _
        MSForms.CommandButton)
End Sub
```

Notice that you need to convert the type of object returned by `FindControl` into a CommandButton type. This is because the Command-Button class exposes a full set of events (Click, MouseDown, DragOver, etc.), while the OLEObject class only provides GotFocus and LostFocus events. Once you've hooked up the control's events, you can write event procedures for that control, as shown below:

```
Private Sub cmdReformat_Click() Handles cmdReformat.Click
    ReformatHTML(ActiveWorksheet)
End Sub
```

Debug Excel .NET Applications

Excel projects do not report errors that occur in Excel the way you might expect. Instead of halting execution when an error occurs, Excel projects just continue on as if nothing happened. This can be *very* confusing since the code exits the procedure where the error occurred and no warning is displayed. A good way to see this behavior is to try to activate a worksheet that doesn't exist. For example:

Runtime errors don't stop Excel—.NET projects run from Visual Studio .NET! You need to change the debug options in order to detect problems while debugging.

```
Private Sub ThisWorkbook_Open() Handles ThisWorkbook.Open
ThisApplication.Sheets("doesn't exist").activate() ' Error! Code exits.
    ' Set the ActiveSheet object
    If ThisApplication.ActiveSheet.Type = Excel.XlSheetType.xlWorksheet Then
        ActiveWorksheet = CType(ThisApplication.ActiveSheet, Excel.Worksheet)
    Endif
    ' Find the control on the sheet and hook up its events.
    cmdReformat = CType(FindControl("cmdReformat"), MSForms.CommandButton)
End Sub
```

In the preceding code, ActiveWorksheet and cmdReformat are never set because Excel can't find the worksheet to activate. The project keeps running, though, and you're just left to wonder why none of your event procedures are working.

You can prevent this by telling Visual Studio .NET to break into the debugger when exceptions are thrown, as described in the following steps:

1. From the Debug menu, choose Exceptions. Visual Studio .NET displays the Exceptions dialog box.

2. Select Common Language Runtime Exceptions and select When the exception is thrown: Break into the debugger, as shown in Figure 5-20, then click OK.

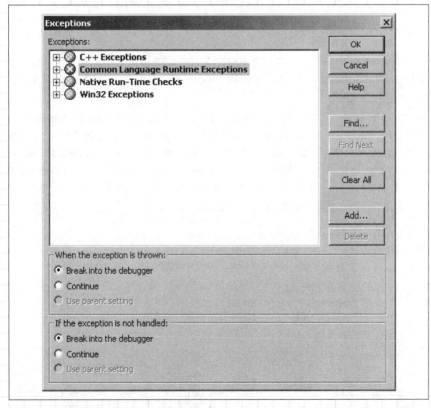

Figure 5-20. Set Break into debugger to detect exceptions in Excel projects

Once you tell Visual Studio .NET to break on all runtime exceptions, you'll start seeing exceptions that are handled as well those that aren't. Two handled file-not-found exceptions occur every time an Excel project starts, as shown in Figure 5-21.

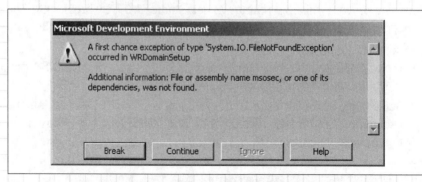

Figure 5-21. This (handled) exception occurs twice every time an Excel project starts

You can ignore these handled exceptions—clicking Continue a couple of times each time you start is a little annoying, but at least you can catch code that doesn't work!

Another way to detect exceptions, without breaking for all of them, is to add Try...Catch blocks to your code. The FindControl method actually does this, but it omits a useful technique for reporting exceptions while debugging. It's a good idea to add a Debug.Fail statement to the code template's FindControl method as shown here (in **bold**):

```
Overloads Function FindControl(ByVal name As String, _
    ByVal sheet As Excel.Worksheet) As Object
    Dim theObject As Excel.OLEObject
    Try
        theObject = CType(sheet.OLEObjects(name), Excel.OLEObject)
        Return theObject.Object
    Catch Ex As Exception
        ' Report the exception.
        Debug.Fail(Ex.Message, Ex.ToString)
    End Try
    Return Nothing
End Function
```

Now, FindControl displays an error message during debugging if a control is not found, rather than just continuing on. Debug.Fail is especially useful since it doesn't affect your released application—the .NET Framework disables the Debug class in code that is built for release.

Display Windows Forms

Excel projects can use Windows forms to gather information and display results. Windows forms are a huge improvement over the forms you can display from Excel VBA.

How to do it

To create a Windows form in Visual Studio .NET for use from Excel, follow these steps:

1. From the Project menu, choose Add Windows Form. Visual Studio .NET displays the Add New Item dialog box.
2. Enter a name for the form and click OK. Visual Studio .NET creates a new Windows form class and displays the class in the Designer.
3. Use the Designer to add controls to the form; then switch to the Code window. Unlike previous versions of Visual Basic, VB.NET describes the entire form in terms of code. The form and control properties are all maintained in the "Windows Form Designer generated code" region of the form's class.
4. In order to enable the form to interact with Excel, add the following lines to the generated code (shown in **bold**):

```
Imports Excel = Microsoft.Office.Interop.Excel

Public Class SimpleForm
    Inherits System.Windows.Forms.Form

    Dim xlCode As OfficeCodeBehind

#Region " Windows Form Designer generated code "

    Public Sub New(ByVal target As OfficeCodeBehind)
        MyBase.New( )

        'This call is required by the Windows Form Designer.
        InitializeComponent( )
```

The forms that .NET displays are true Windows forms with all the bells and whistles available anywhere in Windows programming. You do need to figure out how to communicate between the form and Excel, however, and for that, there's a trick.

```
                        'Add any initialization after the InitializeComponent() call
                        ' Get the OfficeCodeBehind class that created this form
                        ' (used to return responses to Excel).
                        xlCode = target
                    End Sub
                    ' Remainder of class omitted here...
```

5. Within the form's event procedures, use the xlCode object created in Step 4 to interact with Excel. For example, the following code squares each of the values in the active worksheet when the user clicks the Square Values button:

```
        Private Sub cmdSquare_Click(ByVal sender As System.Object, _
          ByVal e As System.EventArgs) Handles cmdSquare.Click
            ' If SquareCells succeeds, then close this form.
            If SquareCells() Then Me.Close()
        End Sub

        Private Function SquareCells() As Boolean
            Try
                ' For each cell in the active sheet's used range...
                For Each cel As Excel.Range In _
                  xlCode.ThisWorkbook.ActiveSheet.UsedRange
                    ' Square the value.
                    cel.Value = cel.Value ^ 2
                Next
            Catch ex As System.Runtime.InteropServices.COMException
                ' Something happened in Excel.
                Debug.Fail(ex.Source & " " & Hex(ex.errorcode), ex.Message)
                Return False
            Catch ex As Exception
                ' Something happened in .NET (display error while debugging)
                Debug.Fail(ex.Source, ex.Message)
                Return False
            End Try
            ' Success.
            Return True
        End Function
```

6. Write code in the OfficeCodeBehind class to create the form and display it. For example, the following code creates a new form based on the SimpleForm class and displays it from Excel:

```
        ' In OfficeCodeBehind class.
        Private Sub cmdSquare_Click() Handles cmdForm.Click
            ' Create a new form object.
            Dim frm As New SimpleForm(Me)
            frm.ShowDialog()
        End Sub
```

How it works

The preceding procedure passes the OfficeCodeBehind class instance to the form's constructor in the code New SimpleForm(Me). The form keeps that instance as the class-level xlCode variable defined in Step 4.

The .NET Framework provides two methods used to display forms: ShowDialog displays forms modally; the form stays on top and must be closed before the user returns to Excel. Show displays forms non-modally; the form may appear in front of or behind the Excel window, depending on which window has focus.

When working with Excel, you'll usually want to display Windows forms modally (using ShowDialog). Exceptions to this rule might include cases where you want to display some output that you want to keep around, such as a floating toolbar or a Help window. In these cases, you can use the Show method combined with the TopMost property to keep the non-modal form displayed on top of Excel.

For example, the following code displays a new form based on the Simple-Form class non-modally, but keeps it on top of the other windows:

```
Private Sub cmdSquare_Click( ) Handles cmdForm.Click
    ' Create a new form object.
    Dim frm As New SimpleForm(Me)
    ' Show the form non-modally but keep it on top.
    frm.TopMost = True
    frm.Show( )
End Sub
```

Distribute Excel .NET Applications

One of the big advantages of Excel .NET applications is that they can be easily distributed through a network. Just set the project Assembly Link Location property to a network address and distribute the Excel workbook that uses the assembly. Whenever anyone uses the workbook, the assembly will then be loaded from that network location.

How to do it

Before you can distribute applications in this way, however, you need to make sure your users meet the following requirements:

Excel .NET applications don't really need to be distributed. The executable component can simply reside on a public server. The tricky part here is checking prerequisites and changing the user's security settings to grant Full Trust to the assembly.

- They must be using Excel 2003. Prior versions of Excel are not supported for Excel .NET applications.
- The Office 2003 PIAs must be installed on the user's machine.
- The .NET Framework Version 1.1 runtime must be installed.
- The user's .NET security policy must specify Full Trust for the network address from which the assembly is distributed.

The first two requirements are best handled using the Office Resource Kit's Custom Installation Wizard or Custom Maintenance Wizard. See Chapter 4 for information on obtaining and using those tools. You can use those tools to create a *chained installation* that calls subsequent installation programs, such as the setup for Excel .NET application prerequisites and security policy settings.

The .NET Setup and Deployment projects detect the Office PIAs and .NET Framework as dependencies of the Excel application. According to the Visual Studio .NET Tools for Office documentation, you shouldn't distribute the PIAs through your setup program (instead, use the Office setup to do this as mentioned above). Special steps for creating an installation program for Excel .NET application prerequisites include:

1. Exclude the PIAs from the setup project. These are added as dependencies by default.
2. Optionally, exclude the Primary Output (*projectname*.dll) from the installation. Usually, you'll want to distribute the assembly from a network address, rather than installing it on client machines where it is harder to update.
3. Create a batch file, script, or Windows installer to set the client's .NET security policy to enable the assembly to load from its network address.

A simple to set security policy on a client is to use a batch file that calls the .NET utility *caspole.exe*. The following batch file assigns FullTrust to the network location \\wombat2\SharedDocs\bin:

```
REM Adds FullTrust for \\wombat2\Sharedocs\bin location.
%WINDIR%\Microsoft.NET\Framework\v1.1.4322\caspol -pp off -m -ag
LocalIntranet_Zone -url \\wombat2\shareddocs\bin\* FullTrust -n "Excel
Project Assemblies" -d "Share point for .NET code running in Office 2003
applications."
%WINDIR%\Microsoft.NET\Framework\v1.1.4322\caspol -pp on
```

You can also use *caspole.exe* to remove a security policy, as shown here:

```
REM Removes FullTrust for \\wombat2\Sharedocs\bin location.
%WINDIR%\Microsoft.NET\Framework\v1.1.4322\caspol -pp off -remgroup "Excel
Project Assemblies"
%WINDIR%\Microsoft.NET\Framework\v1.1.4322\caspol -pp on
```

Another way to distribute security policies is by using the .NET Configuration utility to generate a Windows Installer file (.msi) for a group policy. To do this, follow these steps:

1. Configure you machine with the security policies you want to deploy.
2. Start the .NET Configuration utility for the current version of the .NET Framework.
3. Select the Runtime Security Policy item in the treeview and click Create Deployment Package, as shown in Figure 5-22.

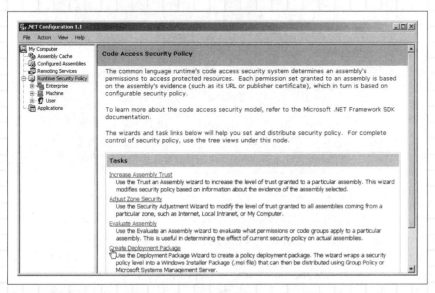

Figure 5-22. Creating a Windows Installer for .NET security policies

4. Follow the steps in the wizard to create an .msi file containing the security policies to deploy (Figure 5-23).
5. Click Next, then Finish to create the Windows Installer file (.msi).

Once you've created the .msi file, you can deploy that policy to your enterprise by using the Group Policy Editor snap-in from the Microsoft Management Console (*mmc.exe*) or by installing the .msi file individually on client computers.

Distribute Excel .NET Documents

If you distribute an Excel workbook that uses .NET code to others who don't have Excel 2003, the .NET code is ignored and programmed features are unavailable. Earlier versions of Excel can open Excel 2003 workbooks, but they can't run .NET assemblies on start-up.

If you distribute an Excel .NET document to an Excel 2003 user who doesn't have access to the assembly location, Excel displays an error message when that user opens the workbook.

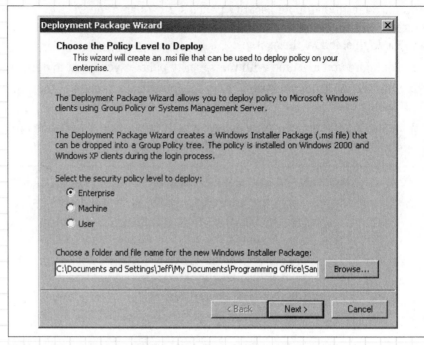

Figure 5-23. Choose the policy level to deploy and enter a filename to create

If you want to distribute a Workbook to Excel 2003 users who don't have access to the .NET assembly, either distribute and install the assembly with the workbook as described in "Distribute Excel .NET Applications" or clear the _AssemblyName0 and _AssemblyLocation0 custom document properties before sending. For example, the following code saves a copy of the current document without the references to the .NET assembly; then sends the workbook via email:

```
Private Sub cmdSend_Click() Handles cmdSend.Click
    Dim _AssemblyName0 As String, _AssemblyLocation0 As String, _
      name As String
    ' Save custom propeperty settings.
    _AssemblyName0 = _
      ThisWorkbook.CustomDocumentProperties("_AssemblyName0").Value
    _AssemblyLocation0 = _
      ThisWorkbook.CustomDocumentProperties("_AssemblyLocation0").Value
    ' Clear custom property settings.
    ThisWorkbook.CustomDocumentProperties("_AssemblyName0").Value = ""
    ThisWorkbook.CustomDocumentProperties("_AssemblyLocation0").Value = ""
    ' Save current name.
    name = ThisWorkbook.FullName
    ' Save a copy of the workbook (without properties).
    ThisWorkbook.SaveAs("Copy of " & ThisWorkbook.Name)
    ' Send the workbook.
```

```
    ThisWorkbook.SendMail("ExcelDemo@hotmail.com", ThisWorkbook.Name)
    ' Set properties and name back to original
    ThisWorkbook.CustomDocumentProperties("_AssemblyName0").Value _
      = _AssemblyName0
    ThisWorkbook.CustomDocumentProperties("_AssemblyLocation0").Value = _
      _AssemblyLocation0
    ThisWorkbook.SaveAs(name)
  End Sub
```

Once the _AssemblyName0 and _AssemblyLocation0 properties are cleared, the workbook no longer runs code from the .NET assembly so the workbook has reduced functionality.

Migrate to .NET

If you are an experienced Visual Basic programmer, you've got a good start on learning VB.NET. However, there are significant language differences so be prepared for a learning curve and don't expect to be able to cut and paste code from a VBA project into VB.NET and have the code run.

Existing VBA code may provide a template for VB.NET code, but VB.NET is really a different language from VBA. There are large as well as subtle differences. If you are new to VB.NET, you will save a great deal of time by buying and reading one of the many books on VB.NET. One of the best, in my opinion, is *Programming Microsoft VB.NET Version 2003* by Francesco Balena—a book that I was proud to work on as technical editor.

The following sections list a few recommendations that may make your transition easier.

> .NET isn't an all-or-nothing proposition. Most businesses will migrate from COM to .NET over a long period of time. In fact, COM will probably never completely go away. Keep those copies of VB 6.0 around!

What you lose: edit and continue

You can't change code while debugging VB.NET applications and then continue execution using those changes. .NET applications must be recompiled each time they are run. This is cumbersome when loading and unloading especially large applications such as Excel, so it is a good idea to have the basic .NET programming techniques down cold before tackling an Excel .NET project.

A good way to learn .NET programming techniques is to start with any of the many tutorials that come with the .NET Framework or to start with Console or Windows Forms projects. Trying to learn .NET while working with Excel can be frustrating.

Be explicit!

I've already mentioned that .NET doesn't support VBA's concept of a default property. If you are going to set the value of an object, you must use the Value property (or its equivalent).

Being explicit also applies to object references. It is much easier to program in .NET if you are using a specific object type, such as Worksheet, rather than the generic Object type. Using the specific object enables Intellisense and autocomplete features of .NET and helps detect inadvertent errors, such as incorrect variable assignments.

In many cases, Excel methods return generic Object types, which should be converted to the expected, more specific type. Use CType to perform this conversion, but be sure to check if the object can be converted before performing the conversion. For example, the following code checks if the passed-in argument Sh is a Worksheet before performing the conversion:

```
Private Sub ThisWorkbook_SheetActivate(ByVal Sh As Object) _
   Handles ThisWorkbook.SheetActivate
    If Sh.Type = Excel.XlSheetType.xlWorksheet Then _
      ActiveWorksheet = CType(Sh, Excel.Worksheet)
End Sub
```

Trying to convert an object to an incompatible type causes a runtime error.

In .NET *everything* is an object, even simple types like strings and integers are their own classes derived from .NET's base Object type. At first this might seem cumbersome, but the consistency and logic of this approach pay huge dividends.

Pass arguments by value

By default in VBA, procedures pass arguments by reference. The default in .NET is to pass arguments by value. If you cut and paste code from VBA, .NET will add ByVal to unqualified argument definitions, thus changing how the arguments are passed.

Collections start at zero

The index of the first element of any .NET collection is zero. In Excel, the first element of any collection is 1.

Data access is through ADO.NET

.NET provides access to databases, XML data, and in-memory data tables through ADO.NET, which is significantly different from prior data access techniques. Backward compatibility is provided for ADO data binding, but the best advice here is to pick up a good book on the subject and start learning.

What about...

To learn how to	Look here
Convert VBA code to .NET	Search *http://msdn.microsoft.com* for "Converting Code from VBA to VB.NET"

Explore Security in Depth

In the physical world, *security* is freedom from danger. There are many dangers in the physical world, but in the world of Excel, dangers relate to protecting data (absent an army of spreadsheet-driven killer robots). Specifically, Excel security is designed to protect you from:

* Unauthorized or accidental changes
* Malicious changes or destruction of data
* Theft or unauthorized distribution of restricted information
* Attack from viruses

This chapter explains approaches to protecting your data from these threats and explains how to implement those approaches within Excel.

Dress in Layers

When it's cold you dress in layers, and security works the same way (Figure 6-1). The outer layer is a firewall, preventing attacks from the Internet. Next, virus detection software scans permitted attachments and other files from bringing in malicious code. Then, operating system security defines users and their permissions. Finally, Excel provides its own security layer.

Data most at risk is that which is shared outside of these layers, such as a workbook posted on a public server. In that case, Excel becomes the primary security layer. Of course, not all data needs the same level (or type) of protection. Therefore, Excel itself provides layers through the following security approaches:

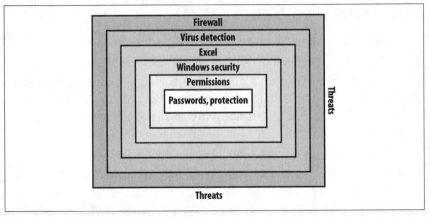

Figure 6-1. Use layers to keep out threats

- Password-protection and encryption controls read and write access to workbooks.

- Worksheet protection password protects items within a workbook and, alternately, can authorize changes to the base of user lists.

- User-based permissions allow authors to limit the rights of others to read, change, print, copy, or distribute a document. Permissions can also set an expiration date for a document.

- Digital signatures identify the author of a document ensuring that a document is the authentic original—not a modified or spoof copy. Signatures can also be applied to macros and ActiveX controls to ensure their code is from a trusted source.

- Macro security levels determine what level of trust is required before Excel will run code included in worksheets, templates, add-ins, or Smart Documents.

- ActiveX control security levels similarly limit which controls Excel will trust.

- Office Anti Virus API provides an interface for anti-virus software to scan documents for malicious code before they are opened.

- Custom installation wizard permits administrators to configure which security options are enabled during installation on user's machines.

Code used in this chapter and additional samples are available in ch06.xls.

These security approaches can be combined to provide a high level of assurance while still allowing files to be shared, macros to be run, and (ultimately) work to be done. The rest of this chapter discusses each of these approaches, along with Windows file security, then provides a list of common security tasks and describes how you complete those tasks by combining Excel security features.

Use Windows Security

Before we talk about Excel security, it is important to explain some general concepts related to the Windows operating system.

Permissions are a set of capabilities that someone has or doesn't have. Permissions apply to files and locations, so someone may be able to open a specific folder, see files, but not write to that folder or edit the files it contains.

Users are identities that Windows uses to control access. When you sign on with a username and password, Windows authenticates that information, and thereafter identifies you as *machinename\username* if your network uses workgroups or *domainname\username* if your network uses domains. Your identity is then used any time you request permission to use a resource, such as open a file or run an application. If your identity has permission to use that resource, you are granted access and the requested file opens or the application runs.

Groups are the security groups to which a username belongs. Windows comes with some groups already configured: Administrators, Users, Guests, Backup Operators, and Power Users. Groups provide an easy way to grant a set of permissions to a set of users rather than having to grant permissions to many individual users.

Certificates and *digital signatures* are small identifiers that can be attached to a data file or executable that identify the author of the file or executable. Certificates are issued by a third-party certificate authority (sometimes called a CA) such as Verisign, which provides the service that authenticates certificates. The idea here is that if a user knows the author of a particular file, she is more likely to trust that it will not harm her computer.

How to set file permissions in Windows XP

How you set permissions is not obvious from the default setup of Windows XP. First, you must disable the Use simple file sharing folder option in Windows Explorer (Figure 6-2).

To set permissions on a folder or file:

1. In Windows Explorer, select the file or folder to set permissions on and select Properties from the File menu.

2. Select the Security tab on the Properties dialog box (Figure 6-3). The top list displays user groups and individual users with permissions for the item. The bottom list shows the permissions assigned to each group or user.

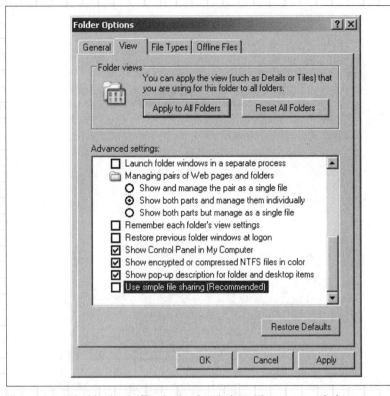

Figure 6-2. Disable simple file sharing in Windows XP to set permissions

3. Select a group or user, then assign or deny permissions by clicking on the boxes in the permissions list. Click OK when done.

If you're not familiar with how this works, it's a good idea to experiment with a file. For example, create an Excel workbook named *Book1.xls* then deny Full Control for your username. Then try to open *Book1.xls* in Excel—you'll get an Access Denied error. Now, change the file permissions to allow read and execute, but deny write access. You'll be able to open the file in Excel, but you can't save it as *Book1.xls*.

These permissions don't have much meaning in the preceding example because you can always change them back to allow writing or whatever. You own the file so you can do whatever you like. Permission settings are truly significant when a file is shared with other users, such as when the file is placed in a public network address.

For example, if you want to allow others to read workbooks but not to make changes, a simple solution is to create a shared folder that denies write permission to everyone but you.

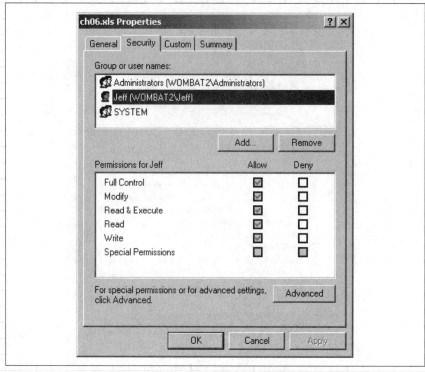

Figure 6-3. Setting permissions

How to view users and groups in XP

When you set up user accounts from the Windows XP Control Panel, you have three types of accounts available: Computer Adminstrator, Limited, or Guest. These accounts correspond to the Administrator, User, and Guest account groups within Windows. These aren't the only groups available, however. To view all the groups:

1. From the Control Panel, run Administrative Tools, then run Computer Management. Windows runs the Microsoft Management Console (MMC).

2. Click Local Users and Groups in the tree view to expand that item.

3. Select the Groups folder to display a list of Groups.

4. Double-click on a group to view a list of the users that belong to that group (Figure 6-4).

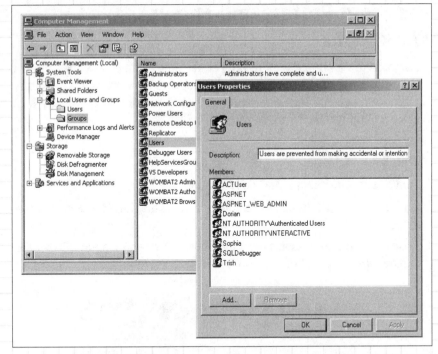

Figure 6-4. Viewing members of a group in MMC

Your list of groups may be different from the list shown in Figure 6-4 because applications often add groups and then add users as members of those groups. If you click around and explore a bit, you'll see that you can't set the permissions of groups or users through the MMC. That's because permissions are set on objects, not on identities.

For example, a folder in Windows may allow users that belong to the Administrators group to read and write files, but only allow Users group member to read those files, and prohibit Guest members from even reading files. In this case, the folder is the security object that defines the permissions for groups that have access.

Applications sometimes check if a user belongs to a certain group before allowing him or her to perform a task. This is referred to as *role-based security*.

What about...

See the chapter sample file for links to the Windows security tools.

Password Protect and Encrypt Workbooks

Passwords are a simple way to protect sensitive data in a workbook. You can use passwords to encrypt a workbook to provide added security. Encryption prevents hackers from being able to read your workbook by disassembling the file in some way.

How to do it

To add a password to a workbook in Excel:

1. Choose Save As from the File menu. Excel displays the Save As dialog box.
2. On the Save As dialog box, click Tools → General Options. Excel displays the Save Options dialog box (Figure 6-5).

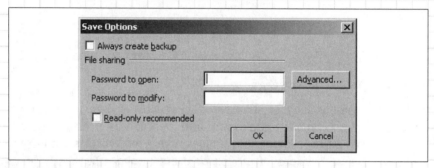

Figure 6-5. Adding a password to a workbook

3. Enter passwords in the Password to open and/or Password to modify text boxes and click OK. To create a workbook that everyone can read but only password holders can edit, set Password to modify and leave Password to open blank.
4. Excel prompts you to confirm the passwords entered in the previous step.

To add encryption to a workbook:

1. Click the Advanced button after Step 2 above. Excel displays the Encryption Type dialog box (Figure 6-6).
2. Select an encryption type from the listed encryption providers, choose an encryption key length, and click OK.
3. Proceed with setting the workbook password.

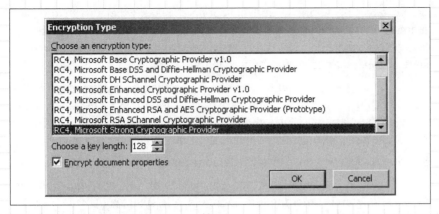

Figure 6-6. Adding encryption to a workbook

The encryption providers you have installed may vary depending on your location. Some encryption providers are not available outside of the United States, so you will want to take that into consideration if you are distributing encrypted files internationally. The longer the encryption key, the harder it is for a hacker to decrypt data. All software-based encryption such as this is potentially reversible without the key.

How secure are Excel Passwords?

It depends.

Encrypting a workbook makes it very difficult to extract passwords from a workbook by peeking inside the file in some way. However, Excel does leave passwords open to guessing attacks. In short, you can write a macro to call the Open method repeatedly with various passwords until you find one that works.

That's because Excel doesn't lock out attempts after a certain number of wrong passwords they way most networks do. Therefore, Excel passwords are only as good as their complexity.

For example, a four-character all-lowercase workbook password takes about 40 minutes to guess using brute-force techniques on my 2.0 Ghz machine. By extrapolation, a mixed-case four-character password would take over 10 hours and a six-character password using any valid character (letters, numbers, or symbols) would take 883 years.

That sounds pretty secure, but remember this is just using brute-force techniques—starting at Chr(33) and working through the valid character set. There are many ways to optimize guessing that reduces these times significantly. The controlling factors are how many attempts are made before guessing correctly and how long it takes Excel to run the `Open` method and return an error if the guess is wrong. Just for example, the Excel Key service on the Web promises password-recovery in four to seven days, regardless of password length.

These same guessing techniques can be applied to password-protected items within a workbook, such as worksheets. It is, in fact, much easier to guess the password for a protected worksheet because the `Unprotect` method returns an error five times faster than the `Open` method.

So what should you do? Here are some recommendations:

- Use strong passwords; strong passwords are at least eight characters long and contain letters, numbers, and symbols.
- Encrypt password-protected files.
- Keep passwords secret; this is obvious, but it is also where most security breaches occur.
- Use Permissions to limit access to the file based on user identities rather than, or in addition to, passwords and encryption.

Permissions or other identity-based approaches are really much better at securing data than password-based approaches.

What about...

To learn about	Look here
Excel Key	*http://www.lostpassword.com/excel.htm*
Permissions	"Use Identity-Based Security"
Strong passwords	Search *http//msdn.microsoft.com* for "Strong Passwords"
Microsoft security news	*http://msdn.microsoft.com/security/*

Program with Passwords and Encryption

You can enforce strong password rules by adding code to a template's Before_Save event.

You can set passwords and encryption options in code using the Workbook object's security members, such as the `Password` property and `SetEncryptionProperties` method. From a security standpoint, it doesn't make sense to hardcode passwords into Visual Basic macros. Instead, the Workbook object's security members are generally used in conjunction with User Forms to set passwords and encryption chosen by the user through a customized interface.

How to do it

For instance, you might create a document template (.xlt) for secure documents that can only be saved using a password and encryption. Such a template might include a User Form to get the password (Figure 6-7).

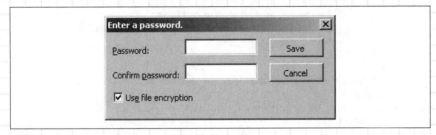

Figure 6-7. Password User Form

The code for the User Form confirms that the password and confirm password text boxes match and allows the user to cancel the operation, as shown here:

```
' Public fields
Public Password As String, Encrypt As Boolean

Private Sub cmdCancel_Click()
    Me.Hide
    Password = ""
End Sub

Private Sub cmdSave_Click()
    If txtPassword.Text <> txtConfirm.Text Then
        MsgBox "Password and confirm password must match.", , _
          "Confirm Error"
    Else
        Password = txtPassword.Text
        Encrypt = chkEncrypt.Value
        Me.Hide
    End If
End Sub
```

Then, the Secure template includes a Workbook-level procedure to intercept the Save event. Whenever the user saves a document based on this template, the following code displays the Password user form and sets the workbook password and encryption options (points of note are shown in **bold**):

```
Private Sub Workbook_BeforeSave(ByVal SaveAsUI As Boolean, Cancel As
Boolean)
    Dim fname As String
    ' Exit if this is a template, not a workbook.
    If ThisWorkbook.FileFormat = xlTemplate Then Exit Sub ' (1)
    ' Cancel default operation.
```

```
        Cancel = True
        ' Get a password if one does not exist.
        If Not ThisWorkbook.HasPassword Then ' (2)
            frmPassword.Show
            ThisWorkbook.Password = frmPassword.Password ' (3)
            If frmPassword.Password = "" Then Exit Sub
            If frmPassword.Encrypt Then
                ThisWorkbook.SetPasswordEncryptionOptions _            ' (4)
                    "Microsoft RSA SChannel Cryptographic Provider", _
                    "RC4", 128, True
            End If
        End If
        ' Save the workbook by enabling the default action.
        Cancel = False    ' (5)
        ' Make sure the user form unloads.
        Unload frmPassword
    End Sub
```

How it works

The key points are:

1. Exit the procedure if saving a template. This allows you to save the template without a password.

2. Use the HasPassword property to determine if a password has already been set. You can't use the Password property to test this, since it always returns asterisks whether or not a password is set (for security reasons).

3. You can set a password by assigning the workbook's Password property or by using the SaveAs method. Using SaveAs in this case would call the Workbook_BeforeSave event procedure again, resulting in an unwanted recursion.

4. Use the SetEncryptionOptions method to choose the type of encryption and the length of the encryption key. This is the only way to set encryption options, since the PasswordEncryption properties are all read-only.

5. Set Cancel to False to allow Excel to complete the save operation. As mentioned in item 3, calling Save or SaveAs would result in unwanted recursion.

What about...

The Workbook object has over 200 members. To help navigate among the various ways to work with passwords from workbooks, Table 6-1 lists the Workbook security members. You can get Help on any of these members from the Visual Basic editor.

Table 6-1. Workbook security members

HasPassword	Password
PasswordEncryptionFileProperties	PasswordEncryptionKeyLength
SetPasswordEncryptionOptions	WritePassword
WriteReservedBy	PasswordEncryptionAlgorithm
PasswordEncryptionProvider	WriteReserved

Protect Items in a Workbook

In Excel, *protection* means preventing changes to parts of a workbook. You can apply protection to worksheets, charts, ranges, formatting, and window layout. Protection can use a password, or it may omit the password if the protection is intended to prevent accidental changes rather than malicious ones.

You can protect multiple items within a workbook and you can use different passwords for each of those items, though that's generally a bad idea. The more passwords you use, the more likely you are to confuse them—especially within a single workbook. It's a good idea to use the same password when protecting multiple items.

How to do it

To prevent changes to a worksheet:

1. Add data to your worksheet and adjust the formatting so it appears the way you want it to.
2. From the Tools menu, choose Protection then Protect a Sheet. Excel displays the Protect Sheet dialog box shown in Figure 6-8.
3. Type a password and select the actions you want to permit on the worksheet from the list. Click OK. Excel prompts you to confirm the password.

After a worksheet is protected, you can't change it without unprotecting it first. To unprotect the worksheet, select Tools → Protection → Unprotect Sheet and enter the password.

Worksheet protection applies to all of the locked cells on a worksheet. To allow users to edit some cells on a worksheet while protecting most of the others, take the following steps *before* protecting the worksheet:

Protection allows users to read, but not change, parts of a workbook. Protection is applied in different ways to different items within a workbook.

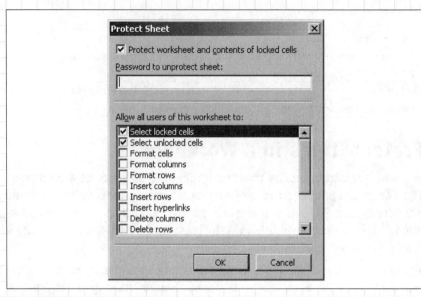

Figure 6-8. Protecting a worksheet from changes

1. Select the cells you want to allow the user to edit.

2. From the Format menu, choose Cells. Excel displays the Format Cells dialog box shown in Figure 6-9.

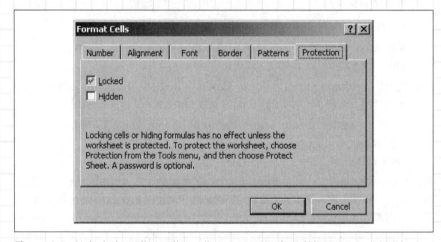

Figure 6-9. Unlock the cells to allow edits on protected worksheets

3. Select the Protection tab and clear the Locked checkbox. Click OK.

4. Protect the worksheet. Now, Excel allows changes in the unlocked cells.

You can also selectively protect ranges of cells by user. This lets some users but not others edit selected cells. To protect ranges by user, take the following steps *before* protecting the worksheet:

1. Select the range of cells to protect.

2. Choose Tools → Protection → Allow Users to Edit Ranges. Excel displays the dialog box shown in Figure 6-10.

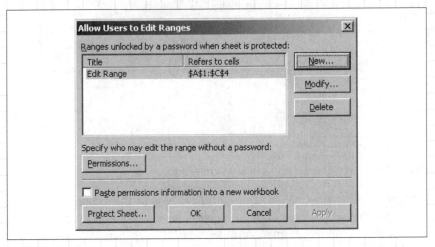

Figure 6-10. Adding an edit range to a protected worksheet

3. Click the New button. Excel displays the New Range dialog box (Figure 6-11) with the range of the selected cells listed in the Refers to cells text box.

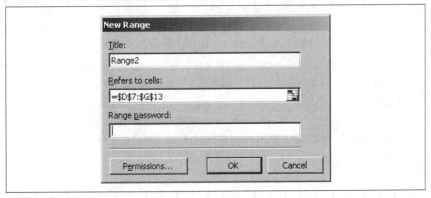

Figure 6-11. Creating the range on which to allow edits

4. Click the Permissions button then click Add on the Permissions dialog box. Excel displays the Select Users or Groups dialog box (Figure 6-12).

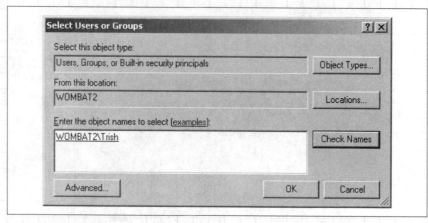

Figure 6-12. Adding users with permission to edit the range

5. Type the names of the users to allow to edit the range. Usernames take the form *machinename\username* for workgroup-based networks or *domainname\username* for domain-based networks. You can also simply type the username and click Check Names to look up a user's machine or domain name if you don't know it. To specify multiple names, separate them with a semicolon. Click OK when done. Excel adds the names to the Permissions dialog box, as shown in Figure 6-13.

6. If you want to require the user to enter a password before editing the range, select the username and click the Deny checkbox. Click OK when done. Excel returns you to the New Range dialog box.

7. Enter a password for the range and click OK. Excel prompts you to confirm the password and then returns you to the worksheet.

8. Protect the worksheet using the steps at the beginning of this section. Protecting the worksheet activates the protection for the range—Excel does not enforce those protections until the worksheet is protected.

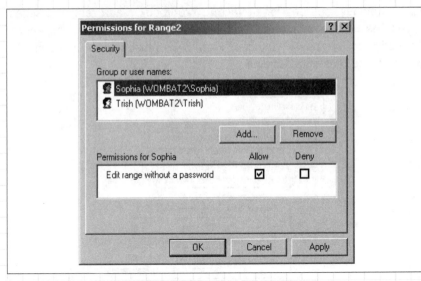

Figure 6-13. Users with edit permissions

How it works

In general, you use the preceding procedure to allow some users to edit ranges without the worksheet-level password. In this case, you would select the Allow checkbox in Step 6, enter a password in Step 7, and probably specify the same password to protect the worksheet in Step 8. Then, all other users would have to enter a password before making changes to the range or the rest of the worksheet.

If you don't enter a password for the range in Step 7, all users can edit the range. This is equivalent to unlocking the range as described in the previous procedure.

You can allow edits for a group of users. In that case, specify the group name in Step 5. For instance WOMBAT1\Administrators allows members of the Administrators group on the machine Wombat1 to edit a range.

In all cases, you must protect the worksheet in order for the range-level protections to take effect.

Program with Protection

Since protecting workbooks, worksheets, and ranges is a multi-step process, it is sometime convenient to automate protection—particularly if you frequently use the same types of protections or if you want to make sure all protections use the same password.

Excel provides methods for protecting Workbook, Chart, and Worksheet objects as well as subordinate objects for controlling various aspects of protection on Worksheet objects. Figure 6-14 illustrates the relationships between the protection objects.

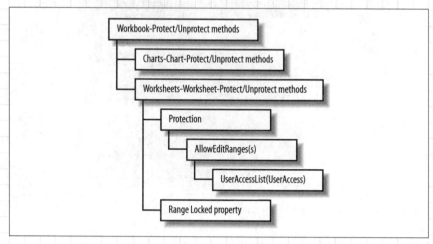

Figure 6-14. Protection object model

The protection objects are organized in a somewhat unusual way: First, the Workbook and Chart objects don't provide a Protection object, because those objects only allow password-protection. Second, the Worksheet object provides a Protection object that allows you to specify a list of users who can edit ranges on the worksheet. Finally, you set which cells on a worksheet are protected by setting the Range object's Locked property.

The protection objects aren't as consistent as other parts of the Excel object model. You need to know where to look to find the right object.

How to do it

You can use the Worksheet object's Protect and Unprotect methods to work together with the Range object's Locked property to conditionally protect cells on a worksheet. For instance, the following code protects all worksheet cells that contain formulas:

```
Set ws = ThisWorkbook.Sheets("Protection")
' Make sure worksheet is not already protected.
ws.Unprotect
' Get each used cell in the worksheet.
For Each rng In ws.UsedRange
    ' If it contains a formula, lock the cell.
    If InStr(rng.Formula, "=") Then
        rng.Locked = True
    ' Otherwise unlock the cell.
```

```
        Else
            rng.Locked = False
        End If
    Next
    ' Protect the worksheet.
    ws.Protect
```

After you run the preceding code, users can edit data on the worksheet but not cells that contain calculations. The `Protect` method above doesn't specify a password, so no password is required to unprotect the cells. This isn't very secure, but it would prevent users from making accidental changes to formulas. An alternative is to hardcode a password into the macro or to prompt for a password, as shown in "Program with Passwords and Encryption." For example, the following code gets a password using the Password user form shown earlier:

```
frmPassword.Show
ws.Protect frmPassword.Password
Unload frmPassword
```

Now, the user will be prompted for a password if he attempts to edit a formula.

How it works

Password protection works well when there is one author for a workbook, but it is not very secure for multiple authors since the password must be shared with anyone who wants to make changes. The more people that know a password, the less secure it becomes.

To solve this problem, Excel provides Protection and UserAccessList objects so that you can apply user-based permissions for ranges on a worksheet. User-based permissions solve the multiple-author problem because users are authenticated by the network when they sign on.

Protection with user-based permissions still requires a password to protect the worksheet, but cells are automatically unlocked for certain users so those users aren't required to enter the password. For example, the following code password protects a worksheet but allows members of the Power Users group to edit the range A1:C4:

```
Dim ws As Worksheet, aer As AllowEditRange
Set ws = ThisWorkbook.Sheets("Protection")
Set aer = ws.Protection.AllowEditRanges.Add("User Range", [A1:C4])
aer.Users.Add "Power Users", True
ws.Protect "Excel2003"
```

The names of edit ranges on a worksheet must be unique. You can remove previously created edit ranges unprotecting the worksheet and using the `Delete` method:

You have to set a reference to the AllowEditRange object in order to add users that are allowed to edit the range without a password. You can't use Excel's Record Macro feature to see how to add allowed users for a range—Excel only records the process of adding the named edit range, not adding the users or setting their permissions.

```
ws.Unprotect
For Each aer In ws.Protection.AllowEditRanges
    aer.Delete
Next
```

Similarly, you can remove users added to an edit range using the Users collection DeleteAll method or the User object's Delete method:

```
ws.Unprotect
Set aer = ws.Protection.AllowEditRanges("User Range")
aer.Users("Power Users").Delete
```

How to get Protection properties

The Protection object provides a set of read-only properties that describe the types of protection in effect on a worksheet. These settings correspond to the settings in the Protect Sheet dialog box and to the arguments used in the Worksheet object's Protect method. For example, the following code displays a report on the Protection property settings in the Immediate window:

```
Set ws = ThisWorkbook.Sheets("Protection")
Set prot = ws.Protection
Debug.Print "Can delete:", "Columns?", "Rows?"
Debug.Print , prot.AllowDeletingColumns, prot.AllowDeletingRows
Debug.Print "Can:", "Filter?", "Sort?", "Use Pivot Tables?"
Debug.Print , prot.AllowFiltering, prot.AllowSorting, prot.
AllowUsingPivotTables
Debug.Print "Can format:", "Cells?", "Columns?", "Rows?"
Debug.Print , prot.AllowFormattingCells, prot.AllowFormattingColumns, _
    prot.AllowFormattingRows
Debug.Print "Can insert:", "Columns?", "Rows?", "Hyperlinks?"
Debug.Print , prot.AllowInsertingColumns, prot.AllowInsertingRows, _
    prot.AllowInsertingHyperlinks
```

You also use the Protection object in order to get a reference to the AllowEditRanges object, which lets you set user-level permissions on a worksheet.

How to add an edit range

Use the AllowEditRanges collection to create ranges that allow edits by specific users. Excel prevents changes to ranges of cells that are protected and locked. The AllowEditRanges settings automatically unlock ranges of cells for the users included in the user access list.

You must remove protection from a worksheet before you can add user-level permissions. For example, the following code unprotects a worksheet, creates a range that allows user-level permissions, and then restores protection:

```
Dim ws As Worksheet, ual As UserAccessList, aer As AllowEditRange, _
    usr As UserAccess
Set ws = ThisWorkbook.Sheets("Protection")
ws.Unprotect "Excel2003"
Set aer = ws.Protection.AllowEditRanges.Add("Edit Range", ws.[a1:c4])
Set usr = aer.Users.Add("Power Users", True)
ws.Protect "Excel2003"
```

How to add users

Use the UserAccessList collection to add users to the user access list of an
edit range on a protected worksheet. You can add individual users or
groups to the user access list, but the names must be valid user or group
names for your system. For example, the following code adds the built-in
Users group to the access list for an edit range:

```
Dim ws As Worksheet, ual As UserAccessList, aer As AllowEditRange, _
    usr As UserAccess
Set ws = ThisWorkbook.Sheets("Protection")
Set aer = ws.Protection.AllowEditRanges("Edit Range")
Set ual = aer.Users
Set usr = ual.Add("Users", True)
```

The UserAccessList collection does not support the For Each construct in
Visual Basic. Instead, you must use a For statement with a counter get
each item in the collection:

```
For i = 1 To ual.Count
    Set usr = ual(i)
    Debug.Print usr.Name
Next
```

What about...

Workbook, Worksheet, and Chart objects all provide protection members.
Each of those objects provides 100 or more other members as well. To
help navigate among the various ways to protect items in code, Tables
6-2 through 6-7 list the protection members and subordinate objects for
each of those objects. You can get Help on any of these members from
the Visual Basic editor.

Table 6-2. Workbook protection members. Use the Workbook object to protect the
order of worksheets, window and pane layout, and to set passwords for shared
workbooks

Protect	ProtectSharing	ProtectStructure
ProtectWindows	Unprotect	UnprotectSharing

Table 6-3. Worksheet protection members. Use the Worksheet object to protect locked cells and other items on the worksheet

Protect	ProtectContents	ProtectDrawingObjects
Protection	ProtectionMode	ProtectScenarios
Unprotect		

Table 6-4. Chart protection members. Use the Chart object to protect chart appearance and data

Protect	ProtectContents	ProtectData
ProtectDrawingObjects	ProtectFormatting	ProtectGoalSeek
ProtectionMode	ProtectSelection	Unprotect

Table 6-5. Protection object members. Use the Worksheet object's Protection method to get a reference to the Protection object

AllowDeletingColumns	AllowDeletingRows	AllowEditRanges
AllowFiltering	AllowFormattingCells	AllowFormattingColumns
AllowFormattingRows	AllowInsertingColumns	AllowInsertingHyperlinks
AllowInsertingRows	AllowSorting	AllowUsingPivotTables

Table 6-6. AllowEditRanges/AllowEditRange members. Use the Protection object's AllowEditRanges property to get a reference to the AllowEditRanges collection

Add	ChangePassword	Count
Delete	Range	Title
Unprotect	Users	

Table 6-7. UserAccessList members. Use the AllowEditRange object's Users property to get a reference to the UserAccessList collection

Add	AllowEdit	Count
Delete	DeleteAll	Name

Use Identity-Based Security (a.k.a. IRM)

Earlier sections discuss protecting workbooks using passwords. The problems with passwords are:

- They are susceptible to guessing attacks.
- There is no secure way to share them among a group.
- They tend to proliferate and become hard to remember. You can use the same password for all items, but that reduces security.

The solution to this problem is identity-based security. The preceding section showed how you could allow specific users to edit protected worksheets without the worksheet password. The larger solution is to define workbook permissions based on the user's identity.

Two key features make IRM worth using: you can add expiration dates to documents and you can prevent users from forwarding, printing, or copying the document. That's great for copywritten or time-sensitive material—like early drafts of this book!

How it works

Identity-based security solves the password problem because users maintain their own password—usually it's the one they use to sign on to the network—and then their identity travels with them wherever they go on a network. You don't have to set workbook passwords, share those with your workmates, and hope you don't lose or forget them.

Excel provides identity-based security through Microsoft Information Rights Management (IRM). This new feature comes at a cost, however. In order to use IRM, you must have a Windows 2003 server running Microsoft Windows Rights Management (RM) Services on your network. If you don't have that, or if you want to share a workbook outside of your network, you can use Microsoft Passport identities instead of network identities. Figure 6-15 shows how IRM works.

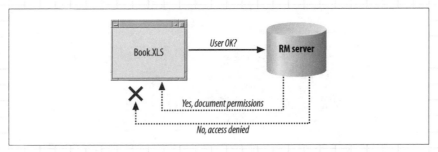

Figure 6-15. IRM uses identities rather than passwords to control access

How IRM compares

There are some huge advantages to IRM over other types of document protection:

- Identities are not susceptible to guessing attacks.
- You can control a wide variety of permissions, such as the ability to print, forward, edit, copy, save, etc.
- Documents can have an expiration date.
- Permissions can be assigned to roles.
- Users can request additional permissions from the author, as needed.

- Users who don't have network accounts inside your organization can use Microsoft Passport accounts for authentication.

The disadvantages are significant, too:

- Using Passports for IRM is a trial service according to Microsoft and so might be discontinued. Microsoft pledges to give 90-days notice before discontinuing support for this.

- The RM service for Windows 2003 requires a significant per client license fee.

- All users need an identity—there's no mechanism for an anonymous user with limited rights.

The following procedures use the Microsoft Passport identities—hopefully that trial service will still be functioning when you read this!

How to do it

To set IRM permissions on a workbook for the first time:

1. Choose File → Permission → Do Not Distribute. Excel starts the Windows Rights Management Wizard, which walks you through creating Rights Management credentials and downloading them to your computer. When you are done, Excel displays the Permission dialog box as shown in Figure 6-16.

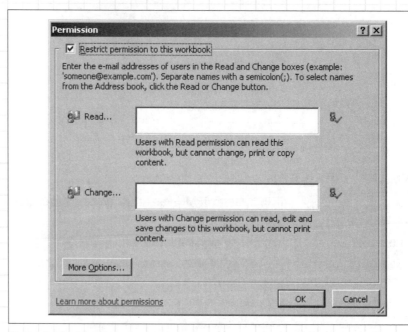

Figure 6-16. Restricting permissions

2. Select Restrict permission to this workbook to set permissions. Excel activates the dialog box so that you can enter data.

3. Enter a list of the users allowed to read and/or change the workbook. Users are identified by email address. Separate multiple addresses with semicolons.

4. To set the expiration date, restrict printing, and other capabilities, click More Options. Excel displays the expanded Permission dialog box (Figure 6-17).

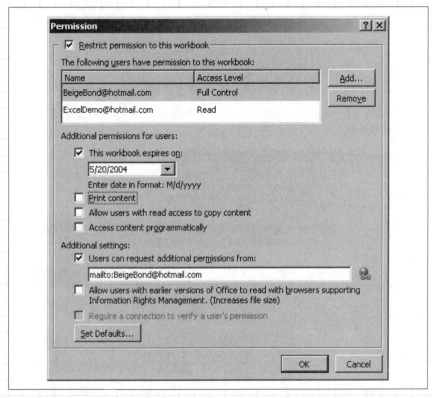

Figure 6-17. Setting an expiration date

5. Set the additional permissions by selecting the user and then changing the permission settings in the Permissions dialog box. Click OK when done.

How it works

As the author of the workbook, you always have permission to open, edit, and distribute your document. The workbook will not expire for you because the author always has full control.

When someone other than the author opens a workbook with permissions enabled, several things may happen:

- If they are included in the workbook's users list and have Office 2003 installed, the workbook opens in Excel and they may perform the actions specified by their permissions.
- If they are not included in the workbook's users list and they have Office 2003 installed, they will see a description of where to send email to get permission to use the workbook (Figure 6-18).

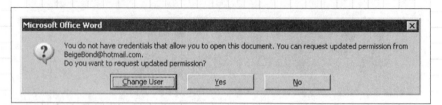

Figure 6-18. Users without permissions are told how to request access to an IRM-protected document

- If they do not have Office 2003 installed, they will see a description of how to get the IRM add-ins for Internet Explorer so they can view the workbook (Figure 6-19).

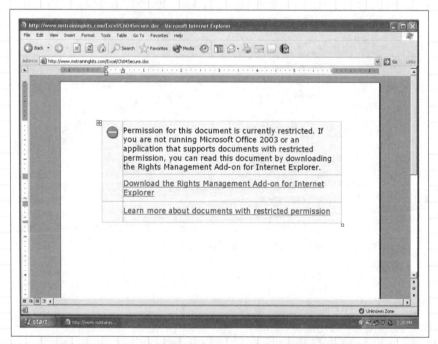

Figure 6-19. Users without Office 2003 are told how to get the IRM-add-ins for Internet Explorer

Chapter 6: Explore Security in Depth

What about...

To learn about	Look here
Information Rights Management	*http://www.microsoft.com/windowsserver2003/ technologies/rightsmgmt/default.mspx*

Program with Permissions

Microsoft provides the permissions objects through the Office object library since permissions can be applied to Excel, Word, and PowerPoint documents. Figure 6-20 illustrates the hierarchy of the permission objects.

You can do some things in code that you can't do through the user interface—like specifying differ- ent permission sets for differ- ent users.

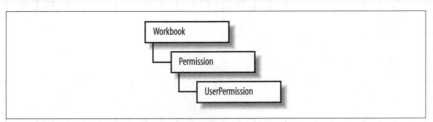

Figure 6-20. Office permisson object model

How to do it

Once credentials are installed, you can restrict access to workbooks by setting the Permission collection's Enabled property to True, as shown here:

```
Dim irm As Office.Permission
Set irm = ThisWorkbook.Permission
irm.Enabled = True
```

The preceding code sets the workbook as Do Not Distribute. You are given full control, but no other users have permissions. Use the Add method to add permissions for other users. You must add each user indi- vidually, even if they have the same permissions, as shown here:

```
Set irm = ThisWorkbook.Permission
irm.Add "ExcelDemo@hotmail.com", MsoPermission.msoPermissionView
irm.Add "someone@microsoft.com", MsoPermission.msoPermissionView
```

Use Or to combine permissions for a user. For example, the following code allows ExcelDemo@hotmail.com to read, print, and copy a work- book:

```
irm.Add "someone@microsoft.com", MsoPermission.msoPermissionView Or & _
    MsoPermission.msoPermissionPrint Or MsoPermission.msoPermissionExtract
```

You must have Rights Manage- ment credentials installed before you can set permissions on a document. Otherwise, most permission methods will cause runtime errors. See the "Use Identity- Based Security" section for instructions on how to install credentials.

When you combine permissions, they may not display in the Excel Permissions options dialog box. Instead, the user may appear as having Custom permissions as shown in Figure 6-21.

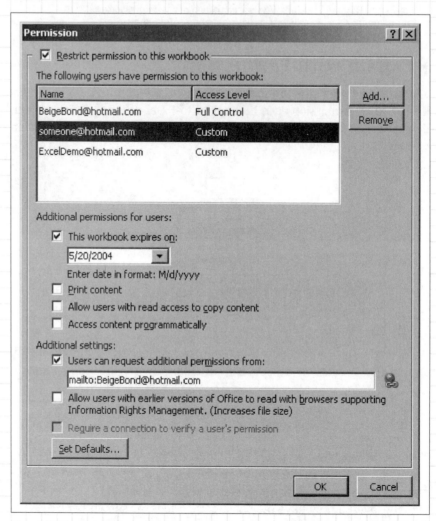

Figure 6-21. User options added in code don't always appear in the Excel dialogs

You can set a date at which the user's permissions to the document expire using an argument in the Add method or by setting the Expiration property as shown here:

```
Set irm = ThisWorkbook.Permission
Set usr = irm("ExcelDemo@hotmail.com")
usr.ExpirationDate = Date + 1
```

Chapter 6: Explore Security in Depth

The preceding code sets the expiration date for the user one day from the current date. Expiration dates are always calendar dates—you can't set permissions to expire at a certain time.

You may also notice from the preceding code that there is no "Users" collection. Instead, you use the Permission collection to get UserPermission objects. For example, the following code displays the permissions for each user in the Immediate window:

```
Dim irm As Office.Permission, usr As Office.UserPermission
Set irm = ThisWorkbook.Permission
For Each usr In irm
    Debug.Print usr.UserId, usr.Permission, usr.ExpirationDate
Next
```

The simplest way to remove permissions from a workbook is to set the Permission collection's Enabled property to False:

```
ThisWorkbook.Permission.Enabled = False
```

Disabling the Permission collection removes all users and their permissions. Use the UserPermission object's Remove method to selectively remove users.

What about...

To learn about	Look here
Permission and UserPermission objects	*C:\Program Files\Microsoft Office\OFFICE11\1033\VBAOF11.CHM*
Deploying and programming with IRM	Subscribe to the newsgroup: microsoft.public.rights_mgmt_svcs

Add Digital Signatures

A digital signature identifies the author of the content or the macros contained in a workbook, template, or add-in. You add a digital signature as the last step before you distribute a file. When others open the a signed file they can see who the author is and therefore decide whether the information in the file is authentic and whether any macros it contains are safe to run.

The signature is overwritten any time a file is saved. Therefore, no one can open a signed file, make changes, save, then send the file on still bearing your signature. Workbooks and macros are signed separately even though they are contained in a single file. If you want to distribute a signed workbook containing macros, you must sign the macros first, then sign the workbook.

The Permission collection and UserPermission object are unusual in that they aren't related by name as are most collections and objects in Office products. (For example, the Add-ins collection contains Add-in objects.) There's no clear reason for this— perhaps the designers felt the need to get creative.

Digital signatures prove that an item comes from a specific author. For VBA code, this may determine whether macros are allowed to run.

Get a Digital Certificate

Before you can sign a document, you must first get a digital certificate, which is also sometimes called a *digital ID* or simply a *certificate*. There are two ways get a digital certificate: create one yourself or purchase one from a Certificate Authority (CA). Self-created signatures are only valid on the machine where they were created, so they are for macros that won't be distributed. CA-created signatures are available from vendors such as Verisign, Inc. and CAcert.org.

To create a digital certificate yourself:

1. From the Windows Programs menu, choose Microsoft Office → Microsoft Office Tools → Digital Certificate for VBA Projects. Windows runs *SelfCert.exe* and displays the Create Digital Certificate dialog box (Figure 6-22).

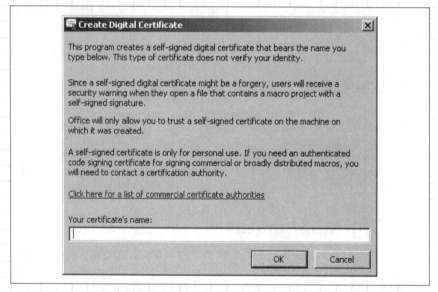

Figure 6-22. Creating a digital certificate

2. Type the name you want displayed within the signature and click OK. *SelfCert.exe* creates a local certificate and displays a success message.

As mentioned previously, this certificate is only valid on the machine where you created it. Therefore, its use is really limited to signing macros on your own machine to avoid the security prompt you get each time you open a workbook containing macros you've written.

To get a much more useful certificate from a CA, click the link on the Create Digital Certificate dialog box to see a list of commercial CAs, select one of them, and purchase a certificate from there. Some vendors, such as Verisign Inc., offer free trial periods so you can see how certificates work before you buy.

Sign Code

To sign a VBA project, follow these steps:

1. Open the VBA Project.
2. Choose Tools → Digital Signature. Visual Basic displays the Digital Signature dialog box (Figure 6-23).

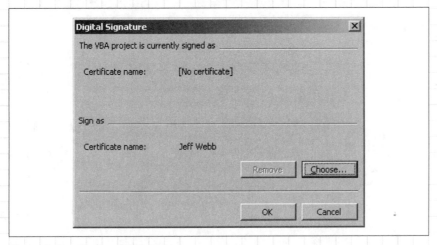

Figure 6-23. Signing a VBA Project

3. Click Choose, Visual Basic displays a dialog box containing all the digital certificates installed on your system (Figure 6-24).
4. Select the certificate to use, and click OK. Then click OK again to close the Digital Signature dialog box.

Visual Basic keeps track of the certificate you are going to use, but doesn't sign the file until you save the project. If your certificate is set up to notify you when it is accessed, you will see a dialog box warning you that the certificate is being accessed any time the workbook is saved—even when it is saved automatically.

Once the code is signed, users may see the security warning in Figure 6-25 when they open a workbook, template, or add-in containing the signed code.

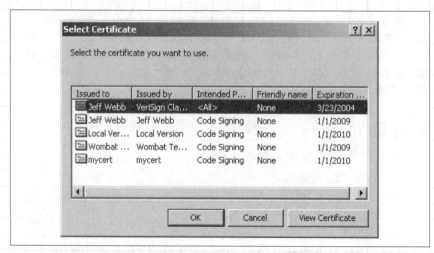

Figure 6-24. Choosing a signature

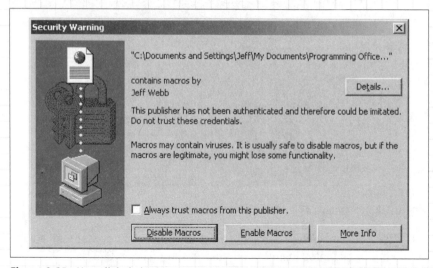

Figure 6-25. Your digital signature now appears in the macro security warning

If the user selects the option to Always trust macros from this publisher, he won't see the warning again. If your certificate is from SelfCert.exe, you can select this option so you won't see this warning every time you open your own workbooks.

Sign Workbooks

You can't use certificates from *SelfCert.exe* to sign workbooks. Since those certificates are valid only on one machine, they don't really make sense for signing workbooks. Instead, digital signatures on workbooks are intended to prove that the content is authentic—that it comes from you and hasn't been altered.

To sign a workbook, follow these steps:

1. Open the workbook in Excel and finish all your edits, formatting, etc. The workbook should be in its final form before signing.

2. Choose Tools → Options then click the Security tab. Excel displays the Options dialog (Figure 6-26).

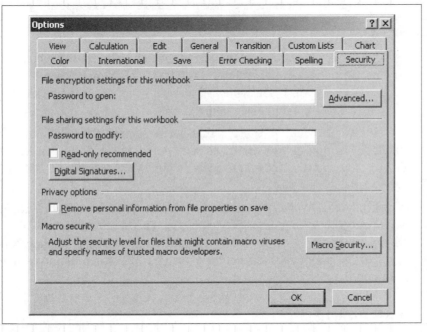

Figure 6-26. Signing a workbook

3. Click Digital Signatures. Excel displays the Digital Signature dialog.

4. Click Add. Excel warns you that it will save the file and then displays the Select Certificate dialog box as shown in Figure 6-27.

5. Select a certificate and click OK, then click OK on each of the remaining dialog boxes.

6. Close, but do not save, the workbook. It was already saved when you added the certificate, and saving it again will remove the digital signature.

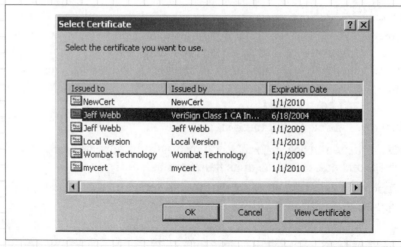

Figure 6-27. Choose a signature to use

When a user receives a signed workbook, he can open the workbook in Excel and view the digital certificate from the Options dialog box to verify that the workbook is authentic. However, if the user then saves the workbook in Excel the digital signature is lost.

If the workbook contains macros that were signed, that signature is maintained as long as the user does not change the code in the workbook. In other words, code and content are maintained separately in Excel.

You can only sign workbooks that are saved in Excel format (.xls). Excel does not support signing other file types, such as XML spreadsheets (.xml). To distribute these types of files as digitally signed documents, you can attach them to an email message, then use your CA-issued digital certificate to sign the message.

What about...

To learn about	Look here
Digital certificates, code, document, and XML signing	*http://www.verisign.com*
Non-profit digital signatures	*http://www.cacert.org* *http://www.onlamp.com/pub/wlg/5142*

Set Macro Security

Excel controls whether workbook macros are allowed to run through security settings. Users may choose to prohibit all macros, allow only signed macros from known sources, allow macros of the user's choosing, or allow all macros. These settings correspond to the Very High, High, Medium, and Low security settings on the Security dialog box (Figure 6-28).

Excel's macro security settings determine how rigorously the user is protected from anonymous and possibly malign VBA code.

How to do it

To set macro security:

1. Open a workbook.
2. Choose Tools → Macro → Security. Excel displays the macro security setting (Figure 6-28)

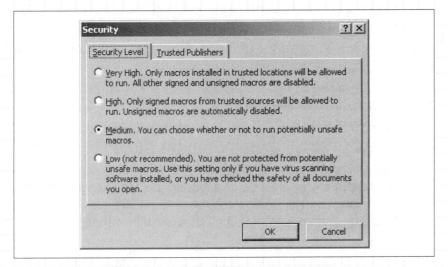

Figure 6-28. Choosing macro security settings

These settings are driven by trust—the user must choose whether or not to trust a publisher or a workbook. There is no way for the user to prohibit certain operations, such as reading or writing to the registry or erasing data files. Users only discover if their trust is misplaced after the damage is done.

For this reason, it is a good idea to encourage users to be suspicious of macros arriving in workbooks. It is a better idea to deploy macros as digitally signed templates or add-ins and to distribute those files from a secure network location.

How to distribute macros

The following scenario demonstrates how to distribute macros in a secure fashion:

1. Set up a public network share. For example, \\Wombat1\Public\Templates.

2. Set Windows security on the Templates folder to allow read-only access to all network users and read/write access to the Administrator (in this case, you).

3. Digitally sign templates and add-ins using a CA-issued digital certificate.

4. Copy the templates and add-ins to the public Templates folder.

5. Add the public Templates location to the alternate startup path for each Excel user.

6. For each user, open one of the signed templates in Excel and select Always trust macros from this publisher on the Security Warning.

7. Select the High or Very High macro security options for each Excel user.

To set the alternate startup path in Excel, set the At startup open all files in: text box in the Options dialog box as shown in Figure 6-29.

To set the alternate startup path in code, use the following line:

```
Application.AltStartupPath = "\\wombat1\public\templates"
```

Now, when users start Excel, templates and add-ins from \\Wombat1\Public\Templates are available automatically. If a file changes, the user will get the latest version. And since the files are digitally signed by a trusted publisher, users won't see the macro security warning every time they open a file.

TIP

SmartTags are provided through a type of add-in, so macro security settings apply to them as well as the other types of files that can contain code (workbooks, templates, etc.).

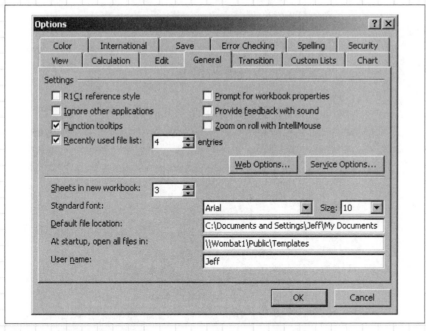

Figure 6-29. Setting the alternate startup path to a secure network location

How to set ActiveX control security

Excel workbooks may contain ActiveX controls that execute code or respond to macros. ActiveX controls may be digitally signed and are marked by the publisher as to whether they are safe to initialize and safe to script. In this case, *safe* means that the control will not harm the user's system.

Whether Excel will download or run any new ActiveX control is determined by security settings in Internet Explorer. To see these settings in Internet Explorer:

1. Choose Tools → Internet Options and click on the Security tab.

2. Select the location that is the source of the ActiveX control and click Custom Level. Figure 6-30 shows the ActiveX security settings for the Local intranet location.

As a rule, you should never install unsigned ActiveX controls from any location. ActiveX controls are software, and you should always be careful when choosing which publishers to trust.

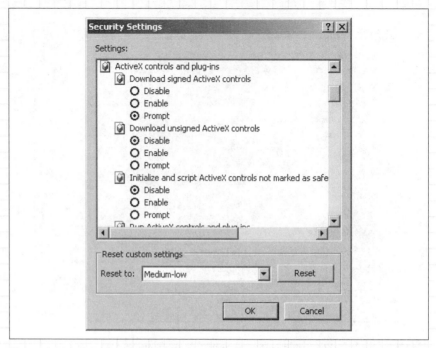

Figure 6-30. Changing ActiveX security settings

Distribute Security Settings

Changing macros security settings on individual computers is fine for personal use, but it doesn't work very well when trying to manage security for an organization. To solve that problem, Microsoft provides the following tools:

- The Microsoft Office Resource Kit provides the Custom Installation Wizard (CIW), Custom Maintenance Wizard, and Profile Template Wizard that automate the installation and configuration of Microsoft Office across your organization.

- The Certificate Manager (*CertMgr.exe*) lets you export, distribute, and install certificates for Trusted Publishers on users' machines.

Use the Install/Maintenance Wizards

The Microsoft Office Resource Kit does not come included with the Microsoft Office product, but is available as a free download from Microsoft (see What about...). Table 6-8 lists the four primary tools that come with the Office Resource Kit.

You probably don't want users within your organization to administer their own security settings. Use these tools to maintain a consistent security policy.

Table 6-8. Office Resource Kit tools

Tool	Use to
Custom Installation Wizard	Create customized installations for your organization. You can remove Office components, add your own components, set default installation paths, and determine Start menu and Desktop items created by Setup.
Custom Maintenance Wizard	Deploy changes to Office installations including new components and updates. This is similar to the Installation Wizard, but it is designed for modifying existing installations rather than creating new ones.
Removal Wizard	Removes previous versions of Office applications.
Profile Wizard	Deploy Office user settings, such as Macro Security settings.

The basic steps for using the Custom Installation and Custom Maintenance Wizards are the same:

1. Set up an administrative installation point on your network. This is the location from which Setup will run, and it includes the Windows installer files (.msi) for Office.

2. Run the Wizard to create a Windows Installer transform (.mst) containing the modifications you wish to make to the Office installation. You can also add components (such as ActiveX controls or Smart-Tags) to the installation by including their .msi files to create chained installations.

3. Execute the installation from the client machines using remote administration, instructions to the user, or installation scripts. See Setup.htm on the Office installation CD for information on Setup command-line options and unattended installation.

The Custom Installation and Maintenance Wizards are important to security because they can remove components that might pose security risks for some users. For example, you may choose *not* to install Visual Basic for Applications and .NET Programmability Support (the Office .NET Primary InterOp Assemblies or PIAs) to impede macros from running at all—that may be an appropriate setting for public workstations, such as those available in libraries.

Use the Profile Wizard to create a file containing the Excel security settings you want to apply to client computers. For example, you may want to make sure all clients use the Very High macro security setting and disable Trust access to VBA projects. To use the Policy Wizard, follow these steps:

1. Set up a computer with the user settings you want to export to all other clients.

2. Run the Profile Wizard on that computer and export the settings to copy to other clients. Figure 6-31 shows the Profile Wizard ready to export Excel security user settings.

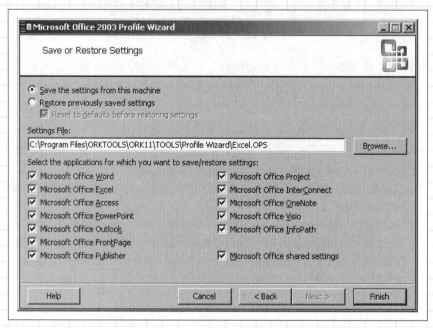

Figure 6-31. Exporting user security settings

3. Run the Profile Template Wizard on client machines using the template exported in Step 2. The wizard can be run from the command-line; run *proflwz.exe /?* to see the command-line options.

Distribute certificates

If you set macro security settings to Very High, Excel will not prompt the user to install certificates from new publishers. The only way the user can run those macros is to lower the security, reload the document, and select Always trust macros from this publisher. If you are using the Very High security setting, you probably don't want users lowering it, installing certificates, then (maybe) raising it again.

To avoid this problem, you can distribute the certificates from trusted publishers beforehand using the Certificate Manager (*CertMgr.exe*). The Certificate Manager is available for download from Microsoft (see What about…) and comes with other certificate-related tools such as *SignCode.exe*.

To use the Certificate Manager to distribute certificates from trusted publishers:

1. Set up a computer with the certificates you want to distribute.
2. Run the Certificate Manager (Figure 6-32) and export the desired certificates *without* their private keys. The Certificate Manager provides a wizard to walk you through the export process.
3. Use the resulting certificate files (.cer or .p7b) with the command-line interface of the Certificate Manager to install those certificates on client machines.

Figure 6-32. Use the Certificate Manager to export and import certificates from trusted publishers

Alternatively, you can manage certificates using the Microsoft Management Console Certificates snap-in (*CertMgr.msc*). Figure 6-33 shows the Certificate snap-in administering certificates on a remote computer.

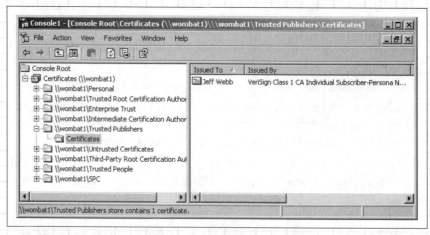

Figure 6-33. Use the Certificate snap-in to administer certificates over the network

What about...

To learn about	Look here
Microsoft Office 2003 Resource Kit	*http://www.microsoft.com/office/ork/2003/tools/ default.htm*
Microsoft Office XP Resource Kit	*http://www.microsoft.com/office/ork/xp/default.htm*
Microsoft Office 2000 Resource Kit	*http://www.microsoft.com/office/ork/2000/default.htm*
Certificate management and code signing tools	*http://office.microsoft.com/downloads/2000/pvkimprt. aspx*

Common Questions

Maintaining security isn't simple or fun. A little Q&A can sometimes help answer difficult questions.

Whew, this chapter is already longer than I planned and (I fear) too complicated. In order to simplify things a bit, I include the following common security problems, with brief descriptions of how to solve them. I hope it helps!

What is partial trust?

The Excel macro security model is based on trust and known publishers. Macro code is digitally signed and that signature identifies the source (publisher) of the macro. At that point, the user makes the decision whether to trust that publisher. The inference here is that if the macro does something bad, the user will no longer trust that publisher and possibly pursue damages through the legal system.

In Excel and other applications that implement the Common Object Model (COM), trust is absolute. You either trust someone or you don't. In fact, this isn't a perfect system for the real world, where you might trust someone but not want to lend them your car keys, or your credit card, or your bank PIN.

There are situations where you might want to *partially trust* an application. Microsoft addresses this in the .NET Framework. Applications written with .NET can be granted partial trust, so they can run but not read the system registry or write to disk, for example.

There are some situations where .NET applications require full trust. For instance, a .NET application must be fully trusted in order to use Excel. You can't use .NET to create partially trusted wrappers for COM applications.

See Chapter 5, "Program Excel with .NET."

What is the Office Anti-Virus API?

Microsoft provides an API for anti-virus software developers so that they can write code to scan documents as they are opened in Excel. Since the scan is focused on the current file being opened, it can be more thorough than general scans of the user's disk. Anti-virus software that uses this API may display settings on the Macro Security options dialog in Excel.

See the web site *http://msdn.microsoft.com/workshop/security/antivirus/overview/overview.asp*.

How do you get rid of the macro security warning?

If you write macros for personal use and get tired of seeing the macro security warning every time you open personal workbooks, you can sign your macros with a personal digital certificate. To do this:

1. Choose Digital Certificate for VBA Projects from the Windows Office Tools menu to run *SelfCert.exe*.

2. Use *SelfCert.exe* to create a personal digital certificate.

3. From the Visual Basic Tools menu, choose Digital Signature.

4. Click Choose to add your digital certificate to the workbook's macros.

5. Repeat Step 4 each time you create a new workbook or template containing macros.

See the section "Add Digital Signatures."

How do you prevent all macros?

You can omit Visual Basic for Applications during installation or remove that component after installation by using Office Setup to perform maintenance. That prevents users from creating their own macros as well as preventing them from running macros in existing workbooks.

Other applications, such as Windows Scripting Host (*WScript.exe*) will still be able to run macros that use the Excel Object Library, however. You can't remove this library—Excel needs it to run and will reinstall it if it is not found. You can remove or disable *WScript.exe* and *CScript.exe*, but other applications can still access the Excel Object Library to perform tasks in Excel.

See "Distribute Security Settings."

How do you secure a workbook?

Security is a sliding scale and I'd hesitate to say *anything* is ever completely secure. You can make Excel workbooks fairly secure by adding password-protection and encryption. Be sure to use a strong password (eight or more characters, upper- and lowercase, include numbers and symbols).

You can also protect access to files through Windows by using the NT Encrypting File System and using the Windows file security settings to prevent access by users other than yourself.

Finally, you can set permissions on a workbook using IRM to prevent any user other than yourself from reading or writing to the workbook in Excel. This last technique also provides a way to share workbooks in a secure way with restricted permissions.

See the sections "Password-Protect and Encrypt Workbooks" and "Use Identity-Based Security."

How do you add a trusted publisher for a group of users?

There are two ways to do this, depending upon your network setup and your distribution needs: you can create a command-line script that uses *CertMgr.exe* to install exported certificate files (.cer) on each user's machine, or you can use the Microsoft Management Console Certificates snap-in (*CertMgr.msc*) to install certificates on user's machines over a network—provided you have administrative privileges to their machines.

See "Distribute Security Settings."

Build InfoPath Forms

InfoPath is a new application in the Microsoft Office System that lets people create and fill in data entry forms. These forms look sort of like a cross between Word documents and web pages (Figure 7-1).

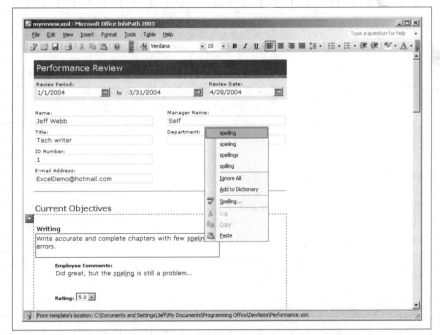

Figure 7-1. InfoPath forms provide spellchecking, suggestions, date picker controls, and RTF formatting for input

Are InfoPath Forms Better?

Creating data entry forms is perhaps the number one programming task today. Years ago, Visual Studio made this task easier with controls and

Code used in this chapter and additional samples are found in ch07.xls.

drag-and-drop design tools; however Windows and Web form design is still much too hard for non-programmers.

InfoPath provides form design tools that can be used by intermediate to advanced Office System users. It simplifies design, distribution, validation, and data collection tasks; plus, InfoPath provides templates for the most common types of forms. This simplification is possible because InfoPath is based on a several assumptions:

- Most forms reflect some underlying data source.
- There is a well-defined set of actions you want to perform on that data source: Query, Refresh, Validate, Submit, Change View.
- Users expect Office-like editing tools such as autocorrect and spell checking.

Because these assumptions are built in to the design of the product, InfoPath makes performing those tasks much easier. Specifically, tasks that were formerly done by programming can now be done by setting control properties or adding predefined actions and rules to controls. This approach is called *declarative programming* and it contrasts with the *imperative* approach most programmers are used to.

Finally, InfoPath forms are based on XML. You can create them from existing XML or XSD files or any XML data source, such as a web service or Access/SQL database. Why is this important? Because it provides a standards-based way to integrate data collected by InfoPath into other systems in an enterprise.

Where to get it

InfoPath is included with the Microsoft Office System Professional Enterprise Edition. That edition is available through volume licensing only. However, you can try InfoPath for 60-days through the InfoPath 2003 Evaluation Kit or buy it as a standalone product outside of the Office System.

What about...

To	Look here
Evaluate InfoPath (60–day trial)	*http://www.microsoft.com/office/infopath/prodinfo/trial.mspx*
Buy InfoPath	*http://www.microsoft.com/office/infopath/howtobuy/default.mspx*

The Version 1.0 release of InfoPath is an interesting first attempt, but the SP1 release provides many more capabilities including additional controls, actions, programmability, links to SharePoint lists, and much more. If at all possible, you should work with the SP1 release—this chapter uses that release throughout, though I do note where key features aren't available in Version 1.0.

The SP1 preview expired July 31, 2004, and is now part of Office 2003 Service Pack 1.

How to do it

InfoPath is both a form designer and a form viewer, so InfoPath tasks can be divided between Designers and Users as shown in Figure 7-2.

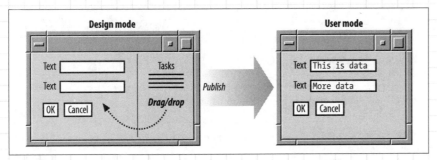

Figure 7-2. InfoPath both designs and views forms

To design a form:

1. Start InfoPath and choose File → Design a Form. InfoPath displays the Design a Form Task Pane.

2. Choose one of the design options. For example, clicking Customize a sample displays a list of the commonly used form templates that come with InfoPath (Figure 7-3).

3. If you select a sample and click OK, InfoPath opens the sample in design mode (Figure 7-4).

You can modify the form by selecting any of the options in the Task pane.

To preview the results of changes:

- Choose File → Preview → Default. InfoPath displays the form in Preview mode (Figure 7-5).

Once you are satisfied with a form, you have a choice: you can save the form for local use or testing, or you can publish the form for others to use. To publish a completed form:

Why doesn't InfoPath have a separate, distributable runtime? I don't know. For now, Microsoft licenses the design and runtime environments together and there's no way to separate the two, though you can disable the design mode (see "Prevent Design Changes").

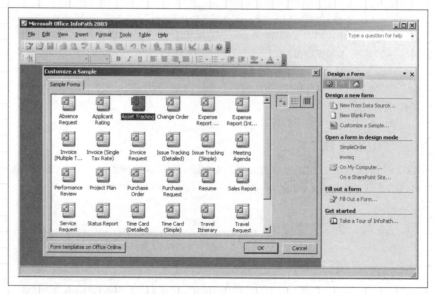

Figure 7-3. Modify an existing sample to get a quick start

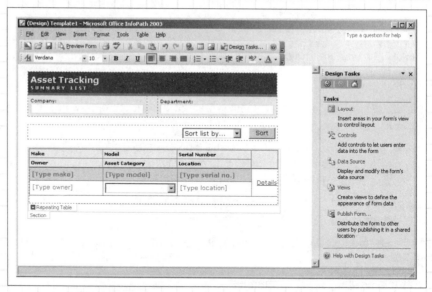

Figure 7-4. The Asset Tracking form in design mode

In preview mode, you can view changes, test controls, but not save data entered on the form.

1. Choose File → Publish. InfoPath starts the Publish wizard to walk you through the process.

2. Click Next to choose the type of location to publish the form (Figure 7-6).

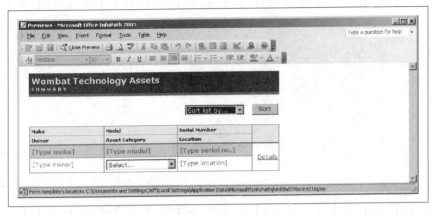

Figure 7-5. Viewing changes in Preview mode

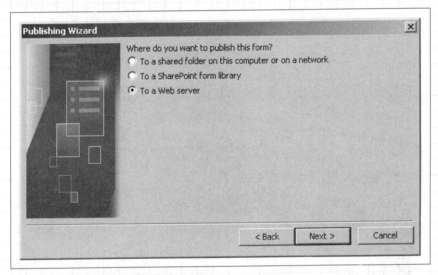

Figure 7-6. Use the Publishing Wizard to deploy a form

3. If you chose to publish to a Web server, the Wizard prompts for the location of the server (Figure 7-7).

4. Finally, the Wizard displays the address of the published form (Figure 7-8).

Once you've published a form, you can open it from the published address. For example, if a form is published to *http://wombat1/assets.xsn* as shown previously, you can open it for data entry by navigating to that address in Internet Explorer or by using the File → Open command in InfoPath.

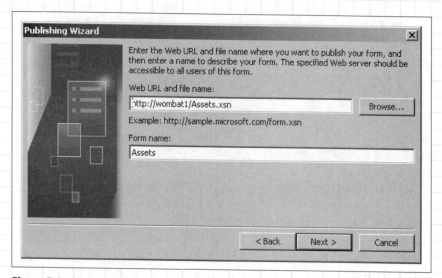

Figure 7-7. You can publish forms to web addresses

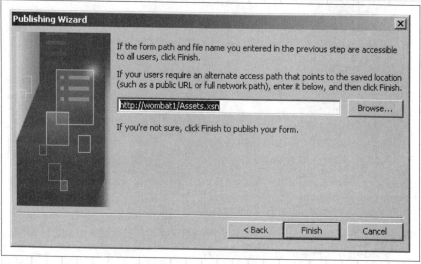

Figure 7-8. The Wizard displays the location of the published form, you can specify an alternate address to publish to another location as well

In either case, InfoPath opens the form template to create a new XML data file. If you enter data and save the form, InfoPath prompts you for a location to save the data with the default set as your local machine (Figure 7-9).

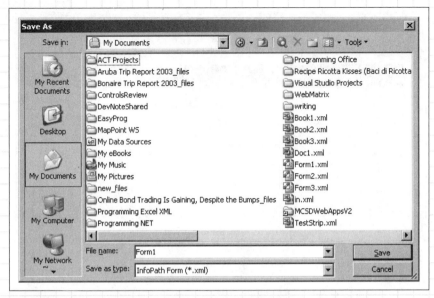

Figure 7-9. Warning: if you open the form template (.xsn), data is saved as a new form (.xml)

Since InfoPath forms are generally intended to collect and share data, saving data locally is not what you usually want to have happen! To solve this problem, follow these steps:

1. Open the form in user mode and save it without entering any data. This creates a "starter" XML file that can receive subsequent data.

2. Copy the XML file created in Step 1 to a public location. This will usually be the same server where the form is published, though it doesn't have to be the same.

3. Tell users to open the XML file from its public location to enter or view data.

How it works

When in design mode, InfoPath creates form template that contains the information InfoPath uses to display the form, collect data, and save that data. When in user mode, InfoPath interprets that form template to create form data files or to exchange XML data with a database, Web service, or other data source.

If you open the form data file in Notepad, you'll see processing instructions that associate that file with InfoPath and with the published location of the form template, as shown in the following XML fragment:

Only one user can have the XML data file open for editing at a time. During that time, other users are allowed read-only access only. For shared access, see the section "Share Data."

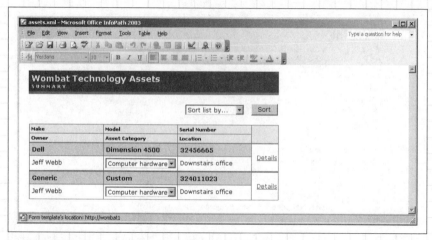

Figure 7-10. Open the XML file to enter or view shared data

```
<?xml version="1.0" encoding="UTF-8"?>
<?mso-infoPathSolution solutionVersion="1.0.0.4" productVersion="11.0.5531"
PIVersion="1.0.0.0" href="http://wombat1/assets.xsn" ?>
<?mso-application progid="InfoPath.Document"?>
<at:assetTracking xmlns:my="http://schemas.microsoft.com/office/infopath/
2003/myXSD" xmlns:at="http://schemas.microsoft.com/office/infopath/2003/
sample/AssetTracking" xml:lang="en-us">
    <at:dateModified xsi:nil="true" xmlns:xsi="http://www.w3.org/2001/
XMLSchema-instance"></at:dateModified>
    <at:owner>
            <at:name></at:name>
```

SharePoint Form Libraries provide a Relink button that can be used to fix this processing instruction if the Form Library is moved.

You must change the href attribute shown above in **bold** if you move the published template to a new location or change its name.

If you open the template file (.xsn) in Notepad, you might be surprised to find that you can't read it—it's just a bunch of gobbledygook! Templates are actually compiled from a collection of different files.

To see the contents of a form template:

1. Open the form template in Design mode.

2. Choose File → Extract Form Files. InfoPath displays a Browse for New Folder dialog to let you create a destination folder for the component files.

3. Click OK to extract the component template files to the folder. Figure 7-11 shows the results in Window Explorer.

Table 7-1 lists the basic file types used by InfoPath.

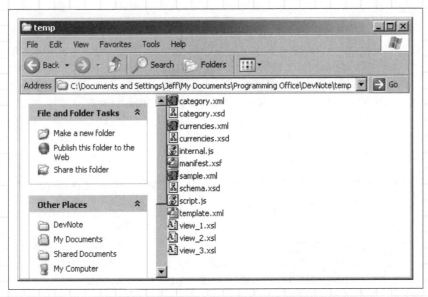

Figure 7-11. Form templates contain many component files

Table 7-1. InfoPath file types

File	Type	Description
Form template	.xsn	Defines the form to display to users.
Form data	.xml	Stores data entered through the form.
Manifest file	.xsf	Describes the contents of the form template. This file brings together all of the internal data (.xml), schemas (.xsd), scripts (.js/.vbs), resource files, and transformations (.xsl) used by the form template. This file also describes the actions and custom data validation rules for the form.
Components used by manifest file (*manifest.xsf*)	.xml	Provides static data displayed in controls on the form. *Template.xml* stores the initial data for new form data files. *Sample.xml* provides sample data used when designing the form.
	.xsd	XML schema descriptions for data items that may appear on the form. These schemas also contain simple data validation rules.
	.js	Contains JScript code that responds to form events and performs other tasks. Code may also be written in VBScript.
	.xsl	Transforms data into different views, such as summary and detail.

InfoPath modifies the component files shown in Figure 7-11 and described in Table 7-1 whenever you work with the form template in design mode. In other words, InfoPath is a visual editor for XML, XSD,

There's no Import Form Files menu item in InfoPath. If you make changes to exported form template components, reload the changes in InfoPath by opening the manifest file (manifest.xsf). Then use Save As to compile the template into a new .xsn file.

and XSL files, although those files are stored in the compiled form template (.xsn).

It is instructive to create a simple template and then extract and examine the generated form files. The *INFREF.CHM* Help file that ships with InfoPath includes descriptions of the elements and attributes used in template component files. Reading these generated files is akin to examining recorded VBA code in Excel.

Some terminology

Before we go too far, I'd like to define a few terms InfoPath uses frequently:

Form template, or just template
The .xsn file that InfoPath uses to generate a form.

Form data file, or just form
The InfoPath .xml document associated with a form template. You open a form template in user mode to create a new form data file.

Design mode, or just design
How you create or edit a form template in InfoPath. From Windows Explorer, you design a template by right-clicking and selecting Design.

User mode, or just open
How you create or edit a form data file. From Windows Explorer, you create a new form data file by double-clicking the template (open is the default action).

Views
What is displayed by a form. One form may have different views – typical examples are detail and summary views or query and result views.

Primary data source
The data that the form is based on. That can be an XML file, database, or a Web service.

Secondary data source
A data provider used to populate controls such as list boxes, and to provide values otherwise used by the InfoPath form.

Actions
Predefined tasks that InfoPath associates with certain controls and menu items. For example, the Button control can have a Submit action that updates a database.

Rules

In SP1, rules provide a way to combine actions in a sequence or set conditions under which an action should occur. Rules and actions provide a way to accomplish tasks that would require programming instructions in most other form tools.

What about...

InfoPath uses the Task pane to display Help. This is sometimes slow and difficult to navigate, and is virtually useless for programming topics. You can get better Help from the following Help files installed with InfoPath.

To get Help on	Look here
Using InfoPath	*C:\Program Files\Microsoft Office\OFFICE11\1033\InfMain.chm*
Programming InfoPath and understanding form template components (.xsf, et al)	*C:\Program Files\Microsoft Office\OFFICE11\1033\InfRef.chm*

InfoPath and Excel

So what does InfoPath have to do with Excel? The two products aren't directly related, but they are both producers and consumers of XML data. You can gather XML data in InfoPath and then import that data into an Excel list for summary or analysis.

You can also start InfoPath from Excel. In that way, InfoPath forms can be the front-end for gathering XML data used by Excel. This chapter discusses those two approaches.

InfoPath collects data in XML format—a format shared by Excel lists. It's not too hard to use InfoPath to edit lists displayed in Excel.

Link Excel to InfoPath through lists

The Excel and InfoPath products interchange data through lists. Lists may be local XML files, XML files posted at a public location, or they may be shared through SharePoint.

The data collected by InfoPath is often a superset of the information you want to analyze in Excel. For example, you want to create an Excel report on the location and value of assets. If you collect that data using the Info-Path Asset Tracker form (described early in this chapter), you create a worksheet from the form's XML but only include a few of the form's nodes in the worksheet list.

The general steps in using an InfoPath form to collect data for display in Excel are:

1. Create the InfoPath form template.
2. Publish the template.
3. Have users fill out the forms.
4. Optionally, use InfoPath to merge the forms into a single XML file.
5. Open or Import the merged XML data into Excel, creating an XML map for the data.
6. Drag the significant nodes from the Excel XML Source task pane to the worksheet to create a list.
7. Update the list from its data source.

Opening an InfoPath-created XML file in Excel may lock the file and prevent others from editing form data. However, once the list is created you can close the workbook (unlocking the form) and then reopen the workbook to analyze the data. Refreshing the data in the Excel list does not lock the form file.

In this scenario, you usually can't edit form data in Excel and then pass it back to the InfoPath form. The schemas of InfoPath forms usually include lists of lists, which you can't export from Excel. It is possible to create forms that collect data that could be edited in Excel, but you are severely limited in how data items may be related and what data types you can collect. As a practical matter, you should consider getting form data into Excel a read-only operation.

Start InfoPath from Excel

You can display InfoPath forms from Excel using VBA code and the Info-Path ExternalApplication object. InfoPath limits what you can do from VBA for security reasons.

To open an existing form:

1. In Excel VBA, create a reference to the Microsoft Office InfoPath 1.0 type library.
2. Create a new InfoPath.ExternalApplication object variable.
3. Call the Open method on the form.

For example, the following code opens a form from within the workbook's folder:

```
pth = ThisWorkbook.Path
Dim ip As New InfoPath.ExternalApplication
ip.Open pth & "\Assets.xml"
```

To close the form, use the Close method:

```
ip.Close pth & "\Assets.xml"
```

To create a new form, use the NewFromSolution method with the form template:

```
ip.NewFromSolution pth & "\Assets.xsn"
```

To close InfoPath, use the Quit method:

```
ip.Quit True
```

Quit closes all instances of InfoPath, not just the current reference. The True argument tells InfoPath to prompt to save changes before closing—a good idea considering that first point.

In SP1, you can also use the Application object from VBA. The Application and ExternalApplication objects are similar, but Application doesn't provide an Open method. Instead, you can open forms through the Application objects XDocuments collection:

```
pth = ThisWorkbook.Path
Dim ip As New InfoPath.Application
ip.XDocuments.Open pth & "\Assets.xml"
```

The Application also provides access to the Windows collection and some InfoPath properties not available from ExternalApplication.

What about...

To learn about	Look here
Excel to InfoPath conversion tools	*http://directory.partners.extranet.microsoft.com/ advsearchresults.aspx?listid=23*

Share Data

Sharing a form template is easy—just publish the template to a public location and InfoPath users can create new XML data files using that form. Sharing data is harder: if you post the XML data file at a public location, multiple users may view the data through the form, but only one can have the file open for changes.

If you want multiple users to be able to edit XML data at the same time, there are a couple of solutions:

- Have each user create a separate, standalone XML data file and then merge those files
- Use InfoPath's Submit feature to manage changes

The simplest InfoPath forms create stand alone XML data files. In order for these files to be of use to others, they've got to be gathered together in some way.

How to merge multiple files

This is the simplest technique for gathering edits from multiple users and it's easy to illustrate using our old Asset tracker form shown earlier. Say, for instance, each department is doing their own asset inventory and each department manager assigns one worker to gather the data for his department. Each of those workers opens *Assets.xsn* to create a new XML data file for their department. When all the work is complete, a supervisor opens *Assets.xsn* to create a new XML data file and merges all of the department files.

In this situation, it is ideal if the form template was published to a Share-Point Site since SharePoint provides a handy interface for creating new XML data files based on an InfoPath form (Figure 7-12).

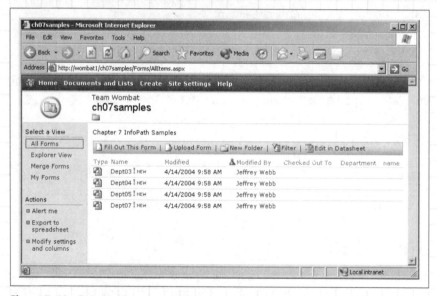

Figure 7-12. Entering department data

Department workers simply click Fill Out This Form to start entering their asset information. When all of the departments are complete, the supervisor clicks Fill Out This Form, then chooses File → Merge Forms to merge the department files (Figure 7-13). Finally, the supervisor saves the merged data file.

This approach works well where individuals are responsible for well-defined tasks. Asset tracking, sales reports, and expense reports all fall into this category. In other cases, live data must be shared in a more interactive fashion.

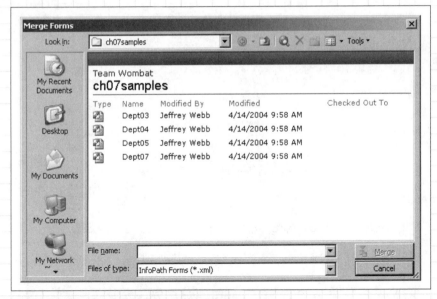

Figure 7-13. Merging data from departments

How to use Submit

Forms that are designed to work with databases or web services can submit their data to the data store rather than saving it as an XML file. In those cases, form data is transmitted to the data store where it is available to other users.

If a form allows Submit, then Submit appears on the File menu when the form is in user mode. Users can still save form data; however, they are prompted to see if they really want to Submit the form (Figure 7-14).

If an error occurs during submit, InfoPath reports it, as shown in Figure 7-15.

The InfoPath errors are not usually clear enough for users to interpret. For example, the error shown in Figure 7-15 occurred because an invalid Customer ID was entered. You should carefully validate data *before* submitting it to a data store.

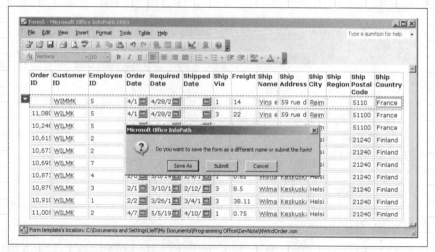

Figure 7-14. Forms that submit data can also save it, but users are prompted first

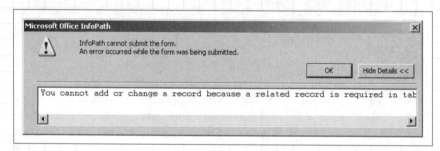

Figure 7-15. Errors are displayed if the data could not be updated

In SP1, you can also use email to submit a form. In that case, the Submit action automatically attaches the form data to a message addressed to a predefined recipient.

How to submit via email

InfoPath also lets you send form data as an attachment in mail. In order for this feature to work, you must have Outlook 2003 installed as the default mail client on your system.

To send form data as email:

- Choose File → Send to Mail Recipient. InfoPath starts Outlook 2003 and creates a new mail message with the form data attached.

When another InfoPath user receives form data via email, she can open, save, or merge that data provided she has access to the published form template.

What about...

To learn about	Look here
Creating a form based on a database table	"Link a Form to a Database"

Link a Form to a Database

InfoPath forms can submit data to Microsoft SQL or Microsoft Access databases. In fact, you can build forms directly from SQL and Access tables or queries. Working with existing data sources is where InfoPath forms really start to shine.

TIP

The following examples use the *NWind.mdb* Access database provided with the Office System 2003.

How to do it

The following procedure is for InfoPath SP1. The Version 1.0 release displays names in the task pane and produces a form containing separate query and data entry views. To build a form from a database table or query:

1. Select File → Design a Form. InfoPath displays the Design a Form task pane.
2. Select New Data Connection. InfoPath starts the Data Source Setup Wizard.
3. Select the Database option and click Next. The Wizard displays the next step.
4. Click Select Database. The Wizard displays a list of the Office Data Connection (ODC) files found in the My Data Sources folder (Figure 7-16).
5. Select a data connection or create a new ODC. The Wizard displays the tables and fields from the data connection (Figure 7-17).
6. Select the fields to include or modify the SQL used to retrieve the data; then click Next. The Wizard displays the final step (Figure 7-18).
7. Click Finish to generate the form template from the data connection (Figure 7-19).

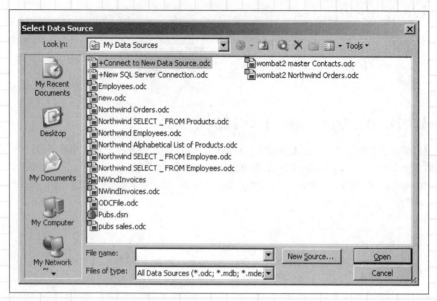

Figure 7-16. Choose a data source

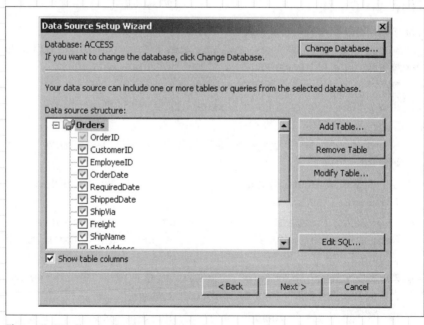

Figure 7-17. Change the query as needed

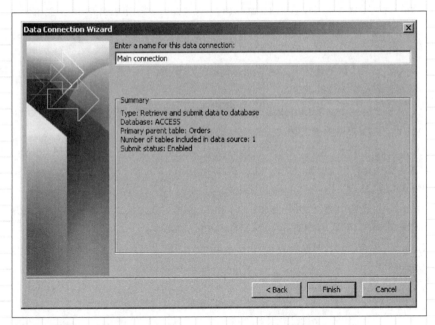

Figure 7-18. Click Finish to create a combined view (SP1)

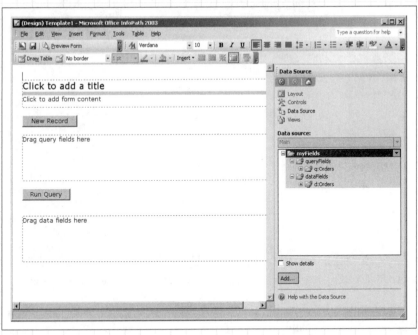

Figure 7-19. Voila! InfoPath SP1 creates a combined query/edit view

The template created by the SP1 release of the Data Connection Wizard is different from the template created by the Version 1.0 release. Version 1.0 created separate query and result views. SP1 combines those views.

The Data Connection Wizard creates two groups within the data source:

- queryFields contain the input parameters used to query the database.
- dataFields contain the results of the query and are also used when adding new records.

To make the form functional, you need to drag fields from the data source to the form. For example:

Drag the :CustomerID and :EmployeeID fields from the queryFields group onto the query fields area on the form. InfoPath creates text boxes and labels for those fields of the form.

Drag the d:Orders group from the dataFields group onto the data fields area of the form. InfoPath displays a pop-up menu.

Select Repeating Table. InfoPath creates a table to display query results (Figure 7-20).

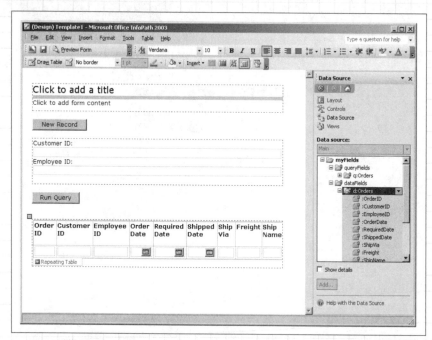

Figure 7-20. Drag queryFields and dataFields onto the form to create a query form

If you add a title, save the form, and then open the form in user mode, Infopath displays results (Figure 7-21).

As with other form templates, opening the template file (.xsn) starts a new, empty form. You may want to set up database forms with some ini-

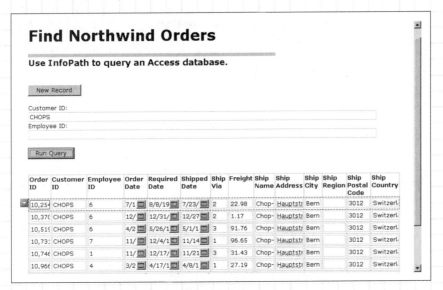

Figure 7-21. Query results for Northwind orders

tial data and save them in user mode as form files (.xml). Then the user can open that XML file to load the database template. This approach displays the name of the XML file (rather than Form1) in the InfoPath titlebar, plus makes it easier for the user to save the results of her query locally.

How it works

InfoPath generates schemas for the fields sent as a query and returned by the data connection. It uses those schemas to generate a tree view of the returned data (shown in the task pane of Figure 7-20).

If you are only trying to create a form to display query results, the process can pretty much end here. You can delete unneeded fields from the generated query form and adjust the column widths of the results table as needed using InfoPath's visual design features. Figure 7-22 shows a database query form modified to display results a little better.

These changes are cosmetic, relatively simple, and require *no code*, so I won't go into detail about how to make them. Messing around in Info-Path's Design mode is half the fun! The two changes that I will briefly mention are:

- I changed the property of the repeating table to prevent new rows because this table is for query results only.

If you click the arrow beside the first record in Figure 7-21, you can add order records to submit to the database. As noted earlier, however, entries aren't validated and may be rejected by the database causing an error. (There's a whole section on validating fields later in this chapter.)

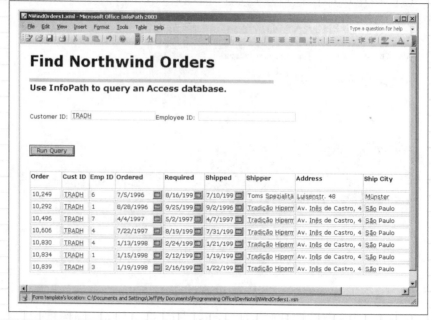

Figure 7-22. Streamlined query form

- I prevented users from submitting changes (choose Tools → Submitting Forms to set those options).

These changes save a world of trouble because any new rows or changes submitted to the database should be validated, and that requires more work. Updating a database is *always* harder than querying it.

What you can't submit

The biggest limitation working with databases is InfoPath's orientation to Microsoft products. InfoPath directly supports only Microsoft Access and Microsoft SQL databases. You can enable access to other types of databases by creating web service frontends to those data sources, generating XML from those data sources in some way, or using the ADO objects provided in the InfoPath object model.

The next biggest limitation is that you can't always submit form data to a database. In general, InfoPath can submit records that come from a single database table and where InfoPath has enough information to maintain the relationships and normal form within the database. In cases where InfoPath is unable to submit changes, the Submit Status field on the summary page of the Data Source Setup Wizard displays the reason for the limitation.

Finally, InfoPath's format for binary data, such as images, is based on XML and so uses base 64 encoding. Database formats for binary data items (BLOBs) is different, so you must convert between the two formats if you want to work with binary data in InfoPath forms. Submitting rich-text format (RTF) data also requires special handling.

What about...

To learn about	Look here
Filling in controls from a database	"Populate a Control from a Data Source"
Validating data items before submitting	See "Validate Data"
What InfoPath requires to enable Submit	*http://msdn.microsoft.com/library/en-us/ ipsdk/html/ipsdkIntegrateWithAccessDB.asp*
Creating and using ODC files	Search Excel Help for "ODC"

Populate a Control from a Data Source

The previous section shows you how to use a database as the primary data source for a form, but you had to know customer or employee codes for the query to work. It would be better if those codes were listed in drop-down list boxes so you could just choose the right criteria (Figure 7-23).

InfoPath's approach to adding items to a list control is very different from other form tools. Don't expect to do this (easily) from code!

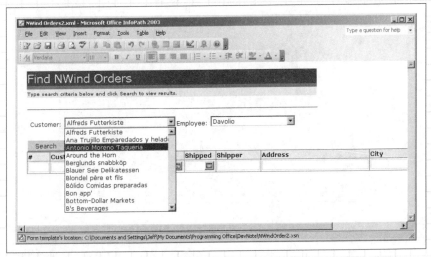

Figure 7-23. Modify the previous sample to populate listboxes from the database

How to do it

In order to populate a listbox from a database, you need to establish a secondary data source. To add a secondary data source to the sample form:

1. In Design mode, right-click the Customer ID text box and choose Change to → Drop-Down List Box from the pop-up menu. InfoPath converts the control to the new type.

2. Display the control's properties (Format → Properties or Alt+Enter) and select Look up in a data connection (Figure 7-24).

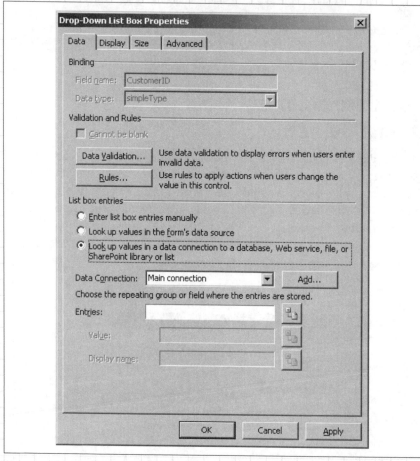

Figure 7-24. Select Look up in a data connection to populate a list from a secondary data source

3. Click Add to select a data source as described in the previous section. In this case, you want to retrieve the Customers table from the Northwind database, as shown in Figure 7-25.

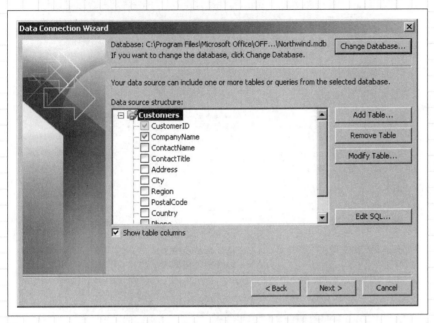

Figure 7-25. Select the fields to retrieve from the Customers table

4. Click the Select XPath button beside the Entries box in Figure 7-24 and select the d:Customers node. Select :CustomerID for Value and :CompanyName for Display name, as shown in Figure 7-26.

5. Click OK and resize the control as needed. When you preview the form, Customer names are displayed in the control (Figure 7-27).

6. Repeat these steps for the Employee ID control using the Employees table from the database and the d:Employees, :EmployeeID, and :LastName XPath settings as shown in Figure 7-28.

How it works

You can have multiple secondary data sources for a form. Each data source may be queried when the form loads depending on the setting in the last step of the Data Connection Wizard (Figure 7-29).

If the data source is not queried at form load, or if it needs to be updated, you can refresh the secondary data source by adding a Button control to the form and selecting the Refresh action as shown in Figure 7-30.

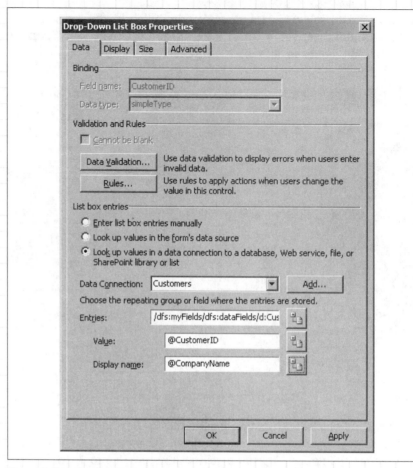

Figure 7-26. Set the XPath for Entries, Value, and Display name fields

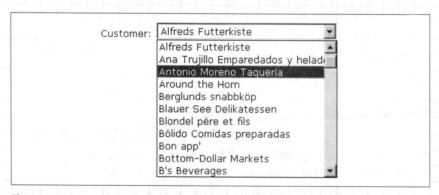

Figure 7-27. List control populated with customers

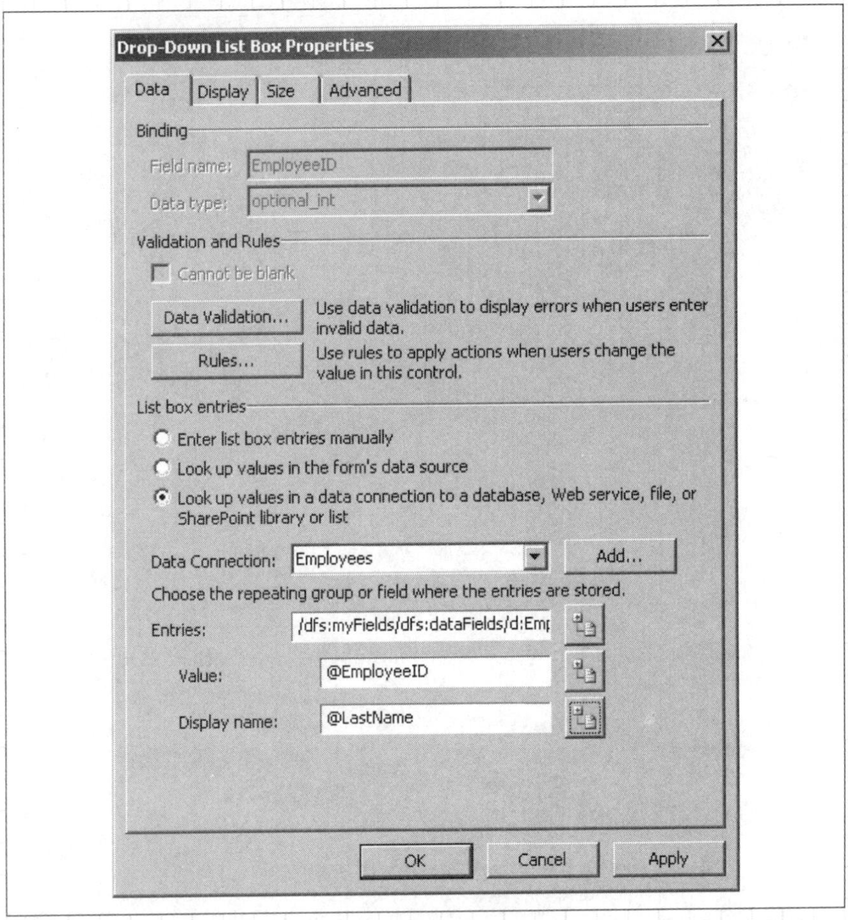

Figure 7-28. Settings to populate the Employee list

InfoPath creates a schema component file in the form template for each secondary data source you use. You can examine those schemas if you extract the form files from the template.

Validate Data

Forms that use a database or web service as their primary data source can send data back to that source through the Submit action. You can call the Submit action by choosing File → Submit or by clicking a button on the form assigned to Submit.

Before submitting, however, you should validate the data to make sure the entries are valid for constraints in the database (or web service).

Validation prevents errors from occurring when data is submitted to a database or web service, and it can prevent invalid entries from being passed on when submitting via email.

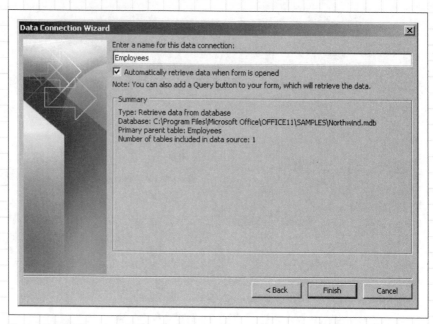

Figure 7-29. Checkbox in this dialog determines whether the database is queried at form load

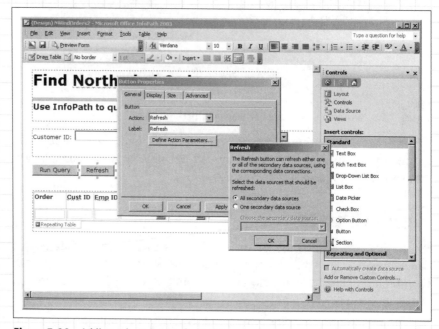

Figure 7-30. Adding a button to refresh lists

InfoPath can validate fields using a variety of criteria. Problems are flagged and must be fixed before continuing, as shown in Figure 7-31.

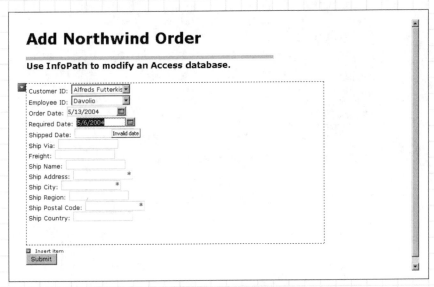

Figure 7-31. InfoPath flags validation errors and highlights required fields

How to do it

To add validation criteria to a control:

1. Display the control's properties and click Data Validation. InfoPath displays the Data Validation dialog, as shown in Figure 7-32.

2. Click Add. InfoPath displays the dialog box for validation criteria. Enter a condition that results in a validation error. For example, the settings in Figure 7-33 make CustomerID a required field.

3. Click OK, then preview the form and test the validation.

You can combine multiple criteria by clicking And > in Figure 7-33; however, you can only have one ScreenTip and Message per control.

How it works

InfoPath stores simple validation rules (required fields and range-checking) in the schema component file of the form template. If you create a simple form with a single required text control, then extract the form files, the schema for the required control looks like the following code:

Any field can have validation criteria—it doesn't have to be linked to a database or web service. Those are just common situations where validation is important.

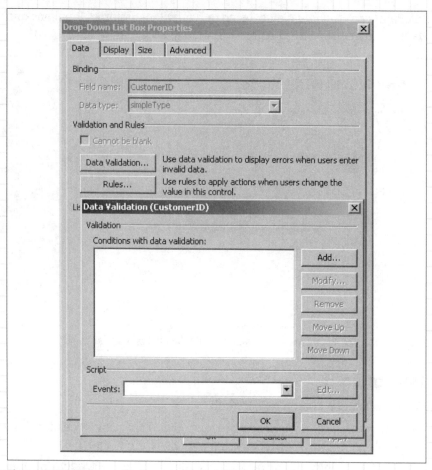

Figure 7-32. Adding validation to a control (SP1)

Figure 7-33. Setting the validation criteria (SP1)

```
<xsd:element name="field1" type="my:requiredString"/>
<xsd:simpleType name="requiredString">
    <xsd:restriction base="xsd:string">
        <xsd:minLength value="1"/>
    </xsd:restriction>
</xsd:simpleType>
```

More complex validation rules, such as pattern matching, are stored in the manifest file (.xsf). For example, the following XML fragment demonstrates a text control that requires a number in social security format:

Pattern-matching validation rules are an SPI feature.

```
<xsf:customValidation>
<xsf:errorCondition match="/my:myFields/my:field1" expressionContext="."
  expression="xdUtil:Match(string(.), &quot;\d\d\d\-\d\d\-\d\d\d&quot;)">
    <xsf:errorMessage type="modeless" shortMessage="Enter SS#.">Not a valid
social security number.</xsf:errorMessage>
    </xsf:errorCondition>
</xsf:customValidation>
```

Validation rules are checked as the user enters data on the form. If an invalid entry is made in a control, that entry is flagged as soon as the focus moves to another control. There is no built-in way to delay validation until the user submits the data.

Forms containing validation errors can't be submitted. Users receive a warning if they save or email a form containing validation errors. There is also no built-in way to prevent the user from saving, emailing without Submit, or printing a form containing validation errors. But you can disable those menu options by choosing Tools → Form Options and changing settings on the Open and Save page of the Form Options dialog.

InfoPath creates an Error object for each validation error on a form. Within script, you can use the XDocument object's Errors collection to check whether or not a form is valid. For example, the following script checks if the form is valid each time the focus changes from one control to another:

```
' Do validation checking.
Sub XDocument_OnContextChange(eventObj)
    If eventObj.Type = "ContextNode" Then
    ' Get check box control
    Set x = XDocument.DOM.DocumentElement.SelectSingleNode("my:chkValid")
        If xdocument.errors.count = 0 Then
            ' Set value to True (valid).
            ' This enables Submit button through
            ' conditional formatting.
            x.text = "true"
        Else
            ' Not valid, set to False (disables Submit).
            x.text = "false"
        End If
```

```
        Exit Sub
    End If
End Sub
```

The preceding code sets a checkbox value on a form to True if the form contains no validation errors. The value from that check box can then be used with conditional format settings to enable other controls that Submit, save, or print the form.

The OnContext Changed event is available in SP1. For Version 1.0, use the OnAfter-Change event instead.

Link a Form to a Web Service

Another way to use a shared data source with InfoPath is to link the form to a web service. You can't just use any web service with InfoPath. If you try to use the Amazon or Google web services, for example, you'll get the error shown in Figure 7-34.

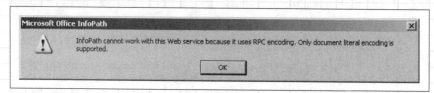

Figure 7-34. InfoPath rejecting an RPC-encoded web service

The InfoPath SDK installs these examples that demonstrate how to write a web service that can be used by InfoPath forms:

- *http://localhost/infopathsdk/infopathwebservicesample/ infopathwebservicesample.asmx*

- *http://localhost/infopathsdk/DataSubmit/SubmitService.asmx*

Web services provide a way to link InfoPath forms to non-Microsoft databases.

TIP

To install the InfoPath SDK web service examples locally, you must be running Windows XP Pro with IIS installed.

How to do it

The SDK has pretty good instructions on how the sample web services work and how to use them from InfoPath. I won't repeat those here, but to make your life a little easier, I've installed those services at *http:// www.mstrainingkits.com/Excel* and modified the sample forms to work with that location. This means that you can run the samples without installing the SDK (Figure 7-35).

Chapter 7: Build InfoPath Forms

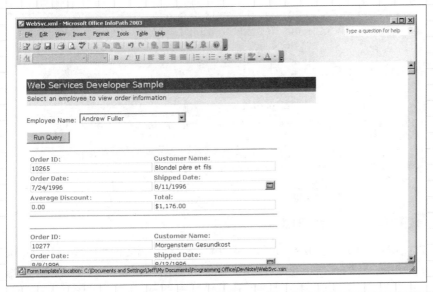

Figure 7-35. SDK web service sample (modified)

In addition to changing the data source for the web service sample, I also:

- Changed the query view to be the default view displayed when the form is loaded.

- Combined the query and data views to simplify the interface; in some cases, performing a query didn't automatically display the data view in the SDK sample.

- Removed the Submit item from the File menu, because the sample didn't actually submit changes to orders, and leaving the Submit item there seemed misleading.

How it works

The SDK sample uses the *InfoPathWebServiceSample.asmx* web service as both a primary data source (to get the Order records) and as a secondary data source (to populate the Employee Name drop-down list).

In this sample, the web service functions as an interface to the Northwind database (renamed *infnwind.mdb*, in this case). This approach allows developers to link forms to any type of data store, including Oracle or MySQL databases—which aren't directly supported by InfoPath—and to access those data stores remotely over the Internet.

It requires a fair amount of knowledge to create a web service, and there are some excellent books devoted to the subject.

What about...

To	Look here
Download the InfoPath SDK	Search *http://www.microsoft.com/downloads* for "Info-Path SDK"
Learn more about creating and using web services with InfoPath	*http://msdn.microsoft.com/office/understanding/ infopath/devdocs/default.aspx*

Script InfoPath

Although InfoPath uses rules and actions for many tasks, there are still a lot of things you have to do with code.

You can write scripts to run within InfoPath forms using JScript or VBScript. These scripts can perform custom actions, such as displaying other forms, send email, or do custom validation.

WARNING

The default language is JScript, so if you'd rather use VBScript (as I would), change the default setting as soon as you create a new form. Once you've opened the code editor, you're stuck with the form setting.

How to do it

To set the default script language in InfoPath:

1. In Design mode, choose Tools → Options. InfoPath displays the Options dialog box.

2. Click the Advanced tab of the Options dialog box and select the default programming language setting. Click OK to close the dialog.

InfoPath, Version 1.0 has slightly different dialog boxes than those shown for the SP1 release in Figure 7-36 and Figure 7-37.

Different types of controls can have code set in different places within InfoPath. Controls that perform actions, such as Button controls, add code through the control properties dialog (Figure 7-36).

Controls that perform validation can add code through data validation events (Figure 7-37).

Once you click Edit, InfoPath displays the Microsoft Script Editor (MSE) (Figure 7-38).

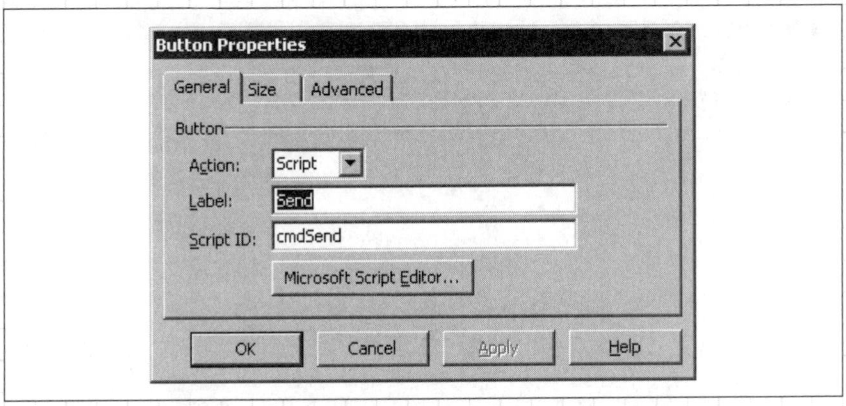

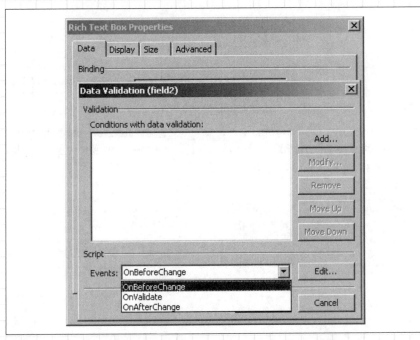

Figure 7-36. For Button controls, use control properties to add scripts (SP1)

Figure 7-37. For other controls, select a validation event and click Edit to add scripts (SP1)

The MSE's debugging tools don't work as you might expect with Info-Path. If you run the script, MSE displays the code in a browser window. To run the code, you must preview the form in InfoPath and then trigger the event. You don't have to exit MSE—you can just switch between it and InfoPath.

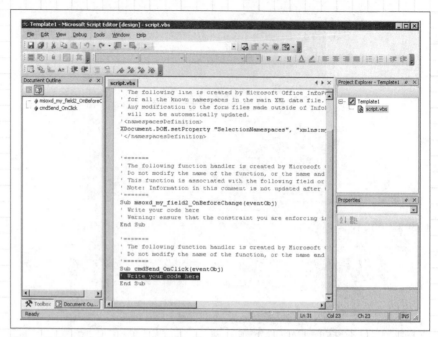

Figure 7-38. InfoPath edits code in the Microsoft Script Editor (MSE)

Even in preview mode, your debugging tools are limited. If your script contains syntax errors, InfoPath won't preview the form and instead displays the error shown in Figure 7-39.

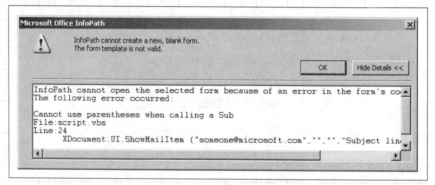

Figure 7-39. Script syntax errors prevent form preview and display this message

If your script contains runtime errors, InfoPath simply stops on the offending line and displays a generic message (Figure 7-40).

Debugging in MSE often means adding message boxes to locate errors and view variables before errors occur.

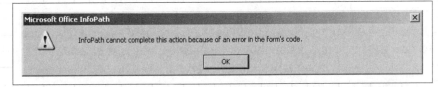

Figure 7-40. Runtime script errors are general and often don't provide line numbers

Why use script?

InfoPath uses VBScript/JScript rather than VBA because of security requirements. VBA code must be fully trusted because it has access to resources on the user's system and can (potentially) do damage. VBScript/JScript can run with limited privileges that prohibit any destructive actions.

Since InfoPath forms may be loaded over the Internet, Microsoft needed to use a language that could run in a restricted mode. The .NET languages (Visual Basic .NET and C# .NET) can also run in this mode, so the SP1 release added the ability to use those vastly superior languages as well.

As a programmer, I find the MSE extremely limiting. It doesn't provide the debugging tools and autocomplete features available from Visual Studio .NET. Still, it does allow you to program InfoPath forms without requiring the .NET Framework to be installed on client machines.

Common script tasks

The following short samples demonstrate some of the common programming tasks in VBScript. Most of the code samples in the InfoPath Help are written in JScript, which isn't much help to VBA programmers.

Display a simple message box

The easiest way to display a dialog box is to create a button control and associate it with the Dialog action (SP1). To display a simple dialog box from a script, use the UI object's Alert method. This script displays a simple message box:

```
XDocument.UI.Alert "This is a message to display."
```

Serious InfoPath applications with more than a few lines of code should use Visual Studio .NET.

Save form data

Users can save forms by choosing File → Save in InfoPath, but if you want to save a form from a script, that script must be fully trusted on the user's machine. The following script saves the form if the data has changed:

```
If XDocument.IsDirty Then XDocument.Save
```

This script saves the form as a specific filename:

```
XDocument.SaveAs "NewForrm.xml"
```

Send form data as an email attachment

You can send a form as an email attachment from a script only if Outlook 2003 is the default mail client on the user machine. The following script creates an email message with the current form as an attachment:

```
XDocument.UI.ShowMailItem "some@example.com", "","","Subject", "Message."
```

Get a value from a control

Use the DOM property to get at items in the form's XML data. The DOM property returns a DOMDocument object, so you need to understand that object's members in order to get the value from any of the form controls. For example, the following script gets the value entered in a text box named "field1" on the form:

```
var1 = XDocument.DOM.getElementsByTagName("my:field1").Item(0).text
XDocument.UI.Alert var1
```

ActiveX controls are a special case in InfoPath. Controls that are specifically written to work with InfoPath return values as shown previously for a text box. Other controls, such as the Slider control, may require you to call the View object's ForceUpdate method before their value is available. For example, the following code retrieves a value from a Slider control on an InfoPath form:

```
XDocument.View.ForceUpdate( )
Set x = XDocument.DOM.DocumentElement.SelectSingleNode("my:field10")
XDocument.UI.Alert x.Text
```

Set a value of a control

You can also use the DocumentElement's SelectSingleNode to locate a control within the form's XML. For example, the following code gets a reference to the node for the chkValid control and sets the control to False (unchecked):

```
Set x = XDocument.DOM.DocumentElement.SelectSingleNode("my:chkValid")
x.text = "false"
```

Get a form's XML data

To get all of the XML data from a form, use the DOMDocument's XML property. When debugging, it is sometimes useful to display the form's XML in order to see the XML node name (XPath) of a control from which you want get or set a value:

```
XDocument.UI.Alert XDocument.DOM.XML
```

Submit data

The easiest way to submit data is to create a button control and associate it with the Submit action (SP1). If the form can submit data, the following script can be used to perform the Submit action:

```
XDocument.Submit
```

Refresh secondary data sources

The easiest way to refresh data is to create a button control and associate it with the Refresh action (SP1). To refresh data from a script, use the DataObject's Query method. InfoPath provides a DataObjects collection containing each of the secondary data sources on a form. You can get a specific DataObject by name or iterate through all DataObjects, as shown here:

```
For i = 0 to XDocument.DataObjects.Count
    XDocument.DataObjects(i).Query
Next
```

Switch form views

The easiest way to switch views is to create a button control and associate it with the Switch views action (SP1). To switch views from a script, use the View object's SwitchView method:

```
XDocument.View.SwitchView "View 2"
```

Display an HTML page

There's no provision in the InfoPath object model for displaying an HTML page in a new browser window. If your form is fully trusted, you can use the Internet Explorer object model to display a new browser window:

```
Set IE = CreateObject("InternetExplorer.Application")
IE.Visible = True
IE.Navigate "http://www.mstrainingkits.com"
```

If the form is not fully trusted, users will see a warning that an ActiveX object on the form may be unsafe to run before the preceding code is run.

Create a new form based on current template

Use the XDocuments collection's New method to create a new form based on the current template:

```
Application.XDocuments.New XDocument.URI
```

The preceding script only works if the form was opened from a form file (.xml). If the form is in preview mode or is a new file created from the template (.xsn), an error occurs. In those cases, you must specify an absolute path in place of the XDocument.URI property.

Create a new form based on a new template

Use the XDocuments collection's NewFromSolution method to create a new form based on a specified template:

```
Application.XDocuments.NewFromSolution XDocument.Solution.URI
```

The preceding script creates a new blank form based on the current form's template.

Open an existing form

Use the XDocuments collection's Open method to open an existing form data file:

```
Application.XDocuments.Open "C:\DevNote\Assets.xml"
```

You must provide the absolute address of the form to open.

Quit InfoPath

Use the Application object's Quit method to close InfoPath (requires full trust):

```
Application.Quit True
```

The preceding script prompts to save changes before closing InfoPath. Calling with False discards any unsaved changes. The Quit method closes all instances of InfoPath that are currently running. Use the XDocuments collection's Close method to close a single form:

```
Application.XDocuments.Close(XDocument)
```

The preceding script closes the current form.

Debug and deploy

Templates that contain scripts may require additional security privileges in order to run on client machines. In SP1, there are two ways to provide additional privileges to a template:

- Sign the template with a digital signature from a trusted publisher
- Install the template on the client's machine

If you are using InfoPath methods that require full trust, you can't easily debug those scripts. Signed templates preview in domain-level security, not full trust. Installed templates preview in full trust, but installing a template that is under development can be cumbersome.

To debug scripts that require full trust:

1. In Design mode, choose Tools → Form Options and select the Security page (Figure 7-41).

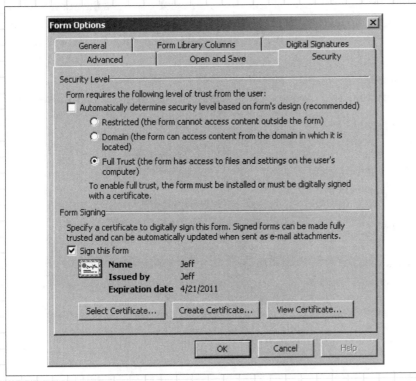

Figure 7-41. Signing a template for full trust (SP1)

2. Deselect Automatically determine security and choose Full Trust, then select Sign this form and select a certificate.

3. If you don't have a certificate, you can create one for self-signing by clicking Create Certificate. Click OK when done.

4. Close InfoPath and open the template in user mode.

5. Save the form to create a dummy form file for debugging purposes.

6. Reopen the template in Design mode.

You can now make changes to scripts in the template, save the template, and then test the code by opening the dummy form. The dummy form will receive full trust, because the template is signed and not running in Preview mode.

When you are finished debugging and testing a template, you can deploy it either as a signed template or as an application installed on the user's machine. Signed templates prompt the user to verify that the signature is from a trusted publisher in the same way as signed VBA code.

To install a template, you must first create a setup program. The InfoPath SDK provides a RegForm tool (*regform.exe*) to help create setup programs for templates. RegForm is a command-line tool that generates a JScript installation script or a Windows Installer package (.msi), depending on the options chosen. For example, the following command line creates a Windows Installer package for a template:

```
regform /u urn:Assets:WombatTech /T Yes /MSI Assets.xsn
```

The resulting Windows Installer package is named *Assets.msi*. Users can install that template by running the package, or that package can be combined with others using Visual Studio .NET.

If you omit the /MSI option, RegForm generates a JScript installation script instead, named *Assets.js*. Users can run that script to install the template on their system.

What about...

To learn about	Look here
Programming InfoPath	*C:\Program Files\Microsoft Office\OFFICE11\1033\InfRef.chm*
Advanced programming techniques	*http://blogs.msdn.com/infopath*
Support from the InfoPath programming community	Visit the newsgroup microsoft.public.infopath
InfoPath SDK	*http://msdn.microsoft.com/library/en-us/ipsdk/html/ipsdkwelcometotheipsdk.asp*
Installing templates using RegForm	*http://msdn.microsoft.com/library/en-us/ipsdk/html/ipsdkUsingTheFormRegistrationTool.asp*
Fully trusted templates	*http://msdn.microsoft.com/library/en-us/ipsdk/html/ipsdkUnderstandingFullyTrustedForms.asp*

Program InfoPath in .NET

With the SP1 preview, Microsoft also released the InfoPath 2003 Toolkit for Visual Studio .NET. This toolkit is similar to the Visual Studio Tools for Office (VSTO) product covered in Chapter 6, but unlike VSTO, it's available as a free download for Visual Studio .NET users.

If you are creating templates that require more than a little script, you should plan to program InfoPath in .NET. Visual Studio .NET is a professional programming tool that gives you far more assistance than MSE. Although the Visual Studio .NET environment is complicated, the command completion, syntax checking, and debugging tools make it a great deal easier to program with InfoPath.

Get the InfoPath .NET Toolkit

You must have the .NET Framework installed before installing InfoPath SPI in order to get the .NET Programmability features. If .NET is not already installed, the InfoPath setup will not be able to install the required components.

To get	Look here
.NET Framework 1.1	*http://msdn.microsoft.com/netframework/ technologyinfo/howtoget/default.aspx*
Visual Studio .NET 2003	*http://msdn.microsoft.com/vstudio/howtobuy/ default.aspx*
InfoPath SP1 preview	Search *http://www.microsoft.com/downloads* for "InfoPath SP1"
InfoPath 2003 Toolkit for Visual Studio .NET	Search *http://www.microsoft.com/downloads* for "InfoPath .NET"

How to do it

To create an InfoPath project with Visual Studio .NET:

1. Choose File → New Project and select InfoPath Form Template from the Microsoft Office InfoPath Projects group (Figure 7-42).

2. Visual Studio .NET starts the Project Wizard (Figure 7-43). Select whether to create a new template or use an existing one, and click Finish.

3. Visual Studio starts InfoPath and creates a new project template in Visual Studio .NET as shown in Figure 7-44.

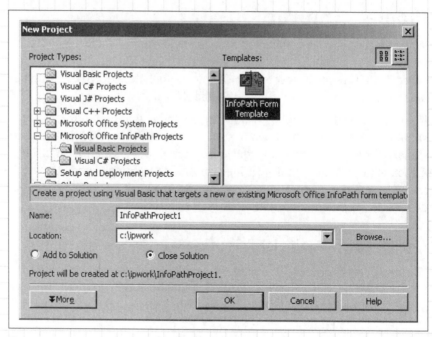

Figure 7-42. Creating a new InfoPath project

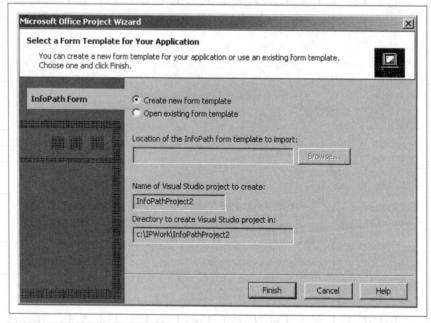

Figure 7-43. Specify a new template or use an existing one

Chapter 7: Build InfoPath Forms

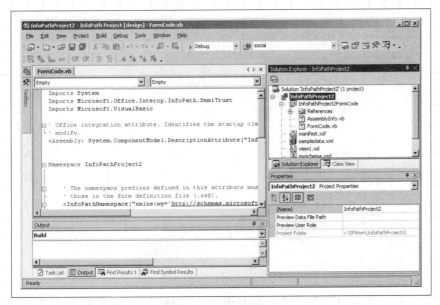

Figure 7-44. The resulting Visual Studio .NET project

InfoPath and Visual Studio .NET are loosely coupled. You edit the template by switching to InfoPath. There, you can design the template's appearance. To write code, click Edit Form Code from control properties (Figure 7-45).

It's a good idea to create a new template in InfoPath first, then specify that template in Step 2. Creating the new template in InfoPath lets you use the Data Connection Wizard or base a new template on an existing one—features which aren't available from Visual Studio .NET.

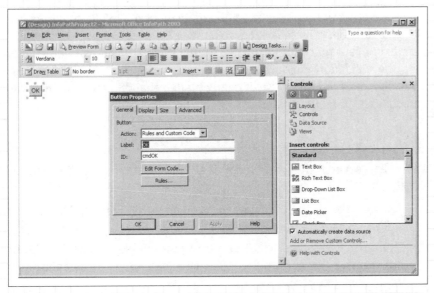

Figure 7-45. Click Edit Form Code to add an event procedure in Visual Studio .NET

Visual Studio .NET creates code templates for any event you create in InfoPath, as shown here (**bold** code is mine):

```
<InfoPathEventHandler(MatchPath:="cmdOK", EventType:=InfoPathEventType.
OnClick)> _
Public Sub cmdOK_OnClick(ByVal e As DocActionEvent)
    ' Write your code here.
    thisXDocument.UI.Alert("This template is " & _
        thisXDocument.Solution.URI)
End Sub
```

To run this code, switch back to InfoPath and click Preview. Visual Studio .NET builds the underlying assembly automatically and then previews the form (Figure 7-46).

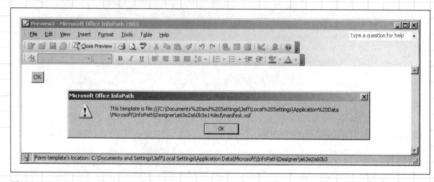

Figure 7-46. Use Preview (not F5) to run the InfoPath project

There are other entry points for creating events from InfoPath. For example, you can select Tools → Programming → On Load Event... to create a form load event procedure in Visual Studio .NET. Or, you can add events from the validation dialog box by selecting an event and clicking Edit. Basically, all of the tasks that formerly started the MSE generate equivalent code in Visual Studio .NET.

How it works

There are several things to note that are illustrated by this simple project:

- You can use InfoPath Preview, as well as Visual Studio .NET's Debug → Start (F5) to run the project.
- The project is copied to a temporary location (see Figure 7-46), not run from the project folder. This can lead to some complications while debugging.
- The InfoPath template is stored as component files, not as a compiled template (.xsn). Those component files are listed in the Solu-

tion Explorer shown in Figure 7-44. If you close InfoPath, you can directly edit those files as XML within Visual Studio .NET.

- If you place a breakpoint within cmdOK_OnClick, you can step through the code using the Visual Studio .NET debugging commands (unlike MSE).

- Visual Studio creates two objects variables: thisApplication and this-XDocument, which you can use in place of the intrinsic Application and XDocument objects used in scripts.

It is fairly simple to convert InfoPath scripts written in VBScript to Visual Basic .NET. Mainly, you need to remember to add "this" before references to the XDocument and Application objects, and remove Set from object assignments (.NET doesn't use Set). For example, the following changes convert some InfoPath VBScript to Visual Basic .NET:

```
Dim x As DOMNode
Set x = thisXDocument.DOM.DocumentElement.SelectSingleNode("my:field1")
x.text = "New value"
```

In the preceding code, **bold** indicates additions and ~~strikethrough~~ indicates deletions.

Debug and deploy

The .NET code running in an InfoPath project inherits its security settings from the InfoPath template. To get some insight into this situation, try to run this code in your new InfoPath project:

```
thisXDocument.Save()
```

InfoPath displays a security exception when you try to execute Save in preview mode. Save requires full trust, and preview runs in domain-level trust by default. Methods that require full trust are flagged in the Info-Path object model reference help as *level 3*. If you use any level 3 methods, you need to sign or install the form template to ensure it runs in full trust.

You face two problems trying to assign full trust to InfoPath templates run from within Visual Studio .NET:

- You can't sign the template since Visual Studio .NET stores the template as component files and InfoPath can only sign compiled templates (.xsn).

- You can't install the template because you are still creating it, and you would need to repeatedly uninstall/reinstall the template every time you made a change.

If you don't use level 3 methods or NET methods that access the local resources, you don't need to worry about ensuring that your code runs in full trust. Domain-level trust is fine. In practice, however, that is pretty limiting.

To solve this problem, follow these steps:

1. Close InfoPath and edit the template's manifest file (*manifest.xsf*) to remove the `publishURL` and `trustSetting` attributes and require full trust:

```
<xsf:xDocumentClass
    solutionVersion="1.0.0.5"
    solutionFormatVersion="1.100.0.0"
    publishUrl="C:\IPWork\FTNet\ manifest.xsf"
    name="urn:schemas-microsoft-com:office:infopath:FTNet2:-myXSD-2004-04-
23T16-52-59"
    productVersion="11.0.6250"
    trustSetting="automatic"
    requireFullTrust="yes"
```

2. Build the InfoPath project in Visual Studio .NET.

3. Run the following script from within the project folder to register the template's manifest file:

```
set ip = CreateObject("InfoPath.ExternalApplication")
Set fso = CreateObject("Scripting.FileSystemObject")
pth = fso.GetFolder(".").path
ip.registersolution pth & "\manifest.xsf"
set ip = nothing
set fso = nothing
```

Now, if you run the InfoPath project, the form previews running in full trust and the Save method (along with any other level 3 methods) will work. This procedure is for debugging only. Once you are ready to deploy the InfoPath project, follow these steps:

1. Run the following script from within the project folder to unregister the template on your development machine:

```
set ip = CreateObject("InfoPath.ExternalApplication")
Set fso = CreateObject("Scripting.FileSystemObject")
pth = fso.GetFolder(".").path
ip.unregistersolution pth & "\manifest.xsf"
set ip = nothing
set fso = nothing
```

The code to register and unregister the form is included with the sample project as the files Register.vbs and Unregister.vbs.

2. From within Visual Studio .NET, choose Project → Publish Form. Visual Studio .NET compiles the component files into a template (.xsn) and builds the assembly (.dll) for the project and starts the InfoPath Publishing Wizard.

3. Both the template and assembly are placed in the destination folder you specified in the Publishing Wizard. You can then open that template (.xsn) in InfoPath to sign it or use *RegForm.exe* to create an installer.

4. Run the signed template or install the unsigned template to test that the form runs in full trust.

What about...

Generate HTML Output

If a user does not have InfoPath and he opens a form data file, that file appears as XML in his browser. The InfoPath SDK provides a down-level tool (XDown) to convert a form file's XML to read-only HTML so others can view InfoPath output.

How to do it

To use XDown:

1. Download and install the InfoPath SDK. By default, the SDK installs XDown in the folder *C:\Program Files\Microsoft Office 2003 Developer Resources\Microsoft Office InfoPath 2003 SDK\Tools\XDown*.

2. Copy the files in the XDown folder to the project folder where you are working, or make them otherwise available for use from the command line.

3. Create a subfolder within the project folder to receive the output of XDown.

4. Run XDown from the command line on your InfoPath template (.xsn). XDown decompiles the template and converts the views from the template into XSL files that can be used to view form files in HTML.

5. Add processing instructions to form files that you want non-InfoPath users to be able to view.

For example, the following command line converts the views from *Assets. xsn* into XSL that can be used to display asset form data; output files are written to the Down subfolder:

```
XDown /d assets.xsn Down
```

You can then use the XSL files written to the Down folder to transform asset form data files into HTML that can be viewed from a browser. The easiest way to do that is to add a processing instruction to the form data file, as shown in the following XML fragment:

InfoPath forms can only be viewed by users who have InfoPath installed, unless you are using the XDown tool to create an HTML view of the form.

```
<?xml version="1.0" encoding="UTF-8"?>
<?xml-stylesheet type="text/xsl" href="view_1.xsl"?>
<?mso-infoPathSolution solutionVersion="1.0.0.4" productVersion="11.0.5531"
PIVersion="1.0.0.0" href="http://wombat1/assets.xsn" ?>
<?mso-application progid="InfoPath.Document"?>
```

If you make the preceding addition to a form, users who don't have InfoPath can view the form in Internet Explorer, but users who do have InfoPath (such as yourself) will still see it in InfoPath. To make sure your transformation worked, remove the mso-application instruction:

```
<?xml version="1.0" encoding="UTF-8"?>
<?xml-stylesheet type="text/xsl" href="view_1.xsl"?>
<?mso-infoPathSolution solutionVersion="1.0.0.4" productVersion="11.0.5531"
PIVersion="1.0.0.0" href="http://wombat1/assets.xsn" ?>
<?mso-application progid="InfoPath.Document"?>
```

Now the file will open in the browser, rather than InfoPath.

How it works

XDown generates an XSL file for each of the views in a template. You can use any of those XSL files to display the form data, but if you want to be able to switch between views you will have to write some code to use the different XSL files. See Chapter 3 for more information on how to perform transformations.

Forms displayed using the XDown-generated XSL files omit buttons and other user-interactive controls. They convert other controls, such as text boxes, into read-only HTML.

What about...

To learn about	Look here
XDown	*http://msdn.microsoft.com/library/en-us/ipsdk/html/ ipsdkUsingTheDownLevelTool.asp*
The InfoPath SDK	Search *http://www.microsoft.com/downloads* for "Info-Path SDK"
Perform XSL transformations	Chapter 3, "Work With XML"

Prevent Design Changes

As mentioned previously, InfoPath both designs and displays forms. In most cases, you won't want your users opening forms in Design mode and tinkering with them. There are two approaches to this problem:

- Enable form protection. This approach discourages users from changing form templates, but does not prevent them from doing so.
- Disable Design mode on your users' systems. This approach keeps users from changing existing form templates and prevents them from creating new ones.

Most developers don't want to expose the inner workings of their applications to the world. InfoPath provides a limited ability to restrict that type of access to form templates.

How to enable protection

To protect a template from changes:

1. Open the template in Design mode.
2. Choose Tools → Form Options, select Enable protection on the General page, then click OK.

Protected templates display the warning shown in Figure 7-47 if the user opens them in Design mode.

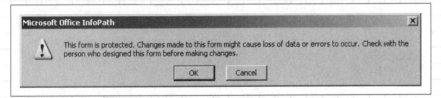

Figure 7-47. Protecting forms discourages users from changing them

That's weak protection at best, but if you sign the protected template with a digital signature, you can both discourage changes and detect changes if they are made (changes overwrite the digital signature, so the template will no longer be trusted).

How to disable design mode

A stronger solution prevents users from designing *any* templates. You can use the Custom Installation Wizard (CIW) to create a customized setup program for Office that omits the design features from InfoPath. In order to do that:

1. Run the CIW, as described in Chapter 6.

2. Open the InfoPath Windows Installer file (*INF11.msi* for SP1) with CIW.

3. Configure Disable InfoPath Designer mode in Step 10 of the Wizard (Figure 7-48).

4. Finish creating the custom installation and then use the generated Windows Installer to install InfoPath on your client machines.

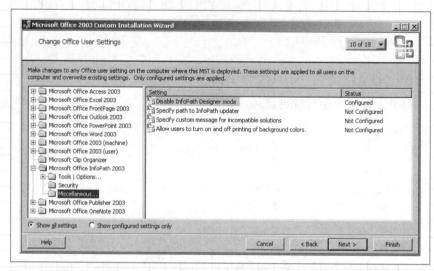

Figure 7-48. Use CIW to create a custom InfoPath installation program that disables design mode

Alternatively, you can disable Design mode by changing the following system registry setting:

```
HKEY_CURRENT_USER\Software\Microsoft\Office\11.0\InfoPath\Designer\
DisableDesigner=0x00000001
```

Editing the system registry requires special knowledge. This is an advanced technique. Disabling Design mode removes InfoPath's Design this Form button, Design a Form task pane, and the File → Design a Form menu option.

Index

We'd like to hear your suggestions for improving our indexes. Send email to *index@oreilly.com*.

elements
    abstract, 99
    calculated, 89
    child, 99
    denormalized, 95
    FieldRef, 64
    index, 179
    repeating, 99
email
    attachments and, 260
    data submission via, 237
    scripts and, 256
    sending workbook via, 176
    validation errors and, 253
Enabled property (Permission), 205,
        207
encryption, 134, 181, 186–190
Encryption Type dialog box, 186
error handling
    Access Denied error, 183
    asynchronous web queries
        and, 117
    COM and, 154
    data submission and, 237
    data validation and, 249, 253
    deleting SharePoint lists, 59
    error code 1004, 155
    namespace prefixes, 75
    runtime errors/exceptions, 170,
        258
    shared data sources, 254
    VB .NET and, 141–144, 154–157
    (see also debugging)
Error object (InfoPath), 253
ErrorCode property, 154, 155
Errors collection (XDocument), 253
events
    debugging and, 256
    handling asynchronous, 117, 118
    responding to XML, 103–104
    VB .NET and, 141–144, 153–154,
        166–168
Excel 11.0 Object Library, 22, 149
Excel 2003, 2, 3
Excel Object Library, 222
exceptions
    defined, 142
    errors as, 154
    handling, 169
    throwing, 142
Exclude property, 159

exclusive access, 38
execute access, 183
expiration dates, 201, 206
Expiration property, 206
Export method (XmlMap), 106
exporting
    denormalized data and, 91, 93
    events and, 103
    lists, 18, 66
    node considerations, 98
    XML maps, 92–99, 104, 105
ExportXml method (XmlMap), 106
Extensible Hypertext Markup Language
        (XHTML), 69
Extensible Markup Language (see XML)
ExternalApplication object, 234, 235

F

F5 shortcut, 268
FieldRef elements, 64
fields, validation criteria for, 251
File › Add Project › New Project, 22,
        144, 147
File › Design a Form, 225, 239
File › Extract Form Files, 230
File › Merge Forms, 236
File › New Project, 265
File › Open, 227
File › Permission › Do Not
        Distribute, 202
File › Preview › Default, 225
File › Save in InfoPath, 259
File › Save Workspace, 32
File › Send to Mail Recipient, 238
File › Submit, 249
file attachments
    adding to lists, 61
    adding to SharePoint, 9
    data submission as, 237, 260
    deleting, 62
    hyperlinks and, 11
    Lists Web service and, 59
    retrieving, 62
File object, 41
File Open dialog box, 36
FileName property, 159
files
    adding to workspace, 35
    checking in, 39
    component, 268

Query method, 261
queryFields group, 239, 242
QueryOptions element, 65
QueryTable object
  error handling, 117
  importing data, 110
  initializing, 118
  Refreshing property, 116
QueryTables collection, 119
Quit method
  Application object, 262
  ExternalApplication object, 235

R

Range object, 18, 152, 196
Range protection member
  (AllowEditRanges), 200
ranges, cell (see cell ranges)
Reader account, 42
read-only access
  anonymous users and, 49
  experimenting with, 183
  form data and, 234
  preventing worksheet
    changes, 191
  Reader account and, 42
  SharePoint and, 36
  Templates folder and, 214
  Users group and, 185
read/write access, 49
Record Macro feature, 197
recursive structures, 98
References dialog box, 138, 139, 150
references (see object references; web
    references)
Refresh action, 247, 261
Refresh method
  Databinding object, 106
  importing data, 114
  ListObject object, 56
  web queries, 116
refreshing
  shared lists, 56, 60
  web queries, 114, 115
Refreshing property
  (QueryTable), 116, 118
RefreshPeriod property, 116
RefreshStyle property, 114
RegForm tool (regform.exe), 264
registering projects, 136

registry settings, 273
Removal Wizard, 217
Remove method (UserPermission), 207
RemoveDocument method, 40
Representational State Transfer
    (REST), 129
requireFullTrust attribute
    (InfoPath), 26
Restrict permission, 203
restricted mode, 259
rich-text format (RTF), 244
RM (Rights Management) Services
    (Microsoft), 201, 202, 205
role-based security, 185
Row node, 81, 83
RTF (rich-text format), 244
rules
  data validation, 251
  InfoPath and, 233, 256
  naming conventions, 52
runtime errors/exceptions, 170, 258

S

Save As dialog box, 70, 186
Save event, 189
Save method (Workbook), 104
Save Options dialog box, 186
SaveAs method (Workbook), 190
SAX (Simple XML API), 68, 69
Schema object, 106
schemas
  inferring, 105
  InfoPath forms and, 234, 243, 247,
    251
  XSLT and, 74
  (see also XML schemas)
Schemas collection, 106
scripts
  converting, 268
  InfoPath and, 253–254, 255–264
  objects used in, 268
security
  anonymous access and, 49
  common questions, 220–222
  digital signatures and, 181,
    207–212
  distributing settings, 216–220
  encryption and, 181, 186–190
  Excel and, 3
  exceptions in preview mode, 269

trust
    ActiveX controls and, 215
    adding trusted sources, 222
    CertMgr.exe and, 216
    considerations, 13
    digital signatures and, 181, 262
    domain-level, 269
    Full Trust, 163, 164, 173, 174
    macros and, 12, 213, 214, 218
    partial, 220
    security and, 14, 210
    templates and, 264
Trusted Sites zone, 32
trustSetting attribute (InfoPath), 26, 269
Try... Catch structure
    End Try construct and, 154
    handling exceptions, 156, 170
    invalid objects and, 157
    New Exception object and, 142
Type attribute (Data node), 83
type library, Visual Studio .NET and, 137, 141, 144

U

UI object, 259
Unlink method (ListObject), 58
Unlist method (ListObject), 58
Unprotect method
    AllowEditRanges object, 200
    Chart object, 200
    Workbook object, 199
    Worksheet object, 196, 200
UnprotectSharing protection member (Workbook), 199
UpdateChanges method, 56
URI property (XDocument), 261
URL property (SharedWorkspace), 39
URLs
    Google web service and, 129
    SharePoint sites and, 31
    SPSITE constant and, 38
    web service access, 122
UsedCells collection, 157
user access lists, 199
user mode (InfoPath)
    defined, 232
    displaying results, 242
    form templates and, 229
    Submit feature and, 237
UserAccessList collection, 199

UserAccessList object, 197, 200
usernames
    forms for, 194
    Windows security and, 182
UserPermission object, 207
users
    adding, 42–44, 199
    adding trusted sources, 222
    anonymous, 45–50, 202
    authentication and, 197
    defined, 182
    editing ranges, 195
    identities and, 182, 202
    IRM and, 201
    permissions and, 180
    viewing in Windows XP, 184–185
users access list, 204
Users group, 182, 184
Users property (AllowEditRange), 200

V

validating data, 245, 249–254, 256
Value property
    Range object, 152
    VB .NET and, 178
variables
    declaring, 150
    declaring types, 152
    responding to events, 153
    Visual Studio and, 268
VB (Visual Basic) .NET
    applications and, 157–160, 173–175
    asynchronous calls and, 131
    authenticating users, 60
    code conversion, 179, 268
    components and, 136–141, 146–148
    debugging, 144–146, 168–170
    documents, 175–177
    events and, 141–144, 153–154, 166–168
    Excel and, 3, 148–151, 157, 161–163
    InfoPath and, 22
    migrating to, 177–179
    objects and, 151–153, 178
    overloading and, 168
    overview, 134–135
    restricted mode and, 259
    security policies, 163–164

Windows Scripting Host, 222
Windows Server 2003, 27, 29, 55
Windows XP, 182–185
WithEvents clause, 166
WithEvents object (.NET)
    declaring variables, 150
    responding to events, 142, 144,
        153, 166
WithEvents qualifier (QueryTable), 117
wizards, 181, 217
    (see also specific wizards)
Word (Microsoft), 205
Workbook collection, 150
Workbook node, 81
Workbook object
    CanCheckIn method, 38
    CanCheckOut property, 38
    CheckIn method, 38
    CheckOut method, 38
    Connected property, 35
    declaring, 166
    events and, 103, 166
    FollowHyperlink method, 39
    HasPassword property, 190
    Open method, 104
    Password property, 188, 190
    protection, 196, 199
    reference example, 152
    Save method, 104
    SaveAs method, 190
    security and, 188, 190
    SetEncryptionOptions method, 190
    SetEncryptionProperties
        method, 188
    SharedWorkspace property, 35
Workbook_BeforeSave event
        procedure, 190
workbooks
    Build Action property, 161
    checking out, 38
    data omitted from, 72
    disconnecting from workspace, 40
    loading assemblies
        automatically, 171
    macros and, 207, 213–215
    protecting, 195
    read-only mode, 36, 49
    saving as XML, 70–73
    security and, 180, 186–195, 221,
        222

setting IRM permissions, 202–205
signing, 211–212
unlocking forms, 234
XML maps and, 85, 91, 105
(see also shared workbooks)
Workbooks collection, 36, 38
workgroups, 182, 194
Worksheet node, 75, 81
Worksheet object
    ListObjects collection, 51
    ListObjects property, 52
    Protect method, 196, 197, 198
    protection, 196, 200
    responding to events, 167
    Unprotect method, 196
    VB .NET and, 178
worksheets
    displaying multi-line text, 6
    errors activating, 169
    macros and, 181
    passwords and, 181
    protecting, 191, 195
    SharePoint and, 60
    unprotecting, 191, 198
    user access lists, 199
    web queries and, 121
Worksheets property
        (Application), 157
workspaces
    anonymous access to, 47, 48
    defined, 2
    folders for, 32, 35
    list access and, 55
    purpose, 3
    removing sharing, 40–42
    shared, 27, 31–33
    /Shared Documents folder, 38
write access, 49, 183, 185
WritePassword security member
        (Workbook), 191
WriteReserved security member
        (Workbook), 191
WriteReservedBy security member
        (Workbook), 191
WScript.exe (Windows Scripting
        Host), 222
WSDL (Web Service Description
        Language), 68, 122
wsm_doGoogleSearch method, 126

X

About the Author

Jeff Webb has written about computers and technology for 20 years. His books include *Using Excel Visual Basic for Applications*; *Visual Basic Developer's Workshop*; and *Developing Web Applications with Visual Basic .NET*. He has also written programming guides, articles, and sample applications for Microsoft and Digital Equipment Corporation.

Colophon

Our look is the result of reader comments, our own experimentation, and feedback from distribution channels. Distinctive covers complement our distinctive approach to technical topics, breathing personality and life into potentially dry subjects.

The *Developer's Notebook* series is modeled on the tradition of laboratory notebooks. Laboratory notebooks are an invaluable tool for researchers and their successors.

The purpose of a laboratory notebook is to facilitate the recording of data and conclusions as the work is being conducted, creating a faithful and immediate history. The notebook begins with a title page that includes the owner's name and the subject of research. The pages of the notebook should be numbered and prefaced with a table of contents. Entries must be clear, easy to read, and accurately dated; they should use simple, direct language to indicate the name of the experiment and the steps taken. Calculations are written out carefully and relevant thoughts and ideas recorded. Each experiment is introduced and summarized as it is added to the notebook. The goal is to produce comprehensive, clearly organized notes that can be used as a reference. Careful documentation creates a valuable record and provides a practical guide for future developers.

Reg Aubry was the production editor and copyeditor for *Excel 2003 Programming: A Developer's Notebook*. Marlowe Shaeffer was the proofreader. Marlowe Shaeffer, Matt Hutchinson, and Claire Cloutier provided quality control. Lucie Haskins wrote the index.

Edie Freedman designed the cover of this book. Emma Colby and Clay Fernald produced the cover layout with QuarkXPress 4.1 using the Officina Sans and JuniorHandwriting fonts.

David Futato designed the interior layout, based on a series design by Edie Freedman and David Futato. This book was converted by Julie Hawks to FrameMaker 5.5.6 with a format conversion tool created by Erik Ray, Jason McIntosh, Neil Walls, and Mike Sierra that uses Perl and XML technologies. The text font is Adobe Boton; the heading font is ITC Officina Sans; the code font is LucasFont's TheSans Mono Condensed, and the handwriting font is a modified version of JRHand made by Tepid Monkey Fonts and modified by O'Reilly. The illustrations that appear in the book were produced by Robert Romano and Jessamyn Read using Macromedia FreeHand 9 and Adobe Photoshop 6. This colophon was written by Colleen Gorman.